"In *Why Workplace Wellbeing Matters*, Ward and De Neve shed light on the crucial relationship between work and wellbeing. The book proves that workplace wellbeing is not just an outcome but a driver of success—impacting productivity, recruitment, retention, and even financial performance. Offering actionable insights for HR practitioners, this book is a must-read for those looking to harness the power of wellbeing as a strategic advantage to attract, engage, and retain top talent."

—**LAFAWN DAVIS**, Chief People and Sustainability Officer, Indeed

"Few topics in management today are more important to understand and master than employee wellbeing. This invaluable new book demystifies what wellbeing really means and why it matters."

—**AMY C. EDMONDSON**, Novartis Professor of Leadership and Management, Harvard Business School; author, *The Fearless Organization*

"What sets this book apart is its scientific rigor, which cuts through subjective definitions and gives practitioners and businesses a practical and evidence-based blueprint for creating real change. It's essential reading for any leader serious about improving employee outcomes and driving tangible business performance."

—**ANDREW GIBBONS**, Group Head of Wellbeing, HSBC

"This is an exciting and inspiring book. Ward and De Neve reorient our thinking about workplaces and wellbeing, providing new frameworks and clear steps for taking effective action."

—**ERIN KELLY**, Sloan Distinguished Professor of Work and Organization Studies, MIT Sloan School of Management; author, *Overload: How Good Jobs Went Bad and What We Can Do About It*

"'Workplace wellbeing' is often discussed but rarely defined with the clarity or depth it deserves. Supported by a unique and impressive body of research, this book provides crystal clarity about why wellbeing at work matters. An essential, illuminating read."

—**SONJA LYUBOMIRSKY**, Distinguished Professor of Psychology, UC Riverside; author, *The How of Happiness* and *The Myths of Happiness*

"Workplace wellbeing has become a strategic imperative for many organizations. This outstanding book highlights the evidence of its positive impact on employee health, productivity, and talent retention. This is a must-read for HR professionals, senior executives, and chief medical officers."

—**SIR CARY COOPER, CBE**, Professor of Organisational Psychology, University of Manchester; Chair, National Forum for Health and Wellbeing at Work

"As this brilliant book shows, wellbeing at work really matters, not just to workers but to productivity and profit. A must-read for any course on management, occupational psychology, or labor economics."

—**LORD RICHARD LAYARD**, Professor of Economics, Emeritus, London School of Economics and Political Science; author, *Happiness: Lessons from a New Science*

"*Why Workplace Wellbeing Matters* is a data-driven yet very readable guide for both managers and employees about the importance of measuring and increasing wellbeing in the workplace, from two of the top experts in the field."

—**MICHAEL NORTON**, Harold M. Brierley Professor of Business Administration, Harvard Business School; author, *The Ritual Effect*

"Authored by two leading researchers on workplace wellbeing, this superb and fact-filled book unpacks the why and how behind the hottest yet often misunderstood trend in managing companies. You'll never think about fostering wellbeing at work the same way again."

—**STEPHAN MEIER**, James P. Gorman Professor of Business, Columbia Business School; author, *The Employee Advantage*

"Drawing on data from over twenty million workers worldwide, De Neve and Ward demonstrate the critical link between employee wellbeing and business success. Their groundbreaking analysis offers leaders an essential, evidence-based road map for creating thriving workplaces. This book should be required reading for every leader and manager."

—**ASHLEY WHILLANS**, Volpert Family Associate Professor of Business Administration, Harvard Business School; author, *Time Smart*

"De Neve and Ward's clear and straightforward approach cuts through the confusion of what wellbeing at work is, how to measure it, and how to make it a strategic priority. We now understand that wellbeing is the result of doing the right things as a company. This is not just about individual benefits but about the organization and design of work. The icing on the cake is the proof that investing in wellbeing literally pays off in better firm performance. A must-read."

—**ANNA BORG**, Head of Psychosocial Health and Well-being, Siemens

"Investing in the wellbeing of your team is essential for your business, and this book is essential in explaining why and how. With data and rigorous research, De Neve and Ward make the serious point that happier employees are good for business, and reveal which factors drive worker wellbeing."

—**CASSIE HOLMES**, Bud Knapp Marketing Professor, UCLA Anderson School of Management; author, *Happier Hour*

"Two superb researchers in the field of workplace wellbeing offer important insights and proposals that, if followed, will dramatically enhance the wellbeing of our world."

—**TYLER J. VANDERWEELE**, John L. Loeb and Frances Lehman Loeb Professor of Epidemiology, Harvard T.H. Chan School of Public Health; Director, Human Flourishing Program, Harvard University

"Finally, a well-researched, science-based approach to measuring, understanding, and improving workplace wellbeing. This book is a game changer for leaders aiming to create happier, less stressful, and more inclusive workplaces—a commitment that, as the authors compellingly demonstrate, is not only the responsible thing to do but also makes solid business sense."

—**SARAH CUNNINGHAM**, Managing Director, World Wellbeing Movement; host, *Working on Wellbeing* podcast

WHY

WORKPLACE

WELLBEING

MATTERS

WHY WORKPLACE WELLBEING MATTERS

▶ The Science Behind Employee Happiness and Organizational Performance

JAN-EMMANUEL DE NEVE

GEORGE WARD

HARVARD BUSINESS REVIEW PRESS
BOSTON, MASSACHUSETTS

Printed in the United Kingdom by TJ Books Ltd, Padstow, Cornwall

10 9 8 7 6 5 4 3 2

The web addresses referenced in this book were live and correct at the time of the book's publication but may be subject to change.

Library of Congress Cataloging-in-Publication Data

Names: De Neve, Jan-Emmanuel, author. | Ward, George (Expert in management science), author.
Title: Why workplace wellbeing matters : the science behind employee happiness and organizational performance / Jan-Emmanuel De Neve, George Ward.
Description: Boston, Massachusetts : Harvard Business Review Press, [2025] | Includes index.
Identifiers: LCCN 2024033264 (print) | LCCN 2024033265 (ebook) | ISBN 9781647826352 (hardcover) | ISBN 9781647826369 (epub)
Subjects: LCSH: Quality of work life. | Work-life balance. | Well-being. | Psychology, Industrial.
Classification: LCC HD6955 .D465 2025 (print) | LCC HD6955 (ebook) | DDC 306.3/6—dc23/eng/20241121
LC record available at https://lccn.loc.gov/2024033264
LC ebook record available at https://lccn.loc.gov/2024033265

ISBN: 978-1-64782-635-2
eISBN: 978-1-64782-636-9

Contents

PART FOUR

The Future of Work and Wellbeing

WHY WORKPLACE WELLBEING MATTERS

Introduction

A quick look at the headlines on workplace wellbeing can leave you spinning with excitement. "Companies reap bigger dividends from happier staff," says the *Financial Times*. "Is happiness the secret of success?" asks CNN. "Proof that positive work cultures are more productive" offers *Harvard Business Review*. "If you want to be productive at work, get happy," declares *Forbes*.[1]

Enthusiasm has begun to reach managers and business leaders too. In a recent survey of executives and managers in the United States, 87 percent agreed that improving workplace wellbeing could give their companies a competitive advantage.[2] Even higher percentages believed that creating happier places to work would make it easier to attract and retain talent, while eight out of ten agreed that unhappiness is likely to harm productivity. Moreover, the vast majority are aware that, through the way they manage and organize work, they have a good deal of influence on the wellbeing of their employees.

In many ways, this is all very encouraging—particularly for those of us who have long studied the topic. But even for those with research backgrounds and time on their hands to sift through the data, sorting out smoke from fire is not always straightforward. Confusion often abounds as to what workplace wellbeing actually is and what it entails. Doubts arise as to how—or even if—we can reliably measure it. And that's before we even begin to look at the causes of workplace wellbeing or the effects it may have on business outcomes like productivity, turnover, or profits. Ultimately, a lot has been written about workplace wellbeing and a lot of claims made. Some have been based on clear definitions and rigorous research; some less so.

Given this confusion, it is perhaps not altogether surprising that, despite all of the apparent enthusiasm, actual progress has been quite limited. Positive attitudes do not necessarily translate into concrete action. In the same survey of managers and executives who were so enthusiastic about the benefits of employee wellbeing, only about a third of them reported that wellbeing was a strategic priority for their organizations. And only half of those went on to say yes to actually having a strategy in place to improve workplace wellbeing.

Along similar lines, recent research looked at the language used on company earnings calls and found that executives talk about customers a great deal more than they do about employees—about eight times as much, in fact.[3] And when they do mention their employees, it is typically associated with risk. So, despite the excitement—and the lip service paid to popular sayings like "our employees are our most important asset"—there is a great deal of room for improvement.

What Is Workplace Wellbeing Anyway?

Workplace wellbeing is how we feel at work and about our work. It has evaluative, affective, and eudaimonic components.[4] These may sound complicated but are actually very straightforward. Evaluative workplace wellbeing refers to how we think about our jobs. It is an overall judgment, an assessment about how things are going, and it is typically measured by job satisfaction—a question many of us have answered on an employer survey at some stage or other during our working careers.

Affective wellbeing, on the other hand, refers to how we actually feel on a day-to-day basis while we are at work. Is work actually enjoyable? This is an emotional or hedonic experience, and it can involve both positive and negative emotions. On the positive side, we often think about how happy we are at work. And on the negative side, one of the most pertinent emotions we study in the workplace—though, of course, not the only one—is how stressed we feel at work.

Finally, eudaimonic wellbeing comes from the Greek word *eudaimonia* and is often traced back to the work of Aristotle. This component of workplace wellbeing is about how much of a sense of purpose we get out of our work. Do we feel like what we do in our work lives is worthwhile? Does it help to improve the lives of others, and do we ultimately find the things we do at work to be meaningful?

So, workplace wellbeing has three components, and each one has a clear definition that is based—as we will see in more detail throughout the book—on decades of research across the social and behavioral sciences, on both subjective wellbeing as a whole as well as on aspects of wellbeing within the workplace.[5] It is sometimes referred to simply as "happiness" at work, in an easier shorthand. This makes sense in some ways, given that it captures relatively quickly the essence of the topic. But it can add an element of confusion. After all, even though happiness is an important part of workplace wellbeing, it is really only one aspect of it—positive affect at work—and so using it as an umbrella term for the whole of workplace wellbeing can add confusion.

Common Conceptual Pitfalls

More confusing still are measures of workplace wellbeing that mix wellbeing with all sorts of other workplace and job characteristics as well as employee behaviors. In our experience talking to managers and executives, many are enthusiastic about workplace wellbeing and often like to show us their data dashboards. Impressive as these often are, the same issue comes up over and over again. Wellbeing ends up being a composite measure of all sorts of things—including wages, flexibility, job satisfaction, work-life balance, stress, paid time off, worker engagement, employee loyalty, turnover intentions, and more. In doing so, these well-meaning indexes at once measure everything and nothing.

To be clear, we are not saying that things like wages and work-life balance are not important. As we will see later in the book, many of these aspects of jobs and workplaces—like paying a living wage, giving workers voice, providing predictable and flexible schedules—are key factors in explaining why some people and companies have higher levels of workplace wellbeing than others. But they are more properly thought of conceptually as drivers of workplace wellbeing, not as aspects of workplace wellbeing itself.

So, we need to distinguish workplace wellbeing from its drivers. Only then can we really analyze what aspects of how work is managed and organized by firms are relatively more important—and, ultimately, make decisions about how to allocate scarce resources within firms. Companies do not have unlimited budgets, and a simple fact of life is that managers have to make choices. If we want to maximize workplace wellbeing, subject to budget constraints, we have to know whether and how much it is shaped by different factors under our control.

On the other side of things, we need to separate workplace wellbeing from what are better seen as its effects, or downstream consequences. This includes measures we often see lumped together with wellbeing, including employee engagement, net promoter scores—such as whether or not you would recommend working there to a friend—and turnover intentions. Again, these are often hugely important measures for firms, but they are not themselves workplace wellbeing. More often they are better thought of as a consequence of it.

Reliable Data and Rigorous Empirical Methods

If the first main goal of this book is to lay out a model of workplace wellbeing—one with a simple definition and conceptual clarity about its drivers and downstream consequences—then the second is to bring the latest data and empirical methods to bear on key questions surrounding the topic. What findings are based on solid data with clear definitions? Which are correlational and which are causal? Which replicate in real-world workplace settings? All sorts of claims are often made in relation to workplace wellbeing, and it is a good time to take stock and assess which stand up and which do not.

When we define workplace wellbeing clearly and simply, then it can be reliably measured—as we will see in more detail—mainly through surveys but also increasingly through other means. In this book we follow the simple strategy of trying to get our hands on as much of the best-quality data as possible. There is an increasing amount of data available to researchers that firms themselves or other entities like polling companies have collected. We also use an exciting new data source we have collected in collaboration with Indeed, the world's largest jobs website, over the past few years, which has crowdsourced data on workplace wellbeing—defined as job satisfaction, sense of purpose, happiness, and stress—from over 20 million workers worldwide (and counting).

Rising Expectations and the Wellbeing Imperative

Even if we accept that workplace wellbeing is a clear concept that we can reliably measure, the obvious follow-up question is: Does it matter? As a manager or executive, is there any reason to care? In other words, is there a so-called business case? While an interesting and important question, and one that we have ourselves worked on extensively, the prospect of financial returns should not be the main reason for genuinely caring about the wellbeing of our colleagues and employees. There is already a very strong human case for workplace wellbeing. Indeed, there are all sorts of good reasons, beyond profits, why firms should care about how they treat their workers and how they manage and organize work in making the lives of employees either more miserable or more enjoyable.

Most of us spend a large portion of our waking hours at work, and it is highly unsurprising that a long line of research has shown that our overall life satisfaction is often shaped to a large degree by how meaningful or enjoyable our work is and how satisfied we are with our jobs.[6] Our experience of work is not something that gets neatly left at the door when we return to our private lives. Mood and satisfaction at work often carry over to how we feel at home. Wellbeing at work is deeply intertwined with our quality of life more generally, even more so for the growing number who work, at least part of the time, from home.

But even with a strong human case, it is still often necessary to put hard numbers on whether there is a return on investment. The evidence on this front is mounting and has been the focus area of much of our own research over the past years. First of all, workplace wellbeing has strong effects on

employee performance—a causal effect that is found both in the laboratory as well as in real-world workplace settings.[7] Second, measures of workplace wellbeing also strongly predict subsequent employee turnover, with
happier workers much more likely to remain in organizations.[8] Finally,
companies with higher levels of wellbeing tend to find it easier to attract
workers in the first place.[9]

As time goes on, firms may have no other option but to start getting serious about workplace wellbeing. Employees' expectations for workplace
happiness are high—and rising. Compared to five years ago, for example,
in a recent study, the majority professed that their expectations had gone
up.[10] This trend—shown in figure I-1—is especially true for younger people,
suggesting that expectations overall are likely to continue to grow.[11]

This strongly indicates that workplace wellbeing matters for business.
But an obvious retort is: What about costs? Even if happier workers are
more productive, that does not necessarily tell us if it is a good idea—
financially speaking, at least—to invest in organizational and management
practices to improve it. It is important that we do not get too Pollyanna-
ish about the benefits of workplace wellbeing.

FIGURE I-1

Expectations about Wellbeing Have Increased

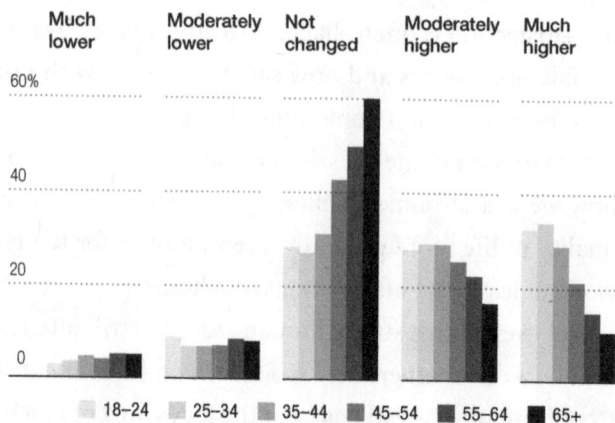

Note: Nationally representative survey of workers in the US, UK, and Canada, carried out in 2023. N = 7,029.

To account for the important issue of costs, we have to look therefore at the relationship between wellbeing and performance at the level of companies. This has been challenging historically. Whereas traditional approaches often limit our analyses to single firms or sectors, the breadth of data collected in collaboration with Indeed enables us to look at company-level wellbeing across tens of thousands of firms, from across the whole of the economy. This means we can, for the first time, link differences across firms in well-defined workplace wellbeing to data on company accounts and stock prices. Focusing on publicly listed firms, we find that those with higher levels of wellbeing are subsequently more profitable and perform better in the stock market.[12] As the then-CEO of Unilever, Alan Jope, observed at a conference we organized in Oxford in 2022, "If we look after our team, then they will look after the business."[13]

All of this makes it imperative to not only see worker wellbeing as a key priority, but also properly understand what drives it. Does it have anything to do with firms? Can it be improved? If so, what sorts of management and organizational practices are most conducive or detrimental to job satisfaction, purpose, happiness, and stress? These are the questions that we focus on and attempt to provide answers.

What's It Got to Do with Managers and Firms Though?

One of the most striking findings from the data is a seemingly simple one. Levels of workplace wellbeing differ significantly and systematically across companies, even within tightly defined industries and locations.[14] Some industries are happier on average than others, of course, but even in the toughest industries and areas, we nevertheless find organizations where people feel good. So, it is possible to improve workplace wellbeing, even in challenging circumstances.

This has important implications. A worker's sense of wellbeing will in part be determined by personal circumstances that are beyond the reasonable control of firms—ranging from fixed genetic dispositions all the way to traffic problems on the way to work. But this does not absolve managers of responsibility. Indeed, when we ask workers in surveys about who is responsible for their workplace wellbeing, they do recognize this fact. They tend to attribute just under half of the responsibility for their workplace happiness to themselves, but over half of it to organizational factors. This includes all levels of the company, from the line manager all the way up to the CEO.[15]

Managing and improving workplace wellbeing is a shared responsibility requiring systemwide thinking and effort. This goes well beyond human resources departments, where it has too often been siloed and thought of as an add-on—rather than a fundamental part of a company's business strategy, as it should be.

Despite all this, both workers and managers do recognize that the way in which work is managed and organized has a significant impact on all facets of workplace wellbeing. When asked about whether it is possible to be happy at work, for example, the overwhelming majority of workers—from a whole range of firm types and sectors—agree that it is possible to a greater or lesser extent to find happiness in work (see figure I-2).[16] Combined with the fact that wellbeing varies significantly across companies that

FIGURE I-2

Wellbeing at Work Is Possible

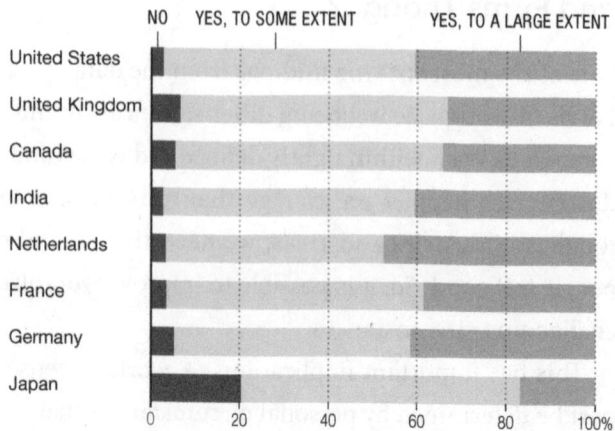

Do you think it's possible for people to be happy at work, most of the time?

NO   YES, TO SOME EXTENT   YES, TO A LARGE EXTENT

United States
United Kingdom
Canada
India
Netherlands
France
Germany
Japan

0   20   40   60   80   100%

Note: Nationally representative survey of workers in 8 countries, carried out in 2023. N = 12,472.

otherwise look very similar and are facing the same business environment, this strongly suggests it is in fact possible to provide conditions conducive to a happier work life.

Of course, we're not saying that there is no role for workers themselves in any of this. Or that there is no role for broader actors, including government and public policy, unions and other forms of organized labor, and industry and employer associations. However, in this book we focus on the important though often overlooked role of managers and firms, which, it turns out, have the potential to improve the wellbeing of society—or hold it back.

Wellbeing beyond Wellness

An additional misperception we increasingly hear when talking to both managers and workers is related to wellness. Wellness and wellbeing are too often conflated. Wellness is somewhat more nebulous as a concept and is often defined more in terms of the wellness programs designed to promote it.

Wellness programs are usually well-meaning initiatives that have the potential to do a great deal of good. Indeed, providing employees with access to resources that can help them to take better care of themselves is something only to be applauded. However, the mistake typically lies in thinking of these kinds of offerings as a solution to workplace wellbeing challenges—and then simply moving on.

Wellness interventions mostly target the individual workers themselves rather than the work or work environment. They can be useful when they effectively address employees' physical or mental health concerns that constitute hurdles to improving workplace wellbeing. Unfortunately, though, it is often not the worker who needs to change, but rather the workplace and the work itself. Wellbeing is a fundamental issue that also relates to how work is designed, organized, and managed. It is not easy, but we need to get beyond the wellness conversation and start to think about workplace wellbeing more holistically—as something that relates to organizational practices and how workers are treated. That goes beyond individualized programs that aim to soften the pain or to improve resilience, but that do not address the root causes of poor workplace wellbeing in the first place.

In order to improve workplace wellbeing, we need to think more clearly about its causes. In this book, we group these drivers of wellbeing into six broad groups: development and security, human relationships at work, independence and flexibility, variety and fulfillment, earning and benefits, as well as risk, health, and safety. While wellness programs aim to improve wellbeing through direct intervention, often bypassing any discussion of how jobs are designed and managed, we argue this alone will never be sufficient. We need to think fundamentally about how to improve the drivers of wellbeing.

As we will see later in the book, what people think is important in determining that workplace wellbeing is not necessarily the same as what actually drives it. When we ask both managers and workers what factors they think are most important, compensation and benefits dominate the discussion. We put together all of the best data available in order to run a large-scale driver analysis. When we did so, we found that wages are important. But they are far from being the most important factors in determining wellbeing. Most significant are more human factors such as a sense of belonging and the quality of relationships, both with colleagues and with management.

Shaping the Future of Work to Benefit Wellbeing

With the world of work in a moment of flux, how does the future look, given the importance of these driving factors? We argue that the defining feature of the much-discussed "future of work" is not whether or not there will be enough jobs—the typical main topic of the conversation. Instead, it is whether those jobs will be any better or worse for people's wellbeing. The discussion needs to move from the *quantity* to the *quality* of jobs.

Ultimately, technology is not deterministic and does not develop according to its own logic or in a vacuum. Tools like robotics, software, and artificial intelligence are not inherently either good or bad. They are developed by humans who make decisions and aim to maximize the outcomes they choose—whether that be productivity, cost-savings, worker wellbeing, or something else.[17] If we are to make the most of technological advances, we need to consider workers when designing and adopting those advances. Labor must have a seat at the table. Not only for the workers but—as we will see in more detail given the latest in a long line of empirical evidence on labor and employment relations—also often for the benefit of firms that also gain from such collaboration.

We argue that firms and managers can and must play an active role, rather than leaving everything to technologists. This can happen by using technology to augment and improve jobs as well as by giving workers a voice and involving them in the process of technology adoption. Ultimately, we can all play a role in shaping a future of work that works for wellbeing.

Plan of the Book

Chapter 1 provides a more detailed overview of the book, which is split into four main parts. In part I, we clarify what workplace wellbeing is. We discuss how important work is for wellbeing as a whole, before developing an integrative model of workplace wellbeing that incorporates a simple definition, a survey measurement module, and a set of drivers and downstream consequences.

Part II delves more deeply into what causes workplace wellbeing. We think about the relative importance of different workplace characteristics and show that wellbeing is an issue that fundamentally has to do with how work is managed and organized. So, to improve workplace wellbeing, we have to think about the drivers and how to improve them. To do so, we survey the best evidence on how to do so and offer a practical guide of best practices.

In part III, we look at the flip side of the coin and think about workplace wellbeing as the cause rather than the outcome. What are the downstream consequences of job satisfaction, meaning and purpose, happiness, and stress? We look at productivity, retention, recruitment, as well as firm financial performance. Finally, in part IV we look to the future and the role of technology in changing the nature of work, with important implications for wellbeing.

Wellbeing at Work: An Overview

Most of us spend around a third of our waking lives at work. But does it make us happy? It certainly seems logical that, given the amount of time we spend in and around our jobs, work-related factors will have a large influence on our overall wellbeing. This is partly what drew us to the study of work and wellbeing in the first place—of all the things that might influence how happy we feel in our lives, work is surely a contender for being very near the top of the list.

The Importance of Having Work for Wellbeing

Although we will focus on understanding the causes and consequences of the wellbeing of people at work, we start from the more basic question: *How important is work for our wellbeing?* We draw from and build on a long line of research in economics, psychology, management, sociology, and elsewhere that has studied human happiness—or "subjective wellbeing," as it is often also known. As it turns out, work is hugely important, and as we will discuss at greater length in chapter 3, the large negative wellbeing effects of being unemployed are one of the most consistently replicated findings in all of the scientific literature.

FIGURE 1-1

Unemployment Is Devastating for People's Wellbeing

Overall wellbeing by employment status

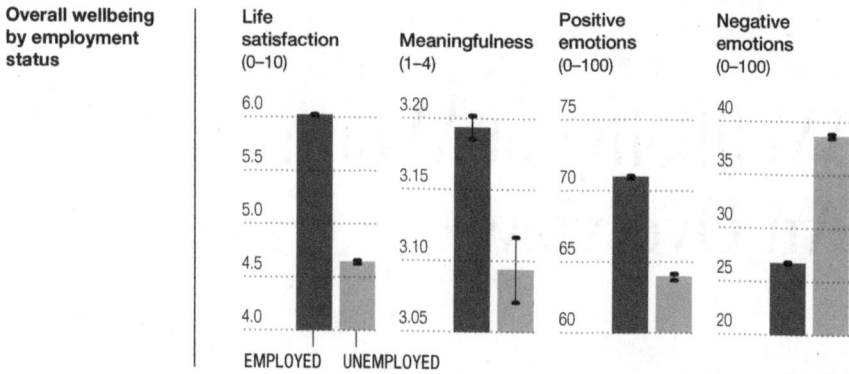

| Life satisfaction (0–10) | Meaningfulness (1–4) | Positive emotions (0–100) | Negative emotions (0–100) |

EMPLOYED   UNEMPLOYED

Note: Employed and unemployed individuals aged 21–64; 95% confidence intervals shown; survey carried out across 166 countries; 2009–2022.
Source: Gallup World Poll.

Figure 1-1 shows the wellbeing differences between full-time employees and the unemployed, using the Gallup World Poll, a vast survey data set collected annually from over 160 countries worldwide since 2006.[1] The data includes questions on all three of the main aspects of subjective wellbeing typically studied in academic literature. Although economists have sometimes conceptualized work as a "disutility," when we look at the data, work instead appears to be an important source of wellbeing.

Evaluative wellbeing refers to an overall evaluation of how things are going. This is typically measured using questions about life satisfaction. It is a cognitive judgment and taps into how we think about the state of our lives as a whole. Worldwide, people in work are over one point more satisfied with their lives, on a scale of zero to ten, than those who are unemployed. This is a huge difference, much larger than almost anything else typically studied in the ever-growing body of scientific work on subjective wellbeing.

The survey also asks people the extent to which they feel the things they do in life are meaningful. On a one-to-four scale—where one is never and four is always—we again see significant differences between those in and out of work. Finally, the survey asks not only about how people think about their lives, but also about how they feel.

How we feel on a day-to-day basis is variously referred to as affective, hedonic, and experienced wellbeing. It has two main components, which are not simply inverses of each other. There are positive emotions that we feel in our everyday lives—things like enjoyment, excitement, and happiness. But there are also negative ones as well, including anger, fear, and stress. In figure 1-1, we show the percentage of people experiencing positive and negative affect around the world, broken down by whether or not they are employed or unemployed. Again, we find significant differences, particularly when it comes to negative emotions.

As we will discuss in more depth in chapter 3, the negative effects of unemployment on wellbeing go well beyond income. Work provides us with not only a wage but also a sense of identity, a daily routine, a sense of purpose, and a set of social connections and regular interactions with others. But as anyone who has held multiple jobs—or even held the same job for any length of time and experienced changes to management and organizational practices—will know, not all jobs are the same.

The Importance of Quality of Work for Wellbeing

We often take it for granted that creating more jobs will improve the wellbeing of those they are created for. There is little doubt that having a stable and reliable source of income is better than not having one. Many, if not most, of our opportunities in life are constrained or determined by our access to financial resources. So, if employers and policy makers can provide us with jobs that provide us with income, have they done their job? Is income all we should expect in return for labor?

In figure 1-2, we zoom in on the life satisfaction of those who are employed full-time, again using worldwide data.[2] Those who report that they enjoy the work they do are more than a full point more satisfied with their lives (out of ten) than those who do not. This is again a huge difference and points to the fact that our work lives are an extremely important factor in

FIGURE 1-2

Wellbeing at Work Is Vital for Wellbeing in Life

Average level of
life satisfaction
(on a 0–10 scale)
by four measures
of workplace
wellbeing

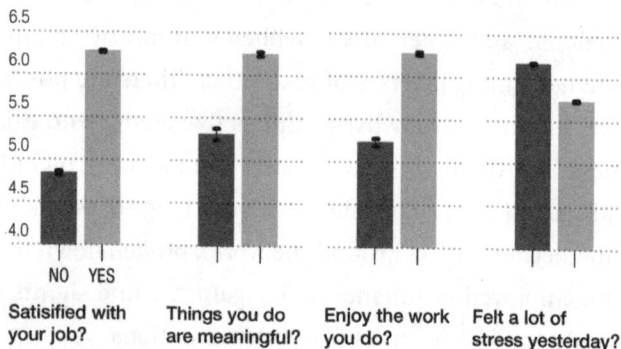

NO   YES

Satisified with your job?   Things you do are meaningful?   Enjoy the work you do?   Felt a lot of stress yesterday?

Note: Survey carried out across 165 countries in 2009–2022. Full-time employed individuals aged 21–64; 95% confidence intervals shown.
Source: Gallup World Poll.

our overall sense of wellbeing. Equally, those who felt stressed yesterday are less satisfied with their lives overall.

These differences go beyond simply how much we enjoy our jobs—that is, how we *feel* at work. They also exist when it comes to how we *think* about our jobs as well. Those who are satisfied with their work are generally much more satisfied with their lives, while those who feel they do meaningful things in life are also more satisfied overall.

So, something important is going on here. We must look at work and wellbeing not simply as an issue of having versus not having, but rather also focus on what's actually going on in workplaces. This is what this book is about—*workplace* wellbeing. Both of us have spent a significant portion of our lives studying wellbeing and work as well as talking to and helping managers in the field.

But before we get into more detail on the causes and effects of workplace wellbeing, we first need to be clear about what it is. Despite widespread interest, different people in different contexts use the term in many—often confusing—ways. At times, they simply conflate it with wages. More often, they see it as an amalgamation of a list of good things about a job, such as working hours, flexibility, pay, belonging, support, enjoyment, satisfaction, and fairness, among others.

How We Think about and Feel at Our Work

We propose a simple and tractable definition that captures how people feel at work and about work. As we will discuss at greater length in chapter 2, workplace wellbeing is a multifaceted concept that incorporates evaluative, affective, and eudaimonic aspects. Many will notice the immediate similarity with the way in which subjective wellbeing as a whole is typically thought about and studied. This is not an accident. While academics are often tempted to come up with new and exciting things they can name after themselves, we see no reason to reinvent the wheel when it comes to workplace wellbeing, and that is why we root our definition of workplace wellbeing purposefully in the science of subjective wellbeing.

Evaluative workplace wellbeing is an overall judgment about a job. This is a cognitive aspect of workplace wellbeing: it is how we think about the work that we do. It is in this sense an overarching assessment and can be thought of most simply as job satisfaction. In addition to how satisfied we are with our jobs, there is how meaningful and purposeful our work is. While purpose has become a key topic of interest for many in the business community, this is most often thought about in terms of corporate purpose—or companies' attempts to make a social impact in the world. In our case, however, what we are referring to is how much meaning and sense of purpose people get out of their work.

Workplace wellbeing goes beyond how people feel about work and also includes how they actually feel while at work. This is where positive and negative emotional experience comes in. Positive affect at work includes things like how much happiness people feel at work and how enjoyable the work they do is. Negative affect at work can encompass a range of feelings, including fear, anxiety, and sadness. In this book we will discuss a range of these negative emotions, but much of the analysis will focus on one in particular, which is acutely important in the workplace context, namely, stress.

Measuring Workplace Wellbeing

With a tractable definition in mind, we turn in chapter 4 to discuss how we can measure workplace wellbeing, including using a novel set of survey measures, and beyond that, in the rest of the book, to the key issues of what determines workplace wellbeing and its downstream consequences for workers and firms.

Are you happy at work? Are you paid fairly? Do you feel your colleagues support you? Does any of this matter for productivity and, ultimately, firm performance? These are empirical questions that we have pored over for most of our research careers. Since 2019, we have had the great fortune to advise and work with an incredible team of people at Indeed, the largest job search platform in the world, with over 350 million unique website visitors per month.

In addition to its core function of hosting job advertisements and facilitating the hiring process, Indeed also serves an increasingly important function—that of collecting and sharing information about what it is really like to work at different firms. In partnership with an excellent team within the company, we posed survey questions on the four main aspects of workplace wellbeing and its potential drivers to over 20 million workers (and counting) worldwide.

We look at the Indeed data in concert with more traditional surveys—like the Gallup World Poll, European Social Survey, World Values Survey, and so on—but none of these allow us to compare wellbeing across companies. Typically, a regular survey will give us insightful data on, say, a few thousand people. This powerful tool allows us to draw a range of inferences, but if we want to think about how individual companies are doing, then we need to get bigger—much bigger. Although there can be some potential drawbacks to crowdsourced data and reasons to analyze it with caution and care, as we discuss in more detail later on in the book, the resulting data set provides a unique and unprecedented insight into the state of workplace wellbeing.

Not only does the Indeed data provide insight into wellbeing across tens of thousands of companies, it does so while allowing us to distinguish between different dimensions of workplace wellbeing. The questions include job satisfaction, purpose, happiness, and stress. These can be thought of as uniquely valuable and distinct domains of wellbeing at work that, together, act as our key wellbeing indicator. While these wellbeing outcome items tend to correlate, scoring highly in one domain is not necessarily indicative of scoring highly in another. People may be satisfied with their jobs and yet feel unhappy at work, or stressed about a project they find to be particularly meaningful. As a result, whenever possible, it is also worth examining each dimension separately and independently. Ultimately, building a sustainable culture of wellbeing at work requires devoting care and attention to all four.

Differences in Workplace Wellbeing across Companies

One of the most important findings from this work is that, across individuals, companies, and industries, there is enormous variation in wellbeing. A detailed study by one of us (George) has shown, for example, that job satisfaction, happiness, stress, and purpose at work all vary significantly across companies, even within tightly defined industries and locations.[3] That might not sound like a very exciting statement, but it has key implications. Two observably similar companies—working in the same place and in the same sector, doing similar things and facing the same business environment—have very different levels of wellbeing among their workers.

Take happiness. On the Indeed website, respondents are asked to report how happy they feel at work on a five-point scale. We can average the responses by firms and show that the resulting variation in company happiness closely resembles a normal distribution. Most companies fall somewhere in the middle, while differences persist at either end. There is thus a huge amount of inequality not only in income but also in the ways in which people experience work in our economy.

FIGURE 1-3

Company-Level Happiness Varies Significantly within and across Industries

Percent by
company-level
happiness
(on a 1–5 scale)

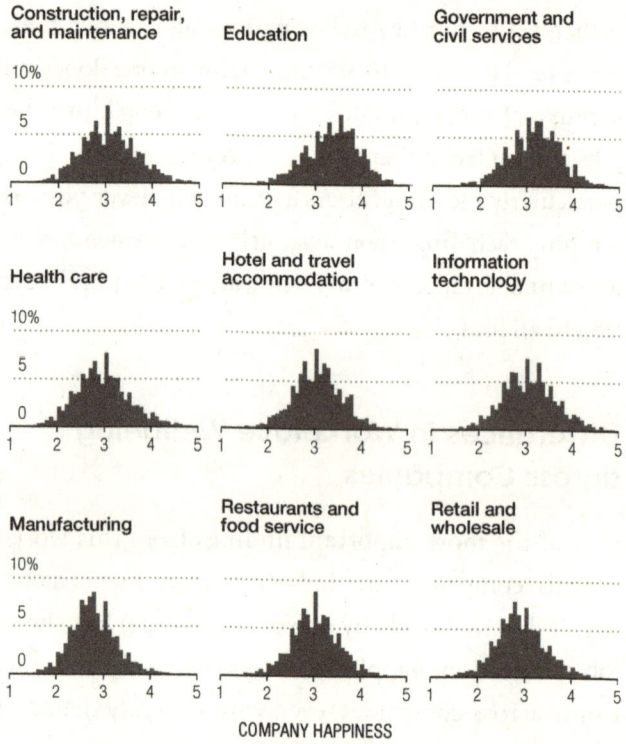

Note: Minimum 10 responses per company to be included. Histograms plot the distribution of average happiness across 68,253 companies in 9 sectors of the US economy.
Source: Data collected from current and former employees on the Indeed platform, October 2019 to May 2024.

In figure 1-3, we break this down by nine of the biggest sectors in the economy. Even within industries, large variations in workplace wellbeing persist. Education is a relatively happy industry, when we compare its average level with others like manufacturing, a relatively more unhappy sector to work in. These average differences across industries are interesting. But much more interesting and important is the fact that there is large variation within them.[4] Even in manufacturing, there are still companies somehow getting things right and having a relatively happy workforce.

Two Sets of Questions

This striking variation across companies in the way employees think about and feel at work—their workplace wellbeing—is what motivates much of this book (and our research agendas and business school teaching more broadly). It raises at least two sets of questions.[5]

First, why do these differences exist? What sorts of management and organizational practices, if any, might be able to explain why some companies have happier workforces than others? Why do some have workers who experience their jobs as having more meaning and purpose than others? And once we know what might explain such differences, what can we do— as business leaders, workers, policy makers, labor representatives, or citizens—to try to improve workplace wellbeing?

Second, does it matter? What are the downstream consequences, for workers and firms, of these stark differences in workplace wellbeing? Are happier workers more productive? Are they any less likely to quit and move to a competitor? Does having a happier workforce help to attract talent in the first place? Ultimately, are firms with higher levels of worker wellbeing any more profitable?

This set of three core issues can be seen more clearly in figure 1-4. Here we present an overall model of workplace wellbeing. In essence, this model

FIGURE 1-4

A Model of Workplace Wellbeing

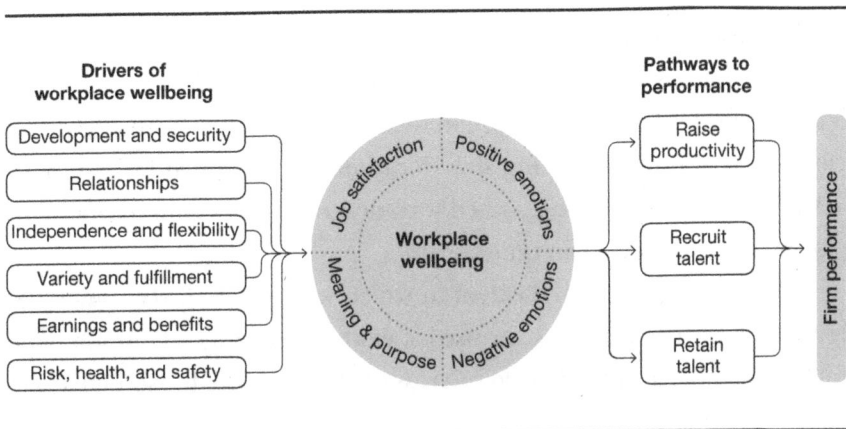

structures how we proceed with the rest of the book. We begin in the middle and define clearly what workplace wellbeing is and how to measure it. Coming from the left, we then try to understand what drives workplace wellbeing and how we might be able to improve it. Moving to the right, we look at the effects of wellbeing on a number of pathways that ultimately lead to firm performance.

Explaining Differences in Wellbeing across Companies

The considerable variation in measures of workplace wellbeing—including job satisfaction, purpose, happiness, and stress—implies stark and profound differences in the quality of workers' lived experience. These differences demand explanation. One potential route would be to appeal to divergent job demands across industries. For example, one might imagine that the demanding manual labor of jobs in agriculture would threaten happiness at work, while the high pay associated with jobs in finance would increase it. In fact, the reality is much more complicated. As we saw in figure 1-3, there is considerable variation even within tightly defined industries and locations. In truth, only about 12 to 15 percent of the variation in company happiness in the United States can be explained by industry differences.[6]

Consider the following two groups of companies. In the first group, we have Walmart—a chain of retail and department stores, Whole Foods—a supermarket for quality foods, and Santander—a large retail bank. In the second group, we have Costco—a chain of retail and department stores, Trader Joe's—a supermarket for quality foods, and HSBC—a large retail bank. These pairings not only are in the same industry, but are also direct competitors. Some competing store locations are separated by mere feet. Yet despite their similarities, when it comes to the wellbeing of their employees, more divides than unites them.

In figure 1-5, we plot the extent to which workers at all six companies report feeling happy at work, stressed at work, satisfied with their jobs, and finding purpose in what they do.[7] Across each dimension, the second group

FIGURE 1-5

Wellbeing Differs Greatly Even among Competitors

Average workplace wellbeing (on a 1–5 scale) across competitors in the same industry

WHOLE FOODS MARKET ■——□ TRADER JOE'S
WALMART ●——○ COSTCO WHOLESALE
SANTANDER ▲——△ HSBC

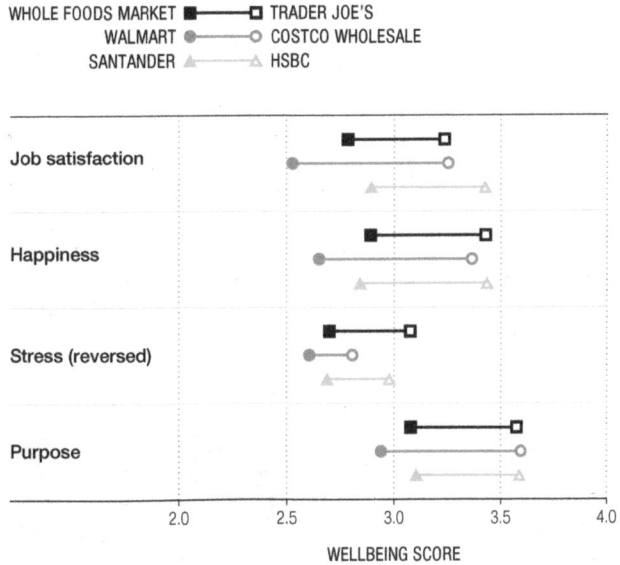

Source: Indeed data, collected October 2019 to May 2024 in the US.

of companies beats the first. Considered from this perspective, the drivers of workplace wellbeing start to become less obvious.

When employee wellbeing at Trader Joe's is more similar to employee wellbeing at HSBC than Whole Foods, accounting for it in terms of objective job characteristics seems unlikely to do the trick. The intuition here is that schedules, salaries, and benefits seem more likely to diverge across industry lines than between direct competitors. This intuition is not entirely misguided, although as anyone who has worked in the same industry long enough can attest, even between direct competitors, there can be substantial variation in working conditions. So as a final exercise, let's go one step further and consider differences in happiness among employees working for the same company.

FIGURE 1.6

Wellbeing varies across US states, even within the same company

Mean happiness levels (on a 1–5 scale) by company by US state

5: Highest
1: Lowest

2.18　2.51　2.59　2.64　2.72　2.77　2.82　2.89　3.08　3.27　3.57

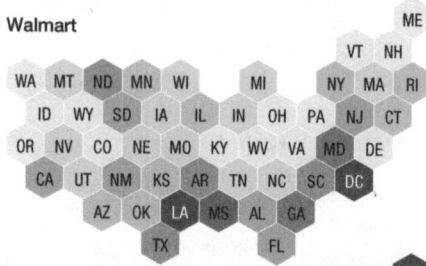

Walmart

UPS

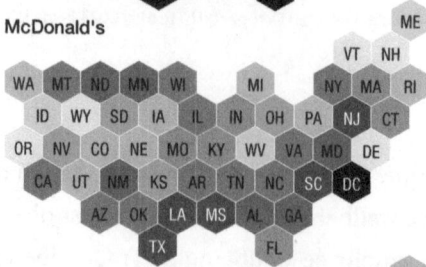

McDonald's

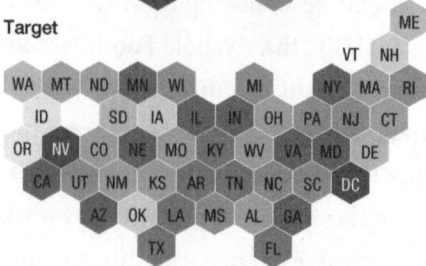

Target

Note: Mean levels are plotted for states. Not plotted if there are fewer than 30 responses to the happiness question in that company-state. Total number of observations: McDonalds=55,732; Target=33,419; UPS=28,841; Walmart=100,768

Source: Indeed data, collected October 2019 to May 2024.

In figure 1-6, we plot average levels of happiness (on a five-point scale) for employees working at Walmart, UPS, McDonald's, and Target locations across the United States. Splitting these company-states into deciles of happiness, we see that, even within companies, there are differences across locations in how happy the workforce is. What's more, these patterns don't necessarily simply match up to statewide differences in subjective wellbeing more generally.[8]

A large part of the variation comes from differences across companies. After all, these are nationwide chains or franchises with many management and organizational practices decided on centrally. But local practices—as well as managers themselves—are likely to matter too. Understanding the underlying drivers of these differences requires looking deeper at job characteristics and workplace conditions.

The Drivers of Workplace Wellbeing

Each of the four domains of workplace wellbeing can be affected by a variety of subjective and objective working conditions, the most important of which we refer to as the six key groups of drivers of workplace wellbeing, namely, development and security, human relationships at work, independence and flexibility, variety and fulfillment, earning and benefits, as well as risk, health, and safety. These are characteristics of the work and the employment relationship, many of which (to varying degrees, as we will see) affect how we think about and feel at work.

In chapters 5 and 6, we leverage multiple data sources and survey the best existing evidence on each of the main drivers. While all these drivers are in some way fundamental to creating positive working environments, some prove to be more important than others. Overall, by conducting a large-scale driver analysis, we find that social drivers—things like feelings of belonging, inclusion, and support—are especially critical for employee wellbeing, in some cases even more so than factors such as pay or flexibility. Throughout the book, we will examine how each one of these drivers can affect workplace wellbeing, comment on their interrelationships, and evaluate interventions to target and improve them.

In chapter 7, we move beyond trying to understand what drives wellbeing, to think about what companies can do to improve it. Here we focus in particular on randomized controlled trials, which provide the best experimental evidence for the kinds of interventions within the workplace that can improve wellbeing.

Improving Workplace Wellbeing

There are two broad approaches to interventions designed to improve workplace wellbeing. Roughly speaking, one is *direct* and the other *indirect*. When we say direct, we mean interventions that are designed to improve the wellbeing of a worker directly—such as through gym membership or access to a mindfulness app. Indirect, on the other hand, means intervening on one or more of the drivers themselves—things like pay, hours, work design, and other management practices. In other words, improving workplace wellbeing by improving work.

Much of the existing discussion surrounding workplace wellbeing tends to describe the direct route. To be sure, there is good evidence for a number of approaches that are focused on the individual employee. As we will see, activities like yoga, mindfulness, and sports have been shown to improve people's wellbeing, while efforts to train and coach managers can also improve their psychological wellbeing directly.[9]

Even more importantly, mental health is a key and ever-present concern. Indeed, mental health issues such as depression and anxiety have a very large impact on people's wellbeing, both in the workplace and more generally.[10] It is vitally important, then, for employers to ensure that workers have proper access to evidence-based mental health care.[11]

There is certainly nothing inherently wrong with providing access to individualized programs and initiatives—and encouraging them. But we need to move this discussion forward in order to more seriously look at how work is managed and organized. One issue with a number of wellness initiatives is that, although there may be good evidence that things like exercise are good for people's wellbeing, when companies provide these programs to their employees, it is usually those who need it the least who take up the opportunity. Using a randomized controlled trial, for example, researchers at the University of Chicago found that when a wellness program was introduced, there was no overall effect on any of the key wellbeing or productivity metrics.[12] It turns out the ones who used the free gym membership, among other things, were those who already regularly went to the gym. The ones who stood to benefit the most did not take advantage.[13]

Any attempts to improve wellbeing directly through wellness programs require careful attention in terms of design and implementation if they are to be successful overall in reaching their goals. Ultimately, we believe that more can be achieved by also looking to the drivers of workplace wellbeing and seeking to address some of the more structural causes of poor wellbeing outcomes.

This is not easy, of course. It would be much more preferable as a manager to be able to continue business as usual and offer a short workshop to solve all of the issues surrounding an unhappy, unsatisfied, stressed-out workforce. But we need to think much more holistically about how we design jobs, how we organize work, how we interact with and give voice to labor, and how, ultimately, we manage the people who do it.

Pathways to Performance

Part III of the book moves from trying to understand the reasons lying behind differences in wellbeing to trying to understand the downstream consequences. In chapter 8, we look at the links between various aspects of wellbeing and productivity before looking at retention and recruitment in chapter 9. We call these pathways to performance the three Rs: raise productivity, recruit talent, and retain talent.

In each case, we survey the evidence and show, using data from large companies such as British Telecom and Indeed, that happier workforces are more productive, suffer less turnover, and find it easier to recruit talent.[14] Overall, we demonstrate that raising employee wellbeing can improve each one of these pathways to performance. But while the impact of wellbeing on productivity, recruitment, and retention is clear, these channels will, of course, work on somewhat different time horizons. The time it takes for these improvements to translate into tangible benefits for the company's bottom line is likely to vary across each of the productivity, recruitment, and retention channels.

This set of issues is often referred to collectively as the "business case" for workplace wellbeing. If we are being perfectly honest, we do not believe there is really a need for one. After all, there is a whole range of very good reasons for why we should care about the wellbeing of workers, and we have each argued elsewhere that wellbeing ought to be seen as a key societal outcome.[15] There is, in other words, already a solid human case for workplace wellbeing. But we nevertheless show there is a strong business case for raising workplace wellbeing.

The Business Case for Wellbeing

Showing that happier workers are more productive or that higher levels of satisfaction reduce turnover provides some initial evidence that there is a business case. But it omits the obvious and hugely important issue of costs. The extent to which intervening to improve workplace wellbeing is likely to be worthwhile depends on how difficult and costly it is to improve it.

Ultimately, to take the issue of costs seriously, it is important to consider performance at the company level. In chapter 10, we look at the best evidence from this "macro" line of work, including some of our own, and also leverage the unprecedented scope of the Indeed data on workplace wellbeing and link it to key firm performance outcomes over time—such as profitability and firm value. With data on over two thousand publicly traded firms in the United States, figure 1-7 shows a strong positive relationship between workplace wellbeing and firm performance.[16] We also find that there is an investment case. Simulating an investment strategy where we build portfolios of stocks based on the workplace wellbeing scores of companies, we find initial evidence of abnormal returns—that is, of beating the market when investing in firms with higher workplace wellbeing.

FIGURE 1-7

Company-Level Wellbeing Contributes to Firm Performance

Firm profitability and firm value by level of company wellbeing (on a 1–5 scale)

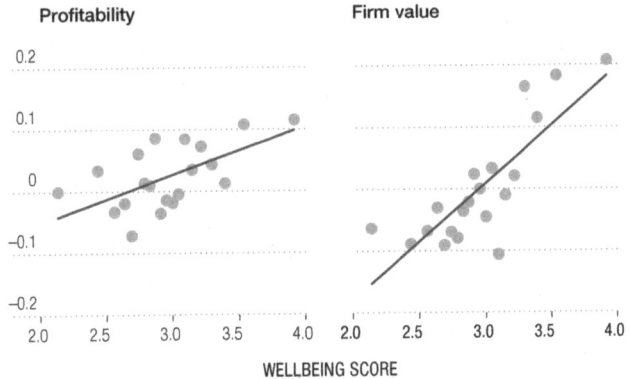

Note: N = 5,573. Both firm outcomes are standardized to have a mean of 0 and standard deviation of 1. Profitability is measured as return on assets (ROA); firm value is measured as Tobin's q. Annual analysis using data from 2020–2023. Wellbeing is the average of company happiness, job satisfaction, purpose, and (reverse-coded) stress. Binned scatterplots are shown, with controls included in each regression for firm size (number of employees), logged assets in the previous year, time-fixed effects, and industry-fixed effects. Source: Indeed and Compustat; Jan-Emmanuel De Neve, Micah Kaats, and George Ward, "Workplace Wellbeing and Firm Performance," University of Oxford Wellbeing Research Centre Working Paper 2304, 2024.

A Future of Work That Works for Wellbeing

In the final part of the book, we discuss the future of the work—including the extent to which automation is likely to have an impact on various aspects of wellbeing. Predicting the future is a decidedly foolhardy task, and doing so in the case of the world of work is fraught with difficulty.

Much of the discussion surrounding automation focuses on the *quantity* of jobs. Will AI take all the jobs? Will it be the end of work? We argue in chapter 11 that this debate is somewhat of a red herring. We instead discuss what automation is likely to do to the *quality* of jobs. Rather than predict what is going to happen, we structure our discussion around the drivers of workplace wellbeing and how they relate to various aspects of automation.

Some types of automation could worsen workplace wellbeing, for example, by stripping out all of the social interaction and the tasks that bring us purpose, lowering wages, and so on. But there are also potential opportunities, to the extent that particularly unpleasant tasks can be automated, leaving more time for workers to spend on more enjoyable or meaningful tasks. Equally, new technologies—including robotics as well as artificial intelligence—have the potential to augment rather than replace some tasks.

Technology is not deterministic. As we will see in chapter 12, we as a society stand at a crossroads and can direct how we develop new technologies and what they are designed to optimize—as well as how managers and firms choose to adopt them and for what. Will technology be a complement to workers, helping to improve their jobs and lives, or rather a complement to capital and used in ways that take the humanity out of work? Left to their own devices, technologists are unlikely to try to maximize worker wellbeing as a key objective. Ultimately, we argue that it is important for a range of stakeholders, including workers and their representatives, to participate in important decisions about the design and implementation of technology.

The world is moving in the direction of wellbeing. Governments worldwide have begun to see subjective wellbeing as a key societal measure of success and performance. Improving how we feel at and about work is by far the most impactful way to improve societal wellbeing, given its importance in our lives and the time we spend at work.

Firms are increasingly recognizing the potential benefits of workplace wellbeing—or, at least, the disastrous downsides to persistently having a miserable workforce. Workers' expectations are changing, while information about what it is like to work at different companies is becoming ever more readily available to people as they decide where and for whom to work. Leaders, both in government and in firms, should take note. Improving workplace wellbeing will need purposeful action; it will not happen by accident. But we know now more than ever about how to improve it, and we know that it can be a win-win.

Part One

DEFINING AND MEASURING WORKPLACE WELLBEING

Chapter 2

What Workplace Wellbeing Is and Is Not

W orkplace wellbeing has long been a topic of interest, in both the academic and business worlds. Major news outlets including *Forbes*, the *Wall Street Journal*, the *Financial Times*, CNN, and *Harvard Business Review*, as well as high-powered consultancies including McKinsey and Deloitte, have all begun to focus increasingly on wellbeing at work.[1]

How people think about and feel at work is hugely important in its own right, but—as we will see later in this book—it also significantly shapes organizational performance and success. It is no surprise then that managers and executives are taking note. Yet, despite this growing interest, it is often widely misunderstood.

Confusion Surrounding Work Wellbeing

Harvard Business Review Analytic Services, with input from us and our colleagues at Indeed, examined more deeply how business leaders currently think about the topic of workplace wellbeing.[2] Managers agree that wellbeing at work is important. In the survey of 1,073 executives and managers in the United States, 87 percent believed that improving workplace wellbeing could give companies a competitive advantage. And similar proportions agreed that happier places to work have better productivity, recruitment, and retention.

But, despite all this, only 19 percent of managers and executives reported having an actual strategy in place to improve workplace wellbeing in their organizations. There are at least two ways of interpreting this disconnect. The first is that, despite paying lip service to the benefits of wellbeing at work, business leaders are unconvinced of its potential benefits. Part III of this book will demonstrate that this belief is misguided. But there is also a second potential reason, which we think may be even more plausible. Managers may be convinced of the importance of employee wellbeing but are confused by the proliferation of different definitions and measurement scales and aren't sure how to improve it, especially in a cost-effective way. Even for those with research backgrounds and time on their hands, sorting out smoke from fire is not always straightforward.

Part of the problem is that people use the terms "workplace wellbeing" (or "workplace happiness") in many different ways. In our discussions with managers and executives, we have come across many different viewpoints. Some managers who come to us essentially conflate the concept of wellbeing with wages and are typically keen to emphasize that their organizations pay employees more than the market rate. As we will see later, wages are indeed an important driver of workplace wellbeing, especially at the bottom of the pay scale, but it is a mistake to assume simply that high-paying jobs are good jobs and that the people doing them must be experiencing high levels of wellbeing. Or that raising wages will solve workplace unhappiness.

Another group of managers is perhaps more common. They are typically much more motivated, interested in, and protective of the wellbeing of their workers. In their zeal to do so, however, they go beyond the wage approach—broadening it, but in doing so, adding confusion and undermining the conceptual clarity they need to be able to act. These managers think of workplace wellbeing as an amalgamation of various positive attributes of a job, which can add up to a long list of variables including flexibility, pay, belonging, support, satisfaction, working hours, psychological safety, purpose, and inclusion, among others. In this list approach, they have often sought to measure all these things in their organization—which is great—but they then often sum them all up into an index and call that wellbeing (or engagement or something similar). It is thus a list of good things about a workplace or a job. But who decides what to put on that list? And how?

What's more, it is unclear if one should take a simple average or give more weight to certain aspects compared to others. This list approach suffers from the arbitrary nature of what is considered and how the variables might be interrelated. We have also found that it does not enable the kind of discussions that are really needed. In most instances, this approach leads senior executives to have unstructured discussions about indicators they have cherry-picked from across the dashboard. These conversations do not lead to a holistic understanding of whether workplace wellbeing across the organization has in fact improved or not—or what may explain it.

For example, over the past period, employees may have appreciated the improvements made in terms of flexibility, but at the same time their sense of belonging may have gone down, which prompts the question what the net impact on workplace wellbeing may have been. The list approach does not normally have an answer for that. Nor do these discussions based on a long list of items allow for an understanding of the relative importance of what may be driving a general change in workplace wellbeing.

A Scientific Approach

So a list approach lacks the conceptual clarity to figure out the most effective ways to intervene and improve workplace wellbeing. But collecting data on the kinds of things typically included in such lists is nevertheless critically important. And with a small but important conceptual tweak, we can get more clarity on the issue.

The key is to separate workplace wellbeing as a clear and well-defined concept on the one hand from the *drivers* of workplace wellbeing on the other. Here, we consider workplace wellbeing as an outcome variable, determined at least in part by the drivers. As we will discuss in more detail, we are certainly not saying that things like pay, hours, belonging, inclusion, and so on are not important. Far from it. But by seeing them as drivers, we are able to think more systematically about how each contributes, in relative terms, to people's overall sense of workplace wellbeing. This is crucial for managers when thinking about how to improve workplace wellbeing, particularly in the face of budget constraints.

For anyone who has been taught economics, mathematics, or statistics, this more structured approach will come naturally, since any equation necessarily has to have a dependent variable (Y) on the left-hand side of the equation and then a set of independent variables (X_1, X_2, X_3, and so on) on the right-hand side that help explain variation in Y. What we have called a driver analysis aims to uncover the relative importance of each of the Xs in explaining workplace wellbeing.

A scientific approach to workplace wellbeing requires a clear outcome measure that can be optimized—something that those in business might call a key performance indicator. We argue strongly that workplace wellbeing is such an indicator for any organization. One of our most important contributions to the Indeed data collection—and the way job seekers now see the measures on the platform—has been to more clearly delineate between workplace wellbeing and its drivers.

At this stage, a scientific approach to workplace wellbeing relies heavily on getting the definition right. We propose a definition of workplace wellbeing that we think is as simple and tractable as possible. We base our approach on the growing science of subjective wellbeing (often referred to as SWB) more broadly. Only after we are clear about what workplace wellbeing is can we move to the practical issues of how to measure and improve it.

The Science of Subjective Wellbeing

We take as our starting point the maturing science of subjective wellbeing, which has grown rapidly over the past few decades across psychology, economics, sociology, management, and beyond. Academics and the public in general often refer to subjective wellbeing somewhat more loosely as "happiness." But more correctly, subjective wellbeing refers to a more multifaceted concept that includes happiness but goes beyond it and captures how we, as individuals and communities, are doing and, in turn, how that makes us feel about our lives.

Here, an eccentric psychologist from rural California enters the picture. Growing up on a farm with working parents, Ed Diener was known to get himself into considerable trouble. By the time he was ten years old, he had built a flamethrower and also taught himself to drive. At twelve, he was spending afternoons reading Tycho Brahe, a Danish astronomer, and developing plans to create a genetically modified animal combining the intelligence of a monkey and the loyalty of a dog. Fortunately, by the time he arrived at the University of Washington to begin his graduate studies, he had given up his ambitions in genetic biology. Instead, he set his sights on human psychology. When it came time to write his dissertation, Diener set out to study the happiness of farmworkers, but his adviser refused to approve the study: "I already know the answer," he opined. "Farm workers cannot be happy." Disheartened, the young psychologist decided to write a paper on conformity instead.[3]

Diener completed his dissertation in 1974, but not until years later—after receiving tenure at the University of Illinois and spending a year on sabbatical in the Caribbean—did he return to the subject of happiness, publishing his first conceptual analysis on what he termed "subjective wellbeing." In the following years, Diener did more than perhaps anyone else to consolidate, conceptualize, and advance the study of human happiness that emerged from the social indicators movement in the 1960s. Many of the concepts he pioneered remain central to how empirical wellbeing researchers conduct their work today. Throughout this book, we too will rely heavily on his concepts.

This may be an appropriate place to clarify terminology.[4] Wellbeing is an overall term for the different valuations people make regarding their lives, the events happening to them, their bodies and minds, and the circumstances in which they live. In this book, we use it to refer to all of the various types of evaluations, both positive and negative, that people make of their lives. These include reflective cognitive evaluations, such as life satisfaction, interest and engagement, affective reactions to life events, such as joy and sadness, and eudaimonic measures, such as purpose and meaning.[5]

Evaluative wellbeing refers to global assessments that people make about their lives as a whole. The most commonly used measure of evaluative wellbeing is life satisfaction. The Cantril Ladder—which asks respondents to imagine life as a ladder with ten steps, the bottom rung representing the worst possible life and the top rung representing the best possible life, and report where on the ladder they feel they currently stand—is a roughly analogous measure of life satisfaction and thus also belongs in the category of evaluative wellbeing. Answers to these kinds of questions represent broad reflective evaluations of life circumstances. They are therefore considered to be unique and distinct from more ongoing assessments of wellbeing, such as positive and negative affect.

Affective wellbeing refers to how people feel, how they experience life on a day-to-day basis. Positive affect denotes pleasant moods and emotions, such as joy. Major categories of positive or pleasant emotions include those of low arousal (e.g., contentment), moderate arousal (e.g., pleasure), and high arousal (e.g., euphoria). They include positive reactions to others (e.g., affection), positive reactions to activities (e.g., interest and engagement), and general positive moods. In the academic literature, "happiness" is itself generally considered to be contained within the broader category of positive affect. When we use the term throughout this book, we also consider it an indicator of affective wellbeing.

Negative affect includes moods and emotions that are unpleasant. Major forms of negative or unpleasant reactions include anger, sadness, anxiety and worry, stress, frustration, guilt and shame, and envy. Importantly, positive and negative affect are generally not thought to exist on a continuum. While both domains are often related, we can, for example, feel stressed and excited simultaneously. The experience of one does not preclude the experience of the other.

Eudaimonic wellbeing refers to feelings of purpose or meaningfulness. The term itself stems loosely from Aristotle's conception of living well or flourishing—though the modern usage of the term in psychology and economics has strayed somewhat from Aristotle's thinking—which he associated with performing virtuous activities that provide us with meaning and purpose. Eudaimonic measures of wellbeing are again typically thought of as distinct from other dimensions. It is possible to find meaning in daily activities without, for example, being satisfied with life overall, or feeling particularly joyful or sad.

Back at the University of Illinois, and armed with this conceptual toolkit, Diener went on to publish more than five hundred papers and books on all manner of topics related to human wellbeing until his death in 2021. His work laid the foundation for much subsequent research on the topic, amassing more than 200,000 individual citations in the process. Since the 1980s, an ever-increasing contingent of economists, psychologists, management scholars, and other social scientists have also joined in to contribute to the ongoing and ever-growing empirical study of human wellbeing. The field today encompasses an array of subfields looking at relationships between wellbeing and income, culture, political attitudes, voting behavior, migration, conflict, crime, academic performance, mental health, physical health—and, most importantly for us, work.

A Working Definition of Workplace Wellbeing

With this extensive existing body of research on subjective wellbeing in mind, we can turn our attention more clearly to the workplace. One of our main contentions here, as we have argued at more length elsewhere, is that while there can be many ways to conceptualize workplace wellbeing, there is no need to reinvent the wheel.[6] It is far more straightforward to think of the workplace as a domain of subjective wellbeing—and to map the main aspects of that body of work to the workplace setting. This has the benefit of conceptual clarity and also means that we can learn from the decades of research that have demonstrated the ways in which it can be measured in valid and reliable ways.

Workplace wellbeing is how we feel at work and about our work. In this way, workplace wellbeing has three main dimensions (see table 2-1). Mapping from the general literature on wellbeing, these dimensions are (1) job

TABLE 2-1

Mapping Subjective Wellbeing to Workplace Wellbeing

Subjective wellbeing	Workplace wellbeing
Evaluative	Job satisfaction
Affective	Emotional experience of work
Eudaimonia	Work purpose and meaning

satisfaction, (2) the emotional experience of work, and (3) work purpose and meaning.

None of the three aspects of workplace wellbeing that we identify is new. Our aim is not to open up a whole new field of scientific inquiry or a school of thought; there are already far too many. Rather, our main aim here is to bring some conceptual clarity to the notion of workplace wellbeing and in doing so, to build on and learn from the extensive existing bodies of research on things like job satisfaction, affect and emotions in the workplace, as well as purpose and meaning. By bringing these topics together under the umbrella of workplace wellbeing, our aim here is to simplify the conceptual terrain.

Job Satisfaction

Scholars from a range of fields including organizational psychology, industrial relations, economics, sociology, management, and elsewhere have studied job satisfaction for many decades. There have by now been multiple generations of scholarship on job satisfaction as an overall concept, including both theoretical and empirical work.[7] Just as "happiness" is often used as a catchall term for subjective wellbeing (despite it actually being one affective component of the overall concept), job satisfaction has come to mean many different things. Indeed, some variously see it as having a range of components—including evaluative, affective, behavioral, and attitudinal ones.

Given this, a range of multi-item scales have been proposed over the years to measure job satisfaction. But the scales frequently attempt to gauge a much broader concept. We argue here instead that job satisfaction should be regarded more narrowly as someone's evaluative, overall assessment of their job. It is an overarching judgment, all things considered, about how things are going with the person's job.

Job satisfaction is how we think about our jobs. How we feel about them, not how we actually feel while working. It is, in this way, a cognitive aspect of workplace wellbeing. It is not related to a particular day or moment, but is rather a more steady, slow-moving variable that changes over time in a job or as we change between jobs and workplaces.

Emotional Experience of Work

Much of the research on workplace wellbeing throughout the twentieth century, as we discussed, focused on job satisfaction. A more recent turn in the literature has occurred in the past couple of decades, however. A greater level of attention is now rightly being paid not only to how we feel about our jobs but also to how we feel while we are doing them.[8]

Affective workplace wellbeing can be split into negative and positive elements. The two are not simple inverses of each other—they do not exist on one continuum. Positive affect at work refers to the positive emotions that people experience while at work, including happiness, enjoyment, and so on. As we will see later, much of this literature has focused on trying to understand the ways in which emotions like happiness shape workplace outcomes of various types, including productivity and creativity.[9]

Negative affect, on the other hand, refers to the negative emotions that people feel while at work, including anger, worry, anxiety, stress, and others. We will spend more time in this book on the sometimes-thorny issue of perceived stress than on the other negative emotions, but all negative affect is relevant to workplace wellbeing. Negative affect at work goes beyond stress, and those looking to understand the full picture of workplace wellbeing should also consider the full range of negative emotional experiences.

Work Meaning and Purpose

There is growing literature across multiple academic disciplines dedicated to the important topic of purpose and meaning at work.[10] An even longer and larger history of thought, dating back thousands of years, has focused on the causes and consequences of meaning in life more generally.[11]

In recent years, though, both academic and popular discussions have addressed the ever-popular idea of corporate purpose. This is often tricky to define exactly, but it usually refers to a company's attempts to make an impact in the world, beyond just making profit. While such efforts have been shown to be important for a range of firm-level outcomes, what we have in mind here is rather the extent to which employees themselves experience the work they do as being meaningful or purposeful.[12]

A long line of research has sought to conceptualize what meaning and purpose at work is, but most often falls into the trap of defining it based on its determinants—for example, by suggesting that purposeful work is that which has a large amount of autonomy. We see it more straightforwardly as a subjective feeling or assessment of how purposeful or meaningful our work is. After all, who better to tell us about how meaningful work feels than the workers themselves, who go to work every day and do the job.

In one sense, having a strong feeling of purpose typically means we feel that our work is contributing to society and improving the lives of others. Having a low sense of purpose means we feel our work is doing very little to make an impact or is perhaps even doing so negatively. In another important sense, however, we can also derive meaningfulness from activities regardless of their social impact. It could come from mastering a skill, or engaging in creative processes, or solving challenging problems. For example, an artist might find deep personal satisfaction in creating art, even if it doesn't reach a wide audience. Similarly, a software developer might find meaningfulness in coding and creating elegant solutions to complex problems, independent of the broader impact.[13] The question of what sort of jobs and work arrangements foster such feelings is a vital question and one that we will explore throughout the book.

Measurement of Workplace Wellbeing

So workplace wellbeing is not a vague or nebulous concept. Still, though, can it actually be measured? If not, it is not likely to be very useful to anyone beyond academic thinkers who like to argue with each other over small points of theory.

One key benefit of basing our definition of workplace wellbeing on subjective wellbeing is that there is, by now, decades of research on the ways in which it can be measured in valid and reliable ways. Indeed, the Organisation for Economic Co-operation and Development (OECD)— which has done a great deal to popularize wellbeing in policy circles to the extent that many countries around the world now collect official national wellbeing statistics to go along with more standard economic indicators like GDP—has noted in the past that "perhaps *because* of concerns about their use, quite a lot is known about how subjective well-being measures behave under different measurement conditions."[14] Not only this, but there are also multiple established lines of research, as we've noted, on various relevant concepts like meaning, purpose, and emotions at work. These are too often siloed from each other, and we prefer to see them brought together under the collective umbrella of workplace wellbeing.

The most obvious and frequently used way to measure workplace wellbeing is through surveys.[15] After all, how better to measure how people feel at work and about their work than asking them? Experts can come up with contextual data and various reasons to believe someone might be happy at work but, ultimately, the most feasible way to do it is by asking the relevant people directly.

Surveys are not the only way, however, and recent research has focused on the use of text-based analysis to codify things like tweets or emails—for example, to learn more about their emotional content through the use of natural language processing techniques.[16] Innovation will surely continue into the future, but for now we offer a simple survey module designed to measure the key aspects of workplace wellbeing in a succinct way.

A Survey Module for Workplace Wellbeing

In table 2-2, there are four questions that we have developed and can be added to standard workplace surveys.[17] Of course, you could expand this survey module and should certainly feel free to do so, particularly when broadening the scope of emotional experiences. But time and space are typically tight, and it is important to make this survey usable as widely as possible. Our goal is to be succinct but also comprehensive, in order to maximize the chances that these questions will be adopted more broadly.

We have sought to follow the best practices of measurement literature on subjective wellbeing more generally and also used, where possible, standard wording that is typical to the workplace literature. Nothing here is revolutionary. The main idea is to see these dimensions—evaluative, affective, eudaimonic—as coming together to constitute workplace wellbeing. In fact, keen readers of wellbeing science may have recognized that our workplace wellbeing survey module mirrors the four-item survey module used by the UK Office for National Statistics to measure general (rather than workplace-specific) wellbeing in the population.

Many companies already conduct regular surveys of their workers, and many readers will have answered such a survey. These often already ask about things like job satisfaction and engagement. Therefore, adding the full set to any such survey should not be a huge step. As we pointed out, it would of course be of great interest and benefit to go into more depth, if

TABLE 2-2

A Survey Module for Workplace Wellbeing

For each of these questions please give an answer on a scale from 0–10, where 0 is "not at all" and 10 is "completely"	QUESTION	ANSWER
	Overall, how satisfied are you with your job?	
	Overall, how purposeful and meaningful do you find your work?	
	How happy did you feel while at work during the past week?	
	How stressed did you feel while at work during the past week?	

possible, but an important goal here is to ensure that these measures are consistent and comparable across workers and companies.

Ultimately, one of our hopes is to have a statistic that is routinely reported in quarterly or annual accounts. In this direction, we collaborated with S&P Global, a major ratings company, which has begun to include workplace wellbeing as a key item in its Corporate Sustainability Assessment (CSA). What's more, by explicitly including our evaluative, affective, and eudaimonic survey items, we hope that these measures will now be more widely collected on a basis that can be meaningfully compared across companies and inform their sustainability ratings.

With all of this in mind, if you are to take nothing else away from this chapter, let it be the importance of measuring and monitoring employee wellbeing. The four questions we highlight in table 2-2 are straightforward to understand, capture the most important distinct dimensions of workplace wellbeing, have been demonstrated as reliable and valid indicators across a wide variety of contexts, and are virtually costless to implement in surveys that many companies already regularly distribute and collect.

Importance of Distinguishing Inputs from Outputs

When considered against other approaches to workplace wellbeing, ours is direct and subjective. It is an approach to workplace wellbeing that we see as being particularly democratic. It asks workers how they feel at work and about their work. After all, who else would be better positioned to judge their wellbeing? There is sometimes a taboo surrounding subjective measures, and people often ask us if we can come up with some sort of proxy for workplace wellbeing that is objective in nature. This is appealing in many ways, but it is also misguided in others. Wellbeing is an inherently subjective concept: it is how we are thinking and feeling about our jobs.

A key benefit of the subjective workplace wellbeing approach is that it is clear about what is an input and what is an output, what is a driver and what is an outcome. The list approach we discussed often conflates outcomes with drivers, leading to a potentially confusing and less practical understanding of wellbeing in the workplace.

Empirical measures that assess the evaluative, affective, and eudaimonic dimensions of wellbeing can provide an overall picture of workplace wellbeing, but they do not necessarily tell us *why* we feel a certain way or what the effects of that feeling are likely to be. We want to be perfectly clear here—when we say that workplace wellbeing is not simply an amalgamation of things like hours, wages, flexibility, belonging, inclusion, voice, and so on, we most certainly do not mean that these things are unimportant or should not be studied.

On the contrary, many of these aspects of the workplace and jobs are hugely important. But they are better seen as drivers of workplace wellbeing, rather than as wellbeing itself. As we will discuss in more detail in part II, managers and executives need to think about the relative importance of these factors in order to decide where to allocate scarce resources. The subjective wellbeing approach provides a clear framework in which to think about such choices. But without a separation of drivers and outcomes, it is impossible to think about which are more important than others.

Data, Data, Data

In addition to our aim to provide a clear definition and model of workplace wellbeing, another major purpose of this book is to bring data to bear on questions surrounding workplace wellbeing. To that end, our goal is to scour the world for the best available data on workplace wellbeing, its drivers, and its effects. And where it doesn't exist, to collect it. Only by amassing a body of evidence on the subject can we collectively start to think about improving people's working lives in a systematic and successful way.

We will have more to say on each of the data sets we use. But as a general principle, we make use of standard surveys such as the Gallup World Poll we discussed in the introduction, as well as others like the International Social Survey Program, European Social Survey, and the World Values Survey. Such data collection efforts typically aim to survey a large, nationally representative sample each year and ask questions on a range of topics including things to do with the workplace.

We also use so-called household panel data sets where respondents typically fill in a survey once a year over a long period, so that we can track key concepts like job satisfaction as they vary over time. While the major national surveys find a new, randomly selected sample each year, in this case we can follow the same people as their lives develop over the years and as they switch between employment statuses, careers, and jobs.

To add to this, we also use data from within firms. For example, we have ourselves gone into companies and administered surveys on workplace wellbeing, some of which we have been able to analyze anonymously for empirical academic research. Moreover, in chapter 10 we report on analyses in partnership with Gallup using its anonymized client database amassed over years of global consulting services. Finally, we use a data set collected together with Indeed, which has been amassed through the power of crowdsourcing (see figure 2-1).

FIGURE 2-1

A Massive Online Survey of Workplace Wellbeing

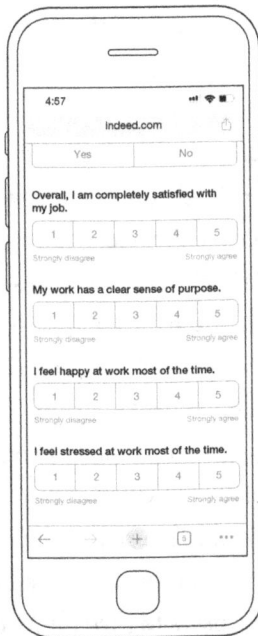

Source: Screenshot of employee wellbeing survey on the Indeed platform.

Big Data: Crowdsourced Workplace Wellbeing Data

Indeed is the world's largest jobs platform, with hundreds of millions of users worldwide. It has at least two main functions. The first is most likely what comes to mind most easily when someone says the words "jobs website"—it hosts job advertisements. But an increasingly important secondary function is to collect and disseminate information. An ever-growing set of platforms has democratized information about the workplace. This began with Glassdoor asking about people's salaries but has since broadened a great deal. Now more than ever, information is able to flow from incumbent to prospective workers.

Indeed's platform already collected text-based reviews of companies, as well as star ratings similar to those you might leave as feedback on websites selling consumer goods. But an enterprising and forward-thinking team working at the company decided to try to measure workplace wellbeing more directly. Led very ably by Janeane Tolomeo—who was and remains a driving force behind the initiative—this team reached out to us following the introduction of our friend and colleague Sonja Lyubomirsky—and we were very excited by the possibility of collecting data on such a scale.[18]

By mid-2024, in partnership with Indeed, we had collected surveys from over 20 million workers worldwide on job satisfaction, purpose, stress, and happiness. Moreover, we have collected data on many of the drivers too. All of this is now shown on the company pages on the website, and interested readers can see how their current and former employers perform.

Of course, as with any crowdsourced data, there are both benefits and drawbacks. The benefit is scale. In no other way can we amass enough data so that we can compare tens of thousands of companies using data that is comparable. But the sample is, of course, not randomly selected. Some people may leave surveys when they are particularly happy or annoyed, for example. To some extent, this can be ameliorated by the company's give-to-get approach, which forces users to give information about their employers in order to be able to continue seeing everyone else's feedback on other companies. This way, it draws people into answering the survey who might not otherwise have done so.

Perhaps most importantly, we are using this data principally as a way to compare companies. Thus, any biases in terms of who answers would have to be different across different industries, occupations, and firms in order to diminish the soundness of any comparisons we make. It may be that unhappy workers at Walmart are more likely to respond, but if this is also true at Costco, then we can still compare the two quite reasonably. In each case, the "true" level of wellbeing might be higher than what is reported on average in our survey, but the data still provides an exciting worker's-eye view of the companies and an unprecedented look at how wellbeing differs across companies.

Finally, as we've noted, we also complement our findings using more traditional data sources, which can provide nationally representative data on a range of issues including workplace wellbeing. Moreover, we will discuss any potential issues surrounding selection biases among others as we move through the book.

A Data-Driven Approach to Workplace Wellbeing

Our goal, by turning not to anecdote or intuition but to the data itself, is to dispel several myths regarding happiness at work. In doing so, we aim to provide a stronger empirical foundation for discussions surrounding the topic moving forward. We draw on several large-scale data sources to do so. The aim is to shine floodlights on the landscape of employee wellbeing where others have been limited to looking with flashlights.

Chapter 3

The Importance of Work for Wellbeing

S ome communities grow around a lake, a church, or a hillside. Marienthal grew around a factory.[1] The industrialist Hermann Todesco first arrived in the region of Lower Austria in 1830 looking for a suitable location to build a flax mill. The setting was ideal. Marienthal was flat and surrounded by even terrain, enabling easy transportation to and from the neighboring city of Vienna. The Fischa River cutting through the landscape was temperate and didn't freeze in winter, making it an ideal power source. The first parts of the mill were constructed on its banks, along with several small houses for the workers who quickly flocked to the region in search of employment.

The factory expanded quickly. Before long, it had transformed into a sprawling industrial complex, employing hundreds of people working in cotton spinning, printmaking, bleaching, and administration. As the factory grew, so did the surrounding village. The roads were dotted with one-story family homes built alongside a plethora of shops, grocery stores, and markets. Despite turbulent times throughout the First World War and fall of the Habsburg Empire, business continued to boom. By 1929, employment at the factory was at its peak, and the town was flourishing.

The Great Depression and *Die Arbeitslosen von Marienthal*

Then came a global economic crisis. In the spring of 1929, the Austrian banking system collapsed, taking with it any businesses reliant on bank loans. Within a matter of months, the factory went bankrupt. In July, the spinning mills closed down. In August, the printing works followed suit. Then the bleaching plant in September. By winter, the looms had stopped, and the turbines had come to a halt. In February of 1930, demolition work began. Only a handful of workers were kept on staff to begin dismantling the plant. The rest lost their jobs. By 1931, only vestiges of the factory remained as piles of debris waiting to be removed.

This was a remarkable turn of events, though sadly not uncommon at the time. Throughout the 1920s, more than 20 million workers around the world lost their jobs—one-fourth of the world's workforce. The story of Marienthal itself may well have been lost to history if not for a small group of researchers from the University of Vienna, including Paul Lazarsfeld and Marie Jahoda (then husband and wife) as well as Hans Zeisel. Recognizing the potential research significance of such a dramatic case study, they arrived in the town in the winter of 1931. Over a period of six months, the researchers—aided by Lotte Schenk-Danzinger—collected data and pored over family histories, time sheets, budgetary assessments, school essays, library records, official statistics, observational accounts, and personal reports from the 1,486 residents still living there. The resulting sixty-six pounds of collected material formed the basis for one of the major early works of modern empirical sociology, which continues to be influential to this day.

Beyond a Wage

You might reasonably expect the dominant effect of mass unemployment to have been financial hardship. This was, indeed, an important part of the story. Almost everyone in the town was shopping, eating, and earning less than they had when the factory was open. A handful of residents even slipped into abject poverty. But, almost immediately, it became clear that whatever ailed the community extended a long way beyond a lack of money. At the time, Austria provided relatively generous levels of unemployment insurance. In Marienthal, the local industrial commission replaced up to 80 percent of factory workers' wages for two to five years after termination.

Residents of the town had more free time than ever, yet increasingly found nothing to fill it with. In her published report on the study, Marie Jahoda documented numerous examples of community life reduced to a state of wistful stillness. The park, once a source of local pride, became an overgrown wilderness. The footpaths no longer staged scenes of romantic strolls or public debates. Almost everyone in town had time to pull the weeds or trim the grass, but no one did. Library records also showed substantial declines in activity. From 1929 to 1931, the number of book loans had dropped by 49 percent, even as borrowing fees were reduced to zero. Local political organizations also shed members at rates of 33 to 62 percent, despite suspending membership fees. Subscriptions to political newspapers and quarterlies declined by more than 60 percent. The local theater, once home to regular productions and a wellspring of community life, became barren and unoccupied.

The stark results of the Marienthal study appeared to demonstrate that employment conferred crucially important benefits to individuals and communities beyond income. Summing up the implications of her research, Jahoda later wrote: "Employment imposes a time structure on the waking day, implies regularly shared experiences and contacts with people outside the nuclear family, links individuals to goals and purposes that transcend their own, enforces activity, and defines aspects of personal status and identity."[2] So, beyond the benefits of income, work confers routine, social ties, and social identity and, as we will see, these nonpecuniary attributes of work end up explaining more than half of the positive effect that employment has on wellbeing in more up-to-date data.[3]

Jahoda and her team published the initial results of their research in 1933. Yet by then, the situation in Europe had changed dramatically. Amid the rise of fascism in Europe and the scourge of rampant book burnings, the German publisher of the Marienthal study left the names of the Jewish authors off the book cover. As for the authors themselves, Lazarsfeld and Jahoda divorced and went their separate ways.[4]

Work and Its Role in Economic Life

The key finding of the Marienthal study stood as a counterpoint to some of the prevailing ideas about work and wellbeing at the time. In mainstream economics, work was increasingly conceptualized as akin to a disutility—a sacrifice of leisure in exchange for income. Adam Smith famously characterized labor as "toil and trouble" in *The Wealth of Nations*.[5] Throughout the nineteenth century, other classical economists extended Smith's interpretation of work as a disutility and further explored the trade-off between labor and leisure—typically emphasizing the unpleasantness of labor and the compensatory role of wages. Given this rather dismal interpretation of work, it was typically argued that no reasonable person would willingly choose to work if they had sufficient resources. Workers, it was often assumed, would happily shirk their duties in favor of leisure.[6]

Not all leading thinkers of the time subscribed to these ideas, of course. Karl Marx critiqued Adam Smith's understanding of work for leaving virtually no room for the value of creative expression. To Marx, the problem was alienation from work, not work itself. He argued that work, when properly oriented and understood, ought to be considered fundamental to the human condition.[7] Other economists, such as William Stanley Jevons and Alfred Marshall, also took issue with what they viewed as an oversimplified understanding of the value of labor. Jevons argued that the satisfaction or dissatisfaction that workers experienced from work could play a crucial role in determining the quality of their output and influence the relative prices of commodities in the marketplace. Marshall defended the central importance of workers' experiences, noting that work could be a source of great pleasure and satisfaction, and that people could be intrinsically motivated by the enjoyment of work itself.[8]

Nevertheless, this relatively small but vocal minority of scholars arguing for a positive, or at least potentially positive, interpretation of work was ultimately (and perhaps somewhat ironically) overshadowed by a group of Austrians. For them, the key economic problem was scarcity. With limited hours in the day, people were forced to decide how to allocate their time. Time spent performing one activity meant time taken away from doing something else. By implication, they argued that the value of any given activity could be defined in terms of the "opportunity cost" of not engaging in another activity.[9] By this account, the value of work could be determined by how much people were willing to sacrifice their leisure time to earn a given level of income—their "reservation wage."

The implications were profound. The Austrian economists rejected the notion that workplace experiences had anything to do with the supply of labor. They assumed that workers were entirely uninterested in the content of work itself, focusing only on the amount of time that work prevented them from engaging in leisure activities. As a result, wages were no longer interpreted to reflect the value of work itself, but rather the value of not working. Understanding the supply of labor meant understanding the price at which workers were willing to give up their leisure time. In a very literal sense, wages could be interpreted as the price of happiness lost.

This framework influenced the dominant understanding of labor supply throughout much of the twentieth century. Labor was considered simply another input to economic production alongside steel, aluminum, or horsepower.[10] However, institutional labor economists and early scholars of industrial relations strongly opposed this view. They pointed out that labor is inherently different from other economic inputs and that the employment relationship is a special form of economic transaction that requires more careful theorizing.[11] Figures such as John R. Commons were at the forefront of this movement and both industrial relations and institutional labor economics grew to become significant fields, with generations of researchers emphasizing the unique and complex nature of labor. They argued that economic behavior, including work, was shaped by social and legal institutions rather than just market forces.[12] Ultimately, this calls for a more nuanced understanding of work and its role in economic life.[13]

Employment Status and Subjective Wellbeing

In 2017, we were asked to write a chapter on the state of the academic literature regarding work and wellbeing for the *World Happiness Report*, a publication one of us (Jan) is an editor of and that readers may have come across for its well-known annual rankings of countries around the world by overall life satisfaction. The obvious place to start our research on the topic was the Gallup World Poll—arguably the most reputable data set on global wellbeing in existence today. As part of the survey, various wellbeing questions have been asked to over 2.5 million respondents in more than 160 countries worldwide since it began in 2006.

So, what does the data tell us about the relationship between work and wellbeing? The survey asks an evaluative wellbeing question (known as the Cantril Ladder), as well as the extent to which people feel that what they do in life is meaningful.[14] Moreover, it asks a series of questions about the different emotions people felt a lot of "yesterday"—including positive ones like happiness and enjoyment and negative ones like sadness, stress, and anger.

Figure 3-1 shows the breakdown of these wellbeing measures by employment status, using data from around 2.1 million people in 2009–2022, using data from 166 countries worldwide.[15] Across all components of wellbeing, people in work are much happier (using the term broadly) than those out of work. And of those not in work, consistently, across all of the measures, the unemployed rank the lowest—with large gaps evident.[16]

Self-employment is a less satisfying experience than working full-time for an employer, and one that entails the experience of more negative emotions. Readers who have worked for themselves may recognize such stress effects. But they experience the most meaning and purpose. This again underscores the need to look carefully at the full concept of wellbeing, including all of its important components.

Those who are out of the labor force—retirees, students, homemakers— are less happy than those in work full-time but fare a great deal better than the unemployed, who are miserable across the board. The extent to which part-time work is associated with wellbeing depends, perhaps unsurpris-

FIGURE 3-1

Employment Status and Wellbeing around the World

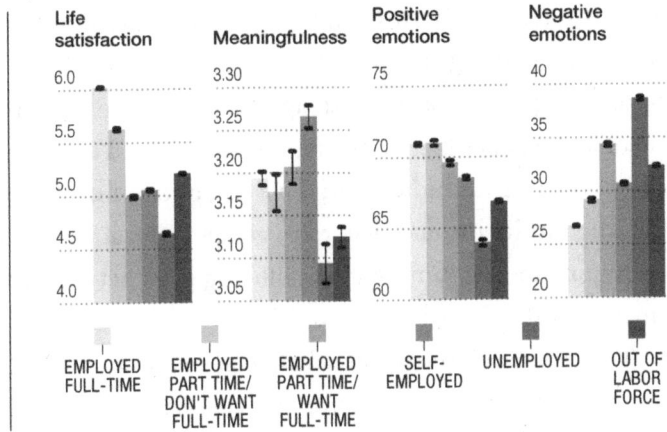

Average level
of subjective
wellbeing by
employment
status

Life
satisfaction

Meaningfulness

Positive
emotions

Negative
emotions

EMPLOYED FULL-TIME — EMPLOYED PART TIME/ DON'T WANT FULL-TIME — EMPLOYED PART TIME/ WANT FULL-TIME — SELF-EMPLOYED — UNEMPLOYED — OUT OF LABOR FORCE

Note: Survey carried out across 168 countries in 2009–2022. Individuals aged 21–64; N = 2,048,604.
Source: Gallup World Poll.

ingly, on whether the individual actually wants to work full-time or not. Are they happily working part-time (around 7 percent of the sample) or are they actually more properly termed underemployed (around 8 percent in our data)?

The Causal Effect of Unemployment

So far, these are raw differences. Quite reasonably, you may object that this omits a lot of detail. People are likely to vary in terms of a range of other relevant characteristics, including income, education, age, and so on (a problem of omitted variables). Moreover, you might think that people experiencing low levels of wellbeing may be more likely to become unemployed in the first place (a problem of reverse causality).

Economists came to the happiness party a little later than psychologists. The field of happiness economics grew largely out of labor economics in the 1990s, though earlier influential work by scholars—such as Richard

Easterlin on happiness and economic growth as well as Richard Freeman on the importance of job satisfaction—laid important groundwork.

Somewhat remarkably, when the first studies on the topic began to be published in the 1990s and early 2000s, by valued colleagues and mentors of ours such as Andrew Oswald, Andrew Clark, and Richard Layard, one of the rarest things in social science started happening. The same result began popping up again and again. The relationship between employment and wellbeing was strong, significant, and consistently in the same direction. These studies were able to control for a range of factors including family income, age, race, gender, education, among others—and continued to find remarkable wellbeing gaps between the employed and unemployed.[17]

To get even closer to causal effects, researchers have also considered so-called natural experiments. In this sense, they have often harked back to the original Marienthal study by considering the wellbeing of workers over time and exploiting factory and plant closures. Across these studies, affected workers report declines in life satisfaction of up to two points on a scale from zero to ten, a drop in wellbeing that has almost no match in any other domain of life, not even serious illness or the loss of a partner.[18] The consistency of these results has led many researchers to consider the negative impact of unemployment to be one of the most robust and reliable results to emerge from the empirical study of human happiness.[19]

(Non-)Adaptation to Unemployment

Crucially, this group of pioneering economists noticed that several household panel data sets had been asking wellbeing questions to the same people over time. The German Socio-Economic Panel, for example, began in 1984 and has since then interviewed and reinterviewed a large sample of households every year on a variety of topics. Fortunately for these researchers, they included a zero-to-ten scale of life satisfaction. Later on, the British Household Panel—now known as the Understanding Society Survey—added a similar question, while the Household, Income and

Labour Dynamics in Australia survey contributed even more data beginning in the early 2000s.

This data is longitudinal, which opens up a lot of empirical opportunities. No longer are we comparing between people, but rather we are now
comparing people's happiness as it develops over time, transitioning in and
out of different employment statuses. In figure 3-2, we go back to the
data from Germany and look at the effect of unemployment—accounting
for other factors that vary over time like household income—on life
satisfaction.[20]

There is a small amount of anticipation effects, lending partial support
to the idea that some of the overall differences can be attributed to reverse
causality. But the sharp decline on becoming unemployed is unmistakable.
Importantly, unlike many other life conditions and circumstances, unemployment can also be exceedingly difficult to adapt to. Once it has
fallen, typically by over a whole point on the scale, which is very large as
an effect size in the literature on wellbeing, it stays at this lower level.

FIGURE 3-2

People Do Not Adapt to Unemployment

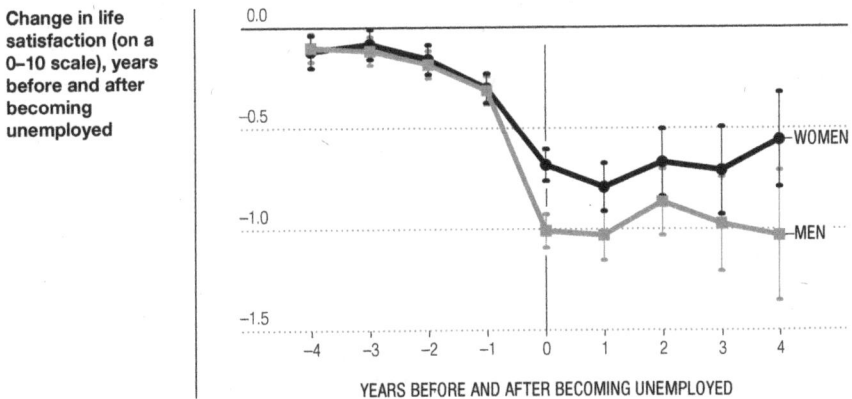

Change in life satisfaction (on a 0–10 scale), years before and after becoming unemployed

YEARS BEFORE AND AFTER BECOMING UNEMPLOYED

Note: Nationally representative survey of workers in Germany. N = 35,626 individuals.
Source: German Socio-Economic Panel (1984–2021); analysis updated from Andrew E. Clark et al.,
The Origins of Happiness (Princeton, NJ: Princeton University Press, 2018).

People do not adapt to unemployment in the way that they have been shown to do in a variety of academic studies to other life circumstances— including at least partial adaptation to events like marriage, divorce, and widowhood.[21]

This inability to adapt to unemployment has been observed in a number of related studies conducted in the United Kingdom, Russia, South Korea, Australia, and Switzerland.[22] In fact, once adaptation is accounted for, the overall effect of unemployment has been found to be greater in size than the effects of becoming divorced, widowed, or having children. For example, in one study of British adults, men who lost their jobs became anywhere between 0.5 and 1.5 points less satisfied with their lives on a scale from 0 to 10, and the effects got worse with time.[23] These dynamics are striking, but not uncommon in the literature. Taken together, they suggest that unemployment presents one of the most pernicious and permanent threats to wellbeing that we currently have evidence of.

Monetary and Nonmonetary Effects of Unemployment

So where does this leave us? We've seen that the unemployed report lower levels of wellbeing than the employed, and by considerable margins. The negative impacts of unemployment are also particularly pernicious and long-lasting. While the general direction of these relationships may not be surprising, their strength and significance do seem to be. Almost no other life circumstance or event seems to present a greater threat to our overall wellbeing than unemployment.

These results already give us some reason to doubt the classical economic understanding of labor. By conceptualizing the decision to work as a trade-off between income and leisure, maybe the unemployed choose not to work because they value their leisure time more than their employed counterparts. But if so, why should they be any less happy? One study in the United States surveyed more than six thousand employed and unemployed adults on a weekly basis.[24] Respondents were asked to report which activities they engaged in on a day-to-day basis, how much time they spent on each one, and the extent to which they enjoyed them. Despite having more time on their hands, the unemployed actually spent less time engaging in leisure activities. More striking still, even while engaging in the exact same activities—like watching television, reading a book, or shopping—the unemployed enjoyed them less. They consistently reported higher levels of sadness, pain, and fatigue. These results were later replicated in another study of German adults.[25] Once again, the unemployed enjoyed their leisure time considerably less than the employed, despite having more of it.

So, if a higher relative value of leisure can't explain the unemployment wellbeing gap, what does? At this point, we suspect many readers would point out the elephant in the room: money. Even in countries with considerable social safety nets and welfare programs, the unemployed generally earn less than working adults. And for better or worse, most of us live in societies that require income to live comfortably. Lower levels of income spell higher levels of insecurity. As a result, it would be reasonable to imagine that lost wages explain the substantial declines in wellbeing for those without work. In fact, they do not. Or at least not completely.

One strong indication that income cannot explain the wellbeing burden of unemployment is that we continue to find significantly negative effects of the latter even after controlling for the former. As a result, the resulting estimate can be interpreted as the impact of unemployment on life satisfaction, over and above what can be explained by declines in income. The fact that we continue to observe significant effects at all, even after controlling for lost wages, suggests that income is not the sole driver of wellbeing differences.

Another way of assessing the role that income plays in explaining gaps in wellbeing is to decompose the effect of unemployment into its constituent parts. The specifics of this approach can vary, but the overall aim is essentially to predict the decline in life satisfaction from unemployment that we might expect if income were all that mattered. In one of the first empirical studies on these dynamics, a team of researchers found that lost wages only explained 9 percent of the decline in wellbeing associated with unemployment for men and 27 percent for women.[26] Similar results were later obtained using large-scale data in the United States and United Kingdom.[27]

In one study using German data, the nonmonetary (or nonpecuniary) effects of unemployment were found to be twice as large as the monetary (pecuniary) effects on the wellbeing of affected workers.[28]

To help visualize these effects, in figure 3-3 we return to the German panel data, spanning over thirty years following thousands of people annually, and we plot the effects of unemployment on German workers. Here we find significant declines in life satisfaction for unemployed adults relative to their employed counterparts, roughly 1.5 points for men and 1.2 points for women on a scale from 1 to 10. Yet in this case, we can also empirically attribute differences in life satisfaction to differences in income between both groups.[29] In unemployment, lower levels of income do lead to lower levels of wellbeing, but it is by no means all that matters. Specifically, the effect of lost wages on life satisfaction amounts to 0.4 points, or roughly 30 percent of the total effect of unemployment. Taken together, all of this evidence indicates that losing a job decreases wellbeing to an even greater degree than can be explained by lost wages. On the other side of the coin, this would also seem to imply that the benefits of work appear to

FIGURE 3-3

Negative Effects of Unemployment Are Only Partly Driven by Loss of Income

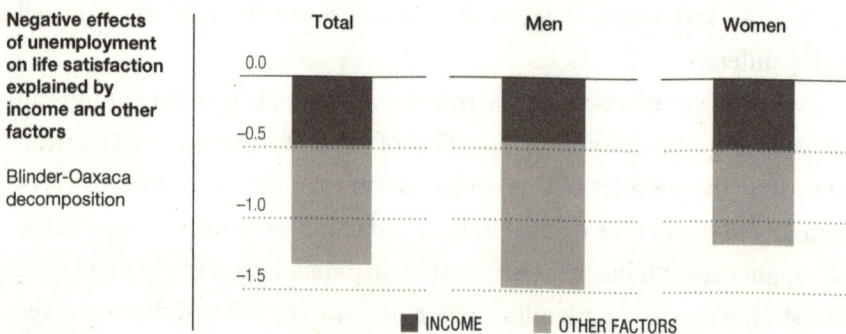

Negative effects of unemployment on life satisfaction explained by income and other factors

Blinder-Oaxaca decomposition

Total   Men   Women

INCOME   OTHER FACTORS

Note: Blinder-Oaxaca decomposition of outcome differentials for life satisfaction across unemployed and employed individuals, by (the natural logarithm of) income. N = 55,991 individuals, Obs = 344,873. Source: Panel data from the German Socio-Economic Panel (1984–2021).

extend far beyond financial gain. We suspect Marie Jahoda would be wholly unsurprised by this finding a century after she first wrote about Marienthal.

Broader Impacts of Unemployment

The negative effects of unemployment have even been found to spill over onto those who remain employed. Rising rates of job loss can signal to others that they may be next in line to lose their jobs. In our own study for the *World Happiness Report*, we found that rising unemployment levels in reference groups—for example, similar ages, genders, and country of residence—significantly lowered the life satisfaction of workers who remained employed.[30] A separate analysis in the United Kingdom and United States confirmed these results, and even purported to show that the negative spillover effects of unemployment on working adults were more severe than the effect on those who lost their job in the first place.[31]

Such are the consequences of job loss for individuals and societies. Unemployment not only threatens the wellbeing of those affected, but can contribute to wellbeing declines among family members, partners, peer groups, and communities. The deep and dynamic relationship between employment and wellbeing is clear in the data. This emerging body of empirical evidence is crucially important not only for researchers interested in the determinants of wellbeing, but also for executives, managers, and policy makers seeking to promote and sustain employee and societal welfare.

Aggregate levels of unemployment may also function as a social norm, to some extent. Interestingly, some of the evidence actually suggests that the effect of unemployment may be less severe if there is more of it around. In one seminal analysis by Andrew Clark, our friend and colleague and a professor at the Paris School of Economics, men who had recently lost their jobs in the United Kingdom reported smaller declines in life satisfaction if they lived in regions with higher levels of unemployment overall.[32] The effect of job loss was still negative and significant, just not quite as severe.

Other analyses have mostly pointed in the same direction. Attenuating effects of surrounding unemployment on job loss have been identified in Australia, South Africa, and Germany.[33] Researchers have often explained these results in terms of the reduced social stigma associated with job loss in more economically distressed environments. Workers who lose their jobs in these environments may be less likely to judge themselves too harshly or be judged too harshly by others. Nevertheless, the overall effects of unemployment are strongly negative regardless, and so we cannot take too much solace from such findings.

Returning to Marienthal

At this point, we come full circle back to Lower Austria and to the town of Marienthal. Two colleagues of ours at the University of Oxford—Lukas Lehner and Maximilian Kasy—began working together with local authorities to trial the effects of a jobs guarantee program.[34] This form of active labor market policy has often been discussed but rarely tested in a robust, experimental way.

The MAGMA job guarantee is a pilot program launched in the municipality that began in 2020.[35] The program provides a guaranteed job to residents who are long-term unemployed or who are at risk of long-term unemployment. These jobs are mostly in social enterprises or local government projects.

Working together with the municipality, Lehner and Kasy managed to persuade them to randomize access to the program, so it's possible to estimate the causal effect of bringing the unemployed of Marienthal back into work. This focus on the average effect of a policy program is quite a different approach from that of the original study ninety years earlier, which did not compare the unemployed to any sort of control group—instead seeking to describe and categorize the unemployed.

At the municipality level, the program almost eradicated long-term unemployment. And at the individual level, Lehner and Kasy found positive effects on the latent and manifest benefits of work, including measures of interactions with others, purpose and meaning, time structure, and social

FIGURE 3-4

A Jobs Guarantee Program in Marienthal Raised Wellbeing

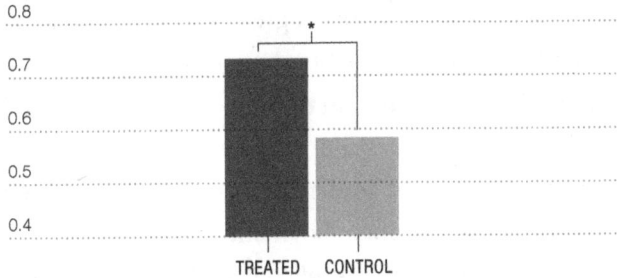

Subjective wellbeing (on a 0–1 scale) of people part of the jobs guarantee program (treated) or not (control)

*Difference is equal to 0.148 (p = 0.033).
Source: Maximilian Kasy and Lukas Lehner, "Employing the Unemployed of Marienthal: Evaluation of a Guaranteed Job Program," IZA Discussion Paper No. 16088, 2023.

recognition. Ultimately, as can be seen in figure 3-4, there was a strong positive effect on wellbeing.[36]

Active Labor Market Policies

The importance of employment for wellbeing and devastating consequences of unemployment confer a great responsibility on those with decision-making power to affect either (1) the dynamics of the labor market writ large, or (2) the employment status of an individual. One obvious lesson at the organizational level is for firms to minimize firing and layoffs, wherever possible. In countries with minimal employment protections, but even in countries with strong unemployment benefits, the negative impacts of unemployment are likely to be felt not only by those who lose their jobs, but also by those who remain at work.

In both small and large companies, the more workers lose their jobs, the more unhappy the remaining workforce is likely to become. As we will see later, this can in turn negatively impact company performance. Promoting and supporting worker wellbeing is therefore likely to be important not only from an ethical perspective, but also from a business perspective. As a result, human resource strategies that seek to minimize worker turnover have the potential to benefit companies and employees alike.

Yet in many cases, this is of course easier said than done. The vast majority of job losses occur in times of financial and economic crisis. As we noted at the outset, there is a great deal to be said about the role of the state and public policy in relation to subjective wellbeing—a topic we have explored elsewhere—and, in this book, we largely focus instead on the role of managers and firms.[37] But it is nevertheless worth noting briefly that in these environments, governments can and should step in to minimize the negative impact of unemployment.

One salient example is, of course, the recent worldwide pandemic. Given the global nature of the crisis, the varying impacts of labor market policies adopted by different countries became particularly salient. Broadly speaking, high-income countries opted for one of two policy approaches—job retention or income replacement. Job retention policies aim to maintain employment contracts by subsidizing firms to keep workers on staff, while income replacement policies generally focus on providing financial relief for workers who have lost their jobs.

Unlike income replacement schemes, policies aimed at keeping workers in their jobs are better poised to keep the nonpecuniary benefits of work intact. So, taking a wellbeing perspective, we may expect the former approach to be preferable to the latter. While empirical research on the topic is still emerging, countries favoring job retention policies did see both lower levels of unemployment and less severe declines in wellbeing in the first year of the crisis. In some of our own work, we evaluated the UK government's furlough scheme, which enabled firms to temporarily suspend workers unable to work because of Covid-19 restrictions while replacing 80 percent of employees' lost wages for up to £2,500 per month. We found that all workers unable to work during that period appeared to suffer a decline in life satisfaction. However, for workers who were furloughed without any income losses (with their organization augmenting the government subsidy), this decline never exceeded 6 percent. On the other hand, the life satisfaction of furloughed and nonfurloughed workers with income losses drops by 10 and 21 percent, respectively.[38]

A Big Responsibility (and Opportunity) for Managers and Executives

It might seem that we have dwelled too much on the importance of having work for wellbeing. After all, this is largely a book about people's wellbeing while at work. The main reason to do so is to emphasize the responsibility that employers have. Work is central to people's lives, and the way in which they are treated in the workplace is likely to have huge implications. But it's also an opportunity. If we want to improve wellbeing generally in society, improving the ways in which work is managed and organized has the potential to have far-reaching results.

Rather than simply viewing work as an inevitable detriment to wellbeing, we ought to think of work as a fundamental determinant of our quality of life. Considered from this perspective, the culture of work itself demands attention. When work is thought of merely as a means to an end, focusing on improving working conditions or monitoring employee wellbeing can seem irrelevant, or at least unnecessary. Yet once we recognize the fundamental importance of work for wellbeing, how businesses and organizations choose to treat and manage their workers when they walk through the door matters—a lot. And it is to this topic the rest of the book is devoted.

Chapter 4

The Current State
of Workplace Wellbeing

I n chapter 3, we saw just how important work is for our general wellbeing, not only as a source of income but even more importantly as a
source of social interactions, meaning, routine, and other nonpecuniary benefits. At the same time, we all sometimes dread getting out of bed to
start a working day. We often see news reports lamenting that attitudes
toward work are deteriorating—think of the apparent Great Resignation,
the rise of so-called quiet quitting, and so on—and suggesting that disen-
gagement with work is widespread.

In this chapter, we explore the data and survey the evidence on just how
unhappy or happy the workforce really is. To do so, we use both traditional
surveys such as those collected by organizations like Gallup and others, as
well as crowdsourced data from Indeed and—importantly—multiple dimensions of workplace wellbeing, including evaluative measures of job satisfaction, eudaimonic aspects such as meaning and purpose, and hedonic
components measuring how we actually feel in the moment while at work.

Measuring How We Feel in the Moment

By the early 2000s, the psychologist Daniel Kahneman was already an academic superstar. He had taken issue with one of the key foundations of
much economic thought—that people act in a rational manner—and won

a Nobel Prize along the way. He now turned his attention to another cornerstone of economics: the notion of utility itself. Economists typically think of the concept as an individual's ability to satisfy their preferences and measure it by observing people's decisions and actions. But if people frequently failed to make rational decisions, then they would fail to act in ways that maximize their individual utility. So, trying to infer someone's utility from their behavior may itself be misguided.

Instead, Kahneman and his colleagues suggested we "go back to Bentham"—the eighteenth-century philosopher whose preserved body still sits at the entrance to University College London, where the two of us first met and began to work together. Kahneman's research suggested we focus not on decision utility but rather on experienced utility, which is how people actually feel. The implications of this cried out for new methods of determining just how much utility (or wellbeing) people really were experiencing on a day-to-day basis.

The standard way to measure people's feelings in the moment is the so-called experience sampling method (ESM), which asks how they are feeling as they go about their lives, typically at random moments during the day. This gives a rich picture but is typically expensive and places a high burden on the respondents. Working together with an all-star cast of researchers—including the Princeton economist and eventual White House adviser Alan Krueger, as well as the noted psychologist Norbert Schwarz—Kahneman started to measure how people are actually feeling, at scale.

They developed a method that involved getting people to recall their previous day's activities and experiences in a structured diary format. Having divided the day into episodes, the researchers asked questions about what people were doing, who they were with, and how they felt in terms of emotions like happiness, stress, and tiredness. This gives a rich description without a heavy burden and does so while giving a picture of the whole day.

Starting with a sample of employed women in Texas, the researchers found experiences and emotions recorded in real time and at the end of each day showed considerable overlap and published their results in the prestigious journal *Science* in 2004. The day reconstruction method (DRM) allows for measurement of affective wellbeing at scale. A decade later, the US Bureau of Labor Statistics incorporated the method into one of its large, nationally representative time-use surveys, so that we could for the first time gain a picture of how an entire population is feeling as it goes about different activities.

Unhappiness in the Workplace

As we will see later, the development of the smartphone has made experience sampling a lot more feasible. What stands out from the original study, therefore, is not just the methodology but some of the results themselves. Measuring both positive and negative emotions, the data showed that work was almost the worst thing people did with their time. The only thing worse was commuting, and even that was only a slightly more unhappy experience. As well as asking people what they were doing during each activity, the researchers also asked who they were with. The worst person to be with in terms of happiness? Their boss.

This is surely quite a shocking indictment of how work is managed and organized. Of course, this was an initial sample of women in Texas in the early 2000s. One might reasonably wonder if this result generalizes. The latest available data from the American Time Use Survey suggests it does.

Figure 4-1 shows average levels of experience (on a 0–6 scale) for employed adults in a representative sample of the United States, collected in 2021.[1] The only activities associated with less happiness than working are education and personal care, which includes things like grooming, taking medications, and taking care of personal emergencies. While the position of work on the list reflects poorly on prevailing management practices, it is not lost on us as university employees that education does so badly.

FIGURE 4-1

Work Is among the Lowest Wellbeing Activities We Do

Average self-reported emotional experience of different activities (on a 0–6 scale)
0: You did not experience this feeling at all, 6: The feeling was very strong

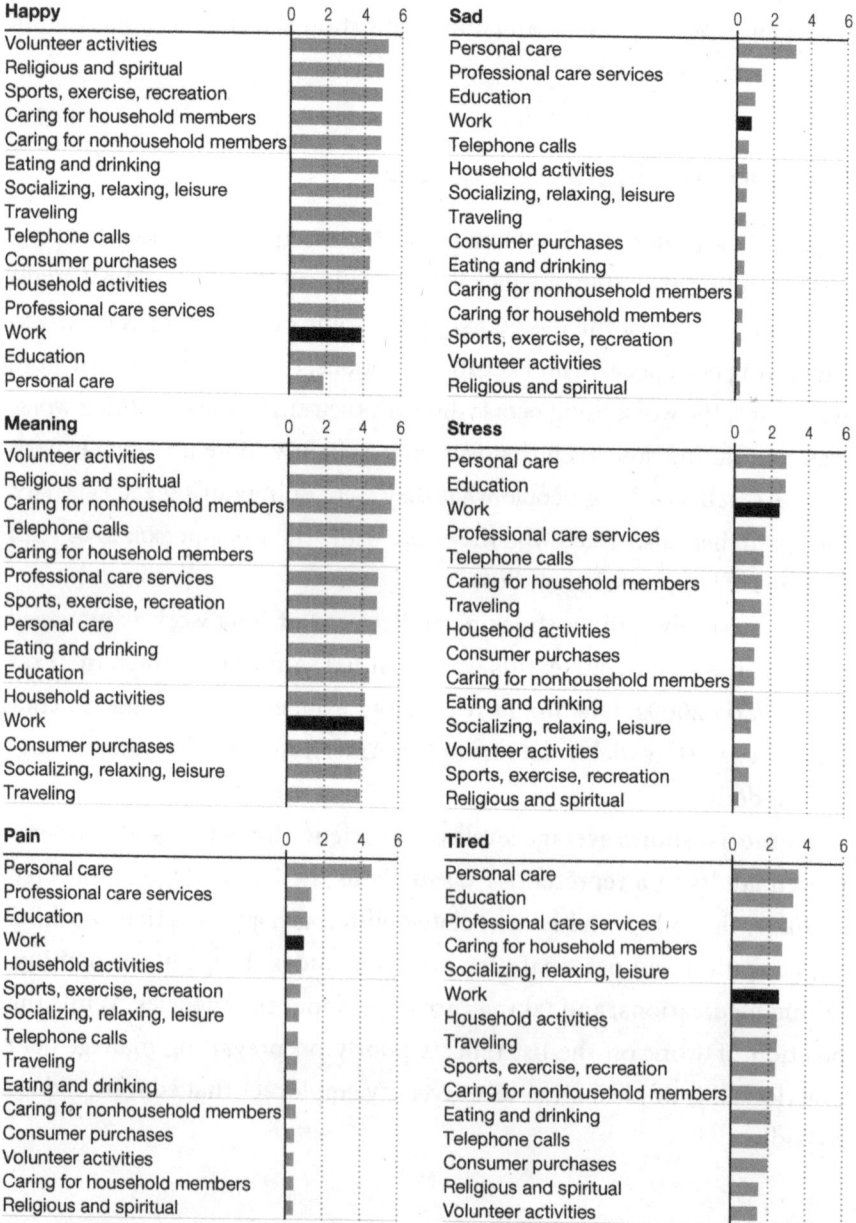

Happy
- Volunteer activities
- Religious and spiritual
- Sports, exercise, recreation
- Caring for household members
- Caring for nonhousehold members
- Eating and drinking
- Socializing, relaxing, leisure
- Traveling
- Telephone calls
- Consumer purchases
- Household activities
- Professional care services
- Work
- Education
- Personal care

Sad
- Personal care
- Professional care services
- Education
- Work
- Telephone calls
- Household activities
- Socializing, relaxing, leisure
- Traveling
- Consumer purchases
- Eating and drinking
- Caring for nonhousehold members
- Caring for household members
- Sports, exercise, recreation
- Volunteer activities
- Religious and spiritual

Meaning
- Volunteer activities
- Religious and spiritual
- Caring for nonhousehold members
- Telephone calls
- Caring for household members
- Professional care services
- Sports, exercise, recreation
- Personal care
- Eating and drinking
- Education
- Household activities
- Work
- Consumer purchases
- Socializing, relaxing, leisure
- Traveling

Stress
- Personal care
- Education
- Work
- Professional care services
- Telephone calls
- Caring for household members
- Traveling
- Household activities
- Consumer purchases
- Caring for nonhousehold members
- Eating and drinking
- Socializing, relaxing, leisure
- Volunteer activities
- Sports, exercise, recreation
- Religious and spiritual

Pain
- Personal care
- Professional care services
- Education
- Work
- Household activities
- Sports, exercise, recreation
- Socializing, relaxing, leisure
- Telephone calls
- Traveling
- Eating and drinking
- Caring for nonhousehold members
- Consumer purchases
- Volunteer activities
- Caring for household members
- Religious and spiritual

Tired
- Personal care
- Education
- Professional care services
- Caring for household members
- Socializing, relaxing, leisure
- Work
- Household activities
- Traveling
- Sports, exercise, recreation
- Caring for nonhousehold members
- Eating and drinking
- Telephone calls
- Consumer purchases
- Religious and spiritual
- Volunteer activities

Note: N = 3,892 individuals, restricted to employed respondents only.
Source: American Time Use Survey, 2021 Well-Being Module.

Measuring Affective Wellbeing with Smartphones

The ESM was originally seen as particularly burdensome, both to researchers and to those they were studying. And it was certainly very difficult to do at any sort of scale. But since the smartphone changed the picture, it is now much more feasible to ping people at random moments of the day and ask how they're feeling, what they're doing, and who they're with.

This brings us to our friend and colleague George MacKerron, a professor of economics at the University of Sussex. While still a PhD student, he was particularly interested in the environment and how it related to wellbeing. For example, how did green space in cities, rolling hills in the countryside, and open bodies of water affect human quality of life? Did they have any effect at all? Unfortunately, the data available at the time to address these sorts of issues, and even the means to collect it, was profoundly limited. As a former software engineer, he saw an opportunity.

Groundbreaking as the first-generation iPhone was, it was not much use to his research agenda. But just one year later, in 2008, the launch of the second-generation iPhone introduced the now familiar App Store, which allowed users to freely download apps directly onto their devices—and not just apps created by Apple itself. Third-party vendors, startups, and even PhD students could now design and develop their own applications to deliver directly to customers. Immediately recognizing the potential of this new platform to conduct just the sort of large-scale experience sampling study he would need to finish his PhD, he ordered as many iPhone developer manuals as he could get his hands on, abandoned a website version of the project he had been working on, and set about developing his first-ever app. He decided to call it "Mappiness."

Users could download the app, complete a short intake study, and then be pinged to complete short surveys at different moments throughout the course of their daily lives. These short surveys would ask what users were doing, who they were with, and—importantly—how they were feeling. All the while, their locations and activity levels were captured using the GPS of their smartphones. In return for their participation, each user received weekly reports about how their wellbeing evolved over time and across different environments.

FIGURE 4-2

Only Feeling Sick in Bed Is a More Unhappy Activity Than Working

Effects of performing each activity on happiness levels	

Percent change in happiness from performing the activity

Intimacy, making love	
Theater, dance, concert	
Exhibition, museum, library	
Sports, running, exercise	
Gardening	
Singing, performing	
Talking, chatting, socializing	
Birdwatching, nature watching	
Walking, hiking	
Hunting, fishing	
Drinking alcohol	
Hobbies, arts, crafts	
Meditating, religious activities	
Match, sporting event	
Childcare, playing with children	
Pet care, playing with pets	
Listening to music	
Other games, puzzles	
Shopping, errands	
Gambling, betting	
Watching TV, film	
Computer, phone games	
Eating, snacking	
Cooking, preparing food	
Drinking tea/coffee	
Reading	
Listening to speech/podcast	
Washing, dressing, grooming	
Sleeping, resting, relaxing	
Smoking	
Browsing the internet	
Texting, email, social media	
Housework, chores, DIY	
Traveling, commuting	
In a meeting, seminar, class	
Admin, finances, organizing	
Waiting in line	
Care or help for adults	
Working, studying	
Sick in bed	

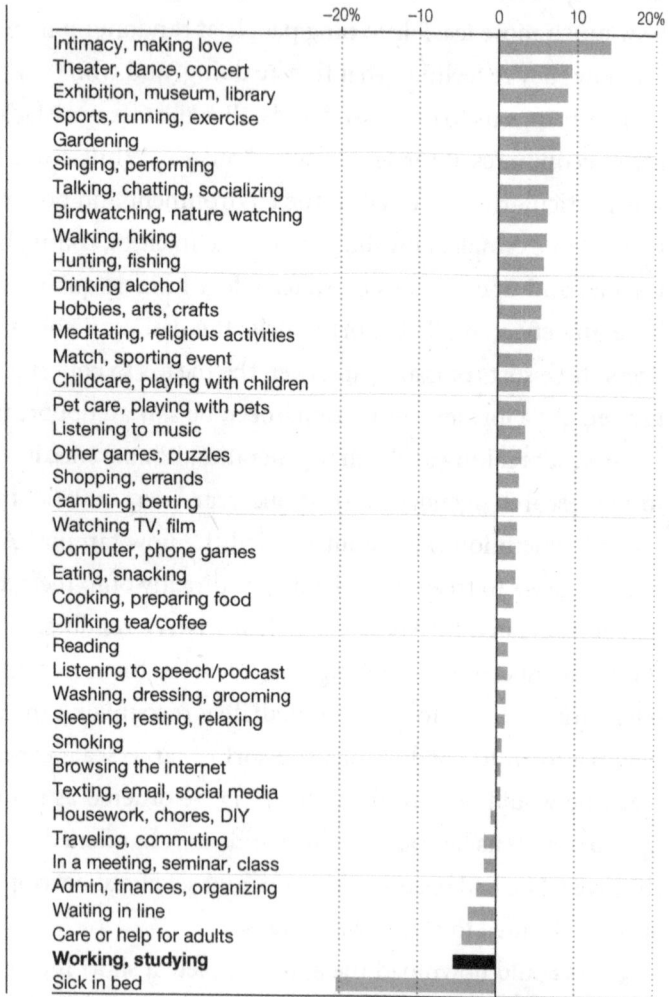

Note: Data gathered in 2010–2011 from N = 20,946 individuals.
Source: Alex Bryson and George MacKerron, "Are You Happy While You Work?," *Economic Journal* 127, no. 599 (2017): 106–25.

Before long, the story of Mappiness had been picked up by multiple large news outlets like CNN, Reuters, and the BBC. Around this time, MacKerron even got an email from Apple saying it would be featuring his app at the top of the App Store to celebrate its launch. All of this meant the app took off. Over the course of the next three months, more than thirty thousand users downloaded the app and completed more than 4.5 million surveys in total.[2] Alex Bryson, a professor at University College London with a history of research on employment and subjective wellbeing, saw its potential and together he and MacKerron put together a study titled "Are you happy while you work?" With data on over twenty thousand people in the UK over the course of a year, they found that—other than being sick in bed—there was one activity that consistently seemed to have negative impacts on users' happiness: work. As can be seen in figure 4-2, working or studying predicted larger declines in happiness than almost any other single activity under consideration.[3]

The Rise of Perceived Stress

Thus far, we have focused on the extent to which people are happy or sad while they work. But the findings from the American Time Use Survey suggest we should be worried about different aspects of negative affect as well, including stress and worry, not to mention other negative emotions like anger and fear. When it comes to the workplace, perceived stress is a particularly relevant affective state, and it seems from figure 4-1 that it is particularly associated with working.

The Gallup World Poll has been asking about a range of emotions in over 150 countries for nearly two decades, as we saw in chapter 1. Focusing on the question whether respondents experienced stress during a lot of the day "yesterday," figure 4-3 reports on how this has changed over that period. No matter what region of the world, the experience of stress has risen dramatically, something that has been something of a blind spot for leaders worldwide, as Gallup CEO Jon Clifton has noted.[4]

It is worth emphasizing that this is stress in general, rather than specifically work-related stress, though we do restrict the sample here to include

FIGURE 4-3

Employee Stress Is on the Rise Worldwide

Percentage of respondents answering "Yes" to feeling stressed during a lot of the day

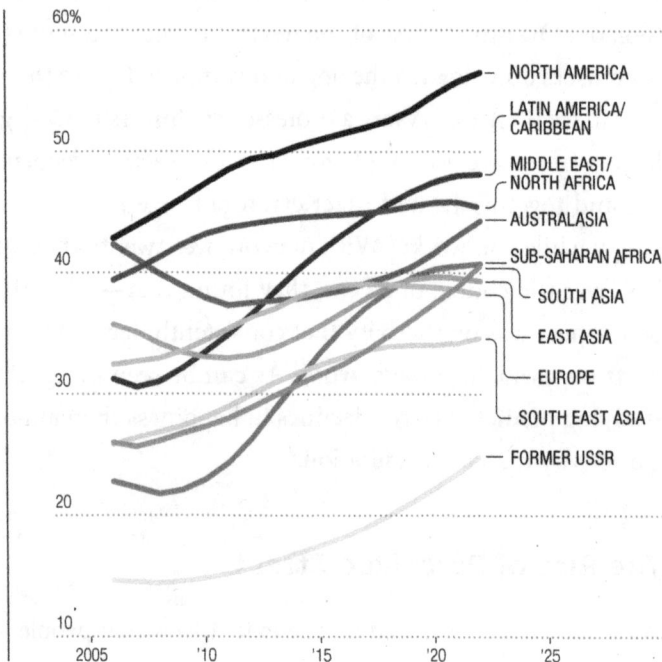

Note: Nationally representative samples of employed individuals (aged 21–64) in countries globally.
N = 1,076,319.
Source: Gallup World Poll.

only people who are employed. Moreover, as the annual Stress in America Survey—run by the American Psychological Association—has repeatedly suggested, work is typically one of if not the biggest sources of stress in our lives.[5] Moreover, not all stress is likely to be harmful. Indeed, some can help drive us forward, and the complete lack of any stress may signal a lack of challenge in our work. But what we are talking about is *perceived* stress—that is, how workers feel—and the fact that it has risen so much and rapidly does give cause for concern.

North America has a particularly toxic relationship with stress, it seems. Though one of the richest areas of the world, it had the highest levels of stress in 2006 when the World Poll began, and the gap has only widened over time. In the latest waves, well over 50 percent of respondents reported feeling stressed during a lot of the previous day.

Is Stress Really That Bad?

A long history of research in psychology has argued that there can be both good and bad types of stress.[6] While distress is clear, eustress is—roughly speaking—an emotional experience that serves to energize and motivate. It might seem odd, then, to include it as a measure of wellbeing if, after all, it might not be all that bad. Indeed, the meaning of feeling stressed may differ in that it may not capture whether someone has the means or ability to cope with the challenges that they are facing but rather that there are challenges in the first place.[7]

As one of us (George) has found in recent work with Ashley Whillans, a colleague at Harvard Business School, the extent to which stress is detrimental to overall levels of subjective wellbeing is at least partially dependent on values and beliefs surrounding work—at both the individual and societal levels. Using worldwide data, we found that for highly work-centered individuals, as well as for those living in cultures where work is particularly central to people's lives, the negative effects of stress on life and job satisfaction were less pronounced.[8]

These cultural factors are quite enduring, too. Drawing on work related to the so-called Protestant work ethic, for example, we showed that the negative effects of stress on life satisfaction in the present day are less strongly pronounced in US counties that had higher percentages of Protestants in the 1930s—even for people in the modern day who are not Protestant. But, even in highly work-centered areas, the effects of stress are still negative— less strongly so, but still negative. Another way to look at this is to return to the Indeed data. In figure 4-4, we use individual-level data from millions of respondents to plot how average levels of job satisfaction, happiness, and purpose vary according to reported levels of stress at work.[9]

The most stressful jobs are more threatening to wellbeing at work than the least stressful ones. Workers who report the highest levels of stress at

FIGURE 4-4

Feeling Stress Is Almost Always Detrimental to Wellbeing

Average levels of work wellbeing (on a 1–5 scale), by stress level

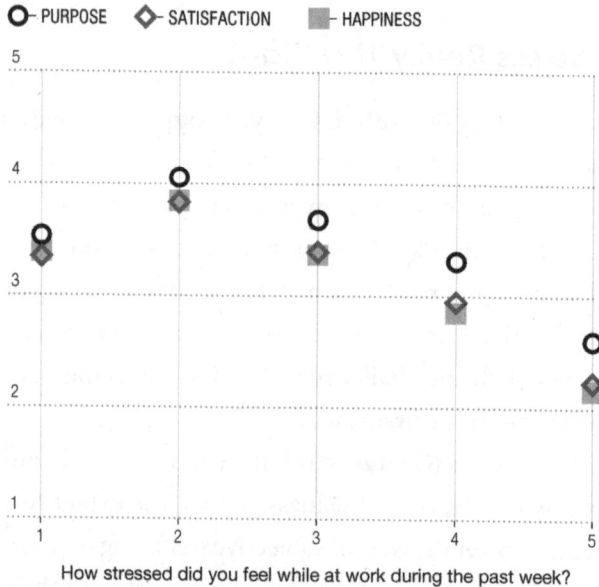

How stressed did you feel while at work during the past week?

Source: Data collected on Indeed, October 2019 to May 2024.

work consistently report lower levels of wellbeing in all other domains. However, in line with some of the intuition we've outlined, a complete lack of stress is not always a good thing. Indeed, those reporting the lowest level of stress (one out of five) report lower levels of satisfaction and happiness than those reporting a two out of five. This suggests that having no work stress at all likely means people are not being sufficiently challenged or are just simply bored. For many of us, being at least a little stressed about our work may actually be an inevitable and even desirable by-product of caring passionately about what we do.[10]

Some stress may be good but going beyond two out of five leads to decreases across the board. So, while it may be true that not all stress is inherently bad, this argument can be pushed too far, and we argue that working to decrease levels of perceived stress is most often beneficial, as we will see later in the book.

Job Satisfaction: Better News?

So far, we have focused on the experience of work—both in terms of negative affect (sadness and stress) and positive affect (happiness). The picture it paints for workplace wellbeing is not an encouraging one. But as we have emphasized, workplace wellbeing is a multifaceted concept, and it is important to measure all the components, both evaluative and hedonic, as well as eudaimonic.

What's more, unhappiness at work does not sit well with the results of chapter 3—that work is fundamentally important to our wellbeing and that being in work is a very significant predictor of how satisfied we are with our lives overall. Why should employed adults be more satisfied with their lives and so seemingly miserable while at work?

When people are asked not to report how they feel while *at* work, but rather how they feel *about* their jobs overall, the reports tend to be more positive. Looking at the International Social Survey Program (ISSP), which asks respondents to rate their overall level of job satisfaction on a scale from one to seven, the average is just over five—not as alarmingly low as we might have expected given the findings on happiness and stress (see figure 4-5).

Similarly, in a broader group of countries, the Gallup World Poll asked a job satisfaction question until 2012. It asked people more simply whether they were satisfied with their job or not. In figure 4-6, we map the percentage saying they were satisfied with their jobs across countries. The numbers range quite a bit between countries but are generally quite high.

How are we to make sense of these high levels of job satisfaction? Why should we be so miserable while working, yet so satisfied with our jobs overall? First, there is nothing inherently contradictory about this dynamic. Thinking outside the arena of work, many of us have likely had days where we feel sad, stressed, or angry, yet remain satisfied with our lives overall.[11] The very reason that wellbeing researchers distinguish between evaluative and affective dimensions of wellbeing is precisely because they are not always perfectly aligned.

Several strands of research demonstrate that we use different mental processes to make these two sorts of judgments—about how we feel in the

FIGURE 4-5

Job Satisfaction around the World

How satisfied are you in your job?					

Mean level, by country

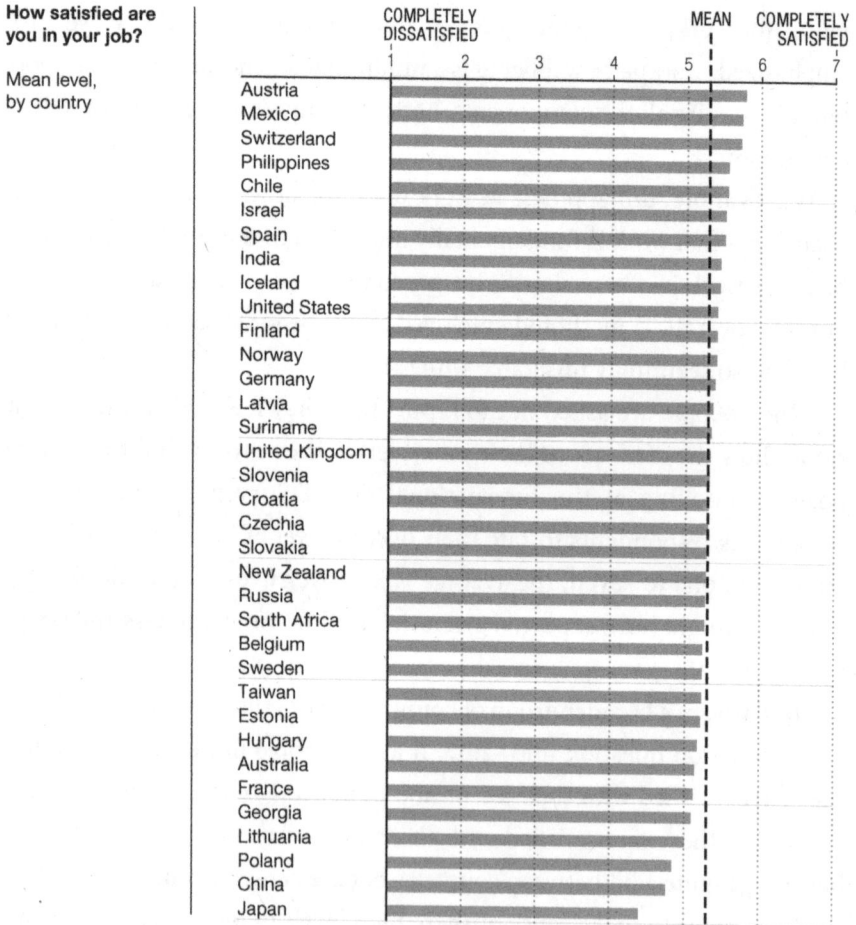

Note: Seven-point scale (from 1–7) asking "How satisfied are you in your (main) job?" N = 24,556.
Employed individuals only, 18–64 years old.
Source: International Social Survey Programme (ISSP), 2015–2017.

moment and how we feel about our lives overall.[12] For all sorts of practical and financial reasons, having a job in most societies around the world is generally preferable to not having one. As a result, when asked how satisfied we are with our jobs overall, if we are likely to compare ourselves to those who are unemployed, it may be unsurprising that most people report

FIGURE 4-6

Most People Have at Least a Basic Level of Job Satisfaction

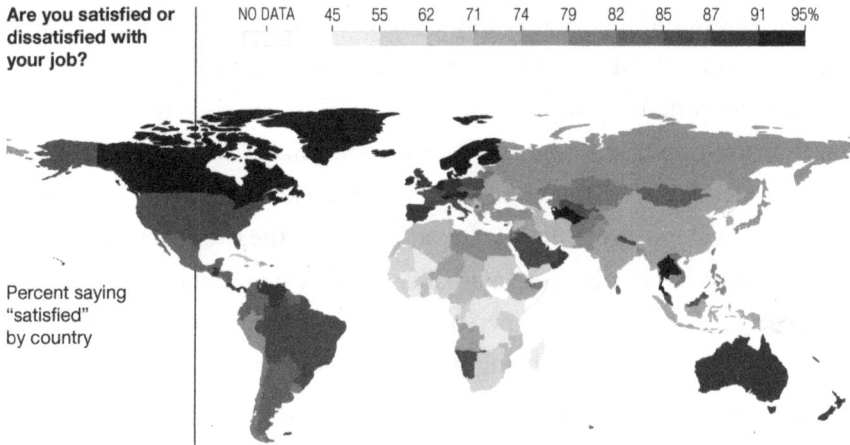

| Are you satisfied or dissatisfied with your job? | NO DATA | 45 | 55 | 62 | 71 | 74 | 79 | 82 | 85 | 87 | 91 | 95% |

Percent saying "satisfied" by country

Source: Gallup World Poll, 2006–2012. N = 460,602.

high levels of job satisfaction, particularly if being unemployed means being unable to afford basic necessities. This is particularly likely if, as in the Gallup World Poll, the question is posed as a binary dissatisfied/satisfied question.

There may also be social and cultural forces driving the relatively high levels of job satisfaction we see around the world. As we discussed in relation to the notion of work centrality, values and beliefs can play a strong role in how we evaluate things. Very often, work is prioritized as a pathway to individual fulfillment and success. This can have a profound impact on how those of us who do work ultimately think about the quality of our lives overall. To illustrate this dynamic, our friend and colleague Paul Dolan—a professor at the London School of Economics—offers the following anecdote in his book *Happiness by Design*: "A few weeks ago, I went out for dinner with one of my best friends, whom I have known for a long time. She works for a prestigious media company and basically spent the whole evening describing how miserable she was at work; she variously moaned about her boss, her colleagues, and her commute. At the end of dinner, and without a hint of irony, she said, 'Of course, I love working at MediaLand.'"[13]

Another explanation is that work is similar to exercise. If we were stopped and asked how happy we felt in the middle of a marathon, it seems hard to imagine we would report anything other than distress. That might just be the two of us, but it does seem to be a mistake to conclude from such a survey that running is a low-wellbeing activity. Even if moments of physical exertion are unpleasant, the overall experience may still be positive, especially in retrospect. In the same way, even if the actual experience of work is demanding and stressful, we may still *evaluate* the overall experience to be positive as it contributes to a broader sense of achievement, purpose, or belonging. Viewed from this perspective, the fact that most people report low levels of emotional wellbeing at work and high levels of job satisfaction may not be paradoxical at all.

In addition to explanations relying on comparisons and potentially rewarding challenges, there may also be more technical reasons lying behind the disconnect that we see. One is that the threshold for being satisfied is lower than for being happy. This is likely to be particularly problematic if the question asks, Yes or no, are you satisfied or not? We thus suggest longer survey scales in our workplace wellbeing module, outlined in chapter 2. Another explanation may be the way in which wellbeing researchers choose to define the very nature and activities of work itself. Consider the variety of activities in the time-use studies mentioned earlier. Work is intertwined with other activities that we may well enjoy, such as reading, socializing, drinking coffee, having lunch, and so on. Each of these activities is often considered separately from work itself in these studies. What we are left with is the "pure" work element, when we are actually carrying out the work tasks.

Workplace Wellbeing over Time

We have already seen in figure 4-3 that stress is on the rise. But what about the other aspects of workplace wellbeing? This turns out not to be a straightforward question to answer, since there are very few regularly repeated surveys that include these kinds of questions. Perhaps the best source is the ISSP, which has been asking a job satisfaction question in OECD countries since the late 1990s.

Overall, as shown in figure 4-7, there has been a small increase over time, though the dispersion of responses has gone up slightly over the same period.[14] That is, although things may be improving overall, this masks a small increase in inequality in workplace wellbeing. But perhaps the most interesting and relevant way to slice and dice the data is by company. As we have seen in chapter 1, there is a great deal of variation, even among competitors, with profound implications for the ways in which work is managed and organized.

FIGURE 4-7

Job Satisfaction Has Increased Only Slightly over Time

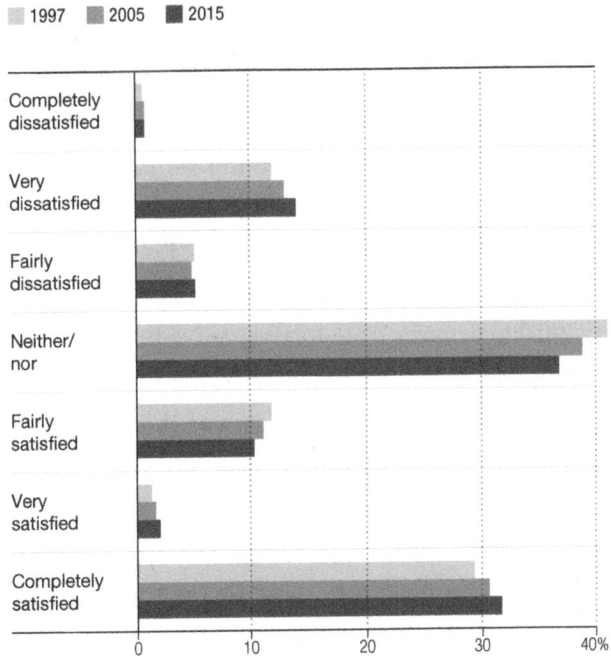

Note: Responses from the 13 OECD countries that appear in all three waves, restricted to employees only.
Source: International Social Survey Programme (ISSP); Andrew E. Clark and Michal Kozák, "Twenty Years of Job Quality in OECD Countries: More Good News?," IZA Discussion Paper No. 16597, 2023.

Meaning and Purpose

Having covered hedonic and evaluative components of wellbeing, we now ask, Do we find purpose or meaning at work? This is, again, distinct from job satisfaction, happiness, or stress. We may be satisfied with our jobs, happy at work, and feel relatively stress-free, yet still find our work meaningless. Or alternatively, we may consider the work we do to be profoundly meaningful, yet still remain unhappy, stressed, and dissatisfied with our jobs overall.

As shown in figure 4-1, work ranks relatively low in terms of meaning among all of the day-to-day activities that people engage in. Beyond a feeling of meaningfulness, we can also think of purpose in terms of how much impact it has or how much it improves the lives of others or is useful to society more broadly.

Figure 4-8 reports data from the European Working Conditions Survey (EWCS) on the extent to which people feel their work is useful. In this case, we are encouraged to find that most people report feeling that they are doing useful work, and this is a source of meaning in their lives. A handful of other studies examining data from the EWCS and ISSP and elsewhere have similar conclusions and found workers reporting high levels of purpose at their jobs.[15]

In a similar vein, Dutch economist Robert Dur, working together with his colleague Max van Lent, found, using a representative data set comprising 100,000 workers from forty-seven countries at four points in time, that only 8 percent of workers reported their jobs to be socially useless, while 17 percent doubted the usefulness of their work.[16] It is difficult to know what a low or high number is here. For those workers who do find little meaning in their work, this can have profoundly damaging effects on their overall levels of wellbeing.[17] Even if just one out of every five workers either finds their jobs meaningless or doubts the usefulness of their work, this should still raise alarm bells.

FIGURE 4-8

Workers Mostly Feel They Are Doing Useful Work

I have the feeling
of doing useful
work

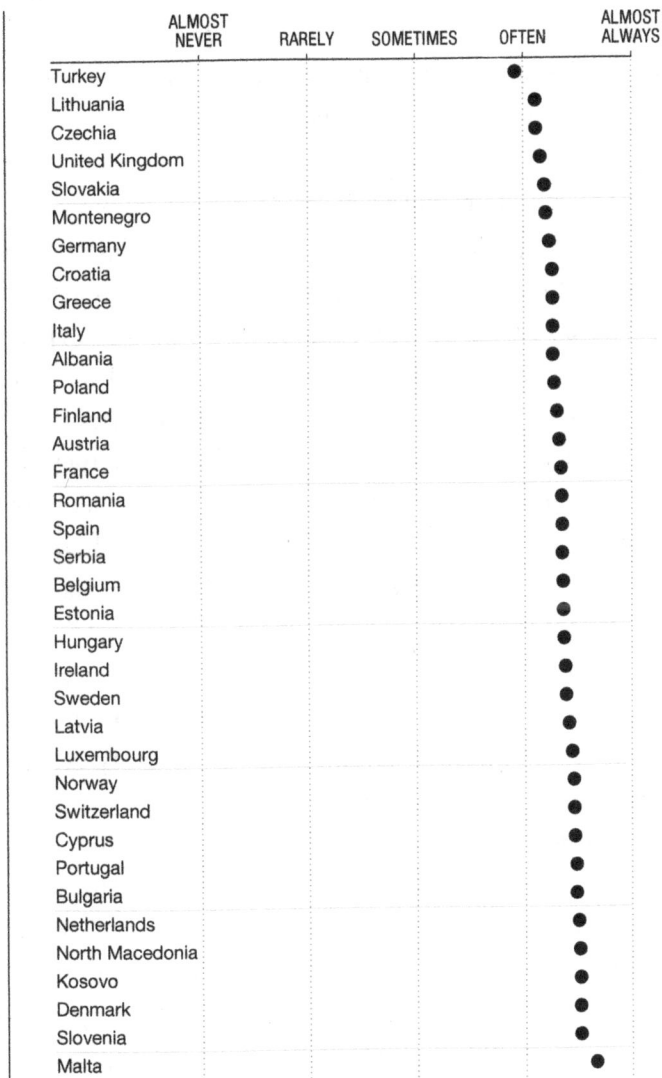

	ALMOST NEVER	RARELY	SOMETIMES	OFTEN	ALMOST ALWAYS
Turkey				●	
Lithuania				●	
Czechia				●	
United Kingdom				●	
Slovakia				●	
Montenegro				●	
Germany				●	
Croatia				●	
Greece				●	
Italy				●	
Albania				●	
Poland				●	
Finland				●	
Austria				●	
France				●	
Romania				●	
Spain				●	
Serbia				●	
Belgium				●	
Estonia				●	
Hungary				●	
Ireland				●	
Sweden				●	
Latvia				●	
Luxembourg				●	
Norway				●	
Switzerland				●	
Cyprus				●	
Portugal				●	
Bulgaria				●	
Netherlands				●	
North Macedonia				●	
Kosovo				●	
Denmark				●	
Slovenia				●	
Malta					●

Note: Average levels of useful work by country on a 1–5 scale. N = 116,018.
Source: European Working Conditions Survey, 2005–2015.

Workplace Wellbeing by Gender, Education, and Age

In order to see the forest from the trees, all of these findings pool everyone together. Yet, we know that an average may end up obscuring meaningful differences among parts of a population. In figure 4-9, however, we return to the Gallup World Poll data, which provides a rich picture of people's workplace wellbeing across the globe and asks how it varies according to gender, education, and age.[18]

On average, women tend to be somewhat happier at work, more satisfied with their jobs, and tend to find more meaning in their work compared to men, in line with previous findings using alternative data sets.[19] Nevertheless, women also feel more stressed at work compared to men. This highlights, first and foremost, the importance of considering the different aspects of workplace wellbeing, since they may not always all point in the same direction. But it also raises a series of questions about why certain types of jobs, companies, or workers have such different levels of wellbeing—a topic we cover extensively in later chapters on the drivers of workplace wellbeing.

While there are relatively small gender differences in workplace wellbeing, starker differentials can be seen when splitting the data by education levels and age groups. Workers with a university degree generally report higher job satisfaction, enjoyment, and meaning at work even if—as was the case for women—they do also report slightly more stress.

As we gain more experience in both work and life more generally, workplace wellbeing tends to rise. Indeed, throughout the course of our working lives, our levels of job satisfaction, enjoyment, and meaning all gradually rise, while stress levels ultimately drop once reaching the final stages of professional life. Although life satisfaction is often thought to be U-shaped in age, with a midlife crisis meaning that we hit low levels of subjective wellbeing in midlife, when it comes to workplace wellbeing, this appears not to be the case.[20] From an age perspective, at least, our workplace wellbeing can only get better.

FIGURE 4-9

Demographic Differences in Workplace Wellbeing

Workplace
wellbeing by
demographic
characteristics

Job satisfaction

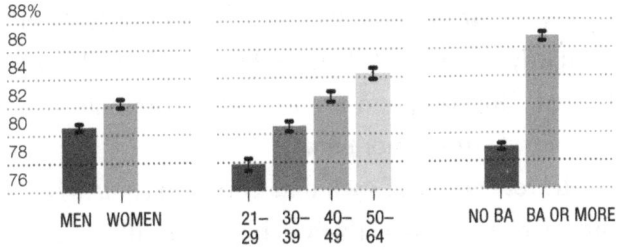

Work meaning

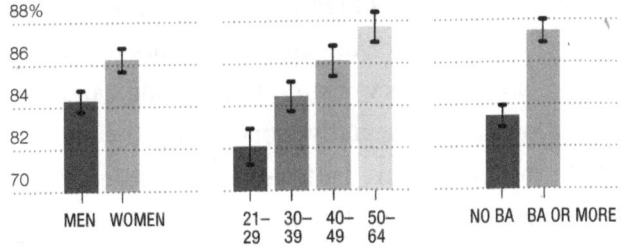

Enjoyment of work

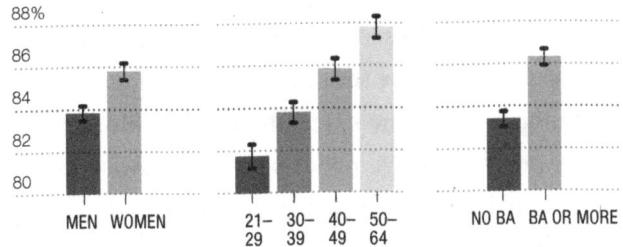

Stress

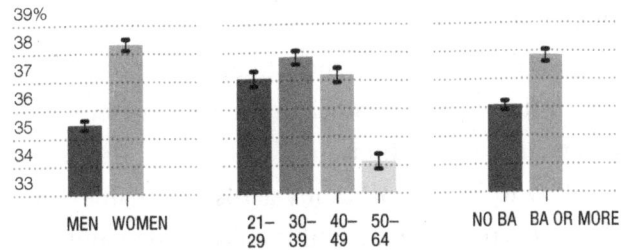

Note: Full-time employed individuals aged 21–64.
Source: Gallup World Poll, 2009–2022.

A Big Data Approach

Using data from Indeed, we can take a different approach. Here we are able to present levels and distributions of job satisfaction, happiness at work, purpose, and stress for the largest sample population of workers ever assembled. Our primary sample includes nearly 20 million working adults, primarily in the United States, but also Canada, Brazil, India, Mexico, the United Kingdom, and France. This represents a considerable step up in sample size from prior efforts.

The real power of such data comes in *comparisons* rather than estimating population *levels*. This wealth of data allows us to look not only at happiness across companies, occupations, and industries, but even within companies and across highly specific geographic regions. We can compare the wellbeing of truck drivers in New York to those in New Jersey, or food service professionals working at McDonald's and Burger King.

Nationally representative surveys like the ones we have looked at thus far in this chapter are better suited to estimating the level of workplace happiness in the population at large. This is because those visiting the Indeed site—and, within that group, those deciding to respond to the survey—may well be different from the general population in multiple ways. As we have discussed before, particularly disgruntled or very happy workers might not be the ones who leave a response, for example. This can be mitigated to some extent by the website's give-to-get model that induces people to leave reviews who otherwise might not have done. But ultimately it is unlikely to ever be a sample that can be seen as representative of the workforce.[21] When we have posed the same or similar questions in national-representative samples, we have tended to find levels that are slightly above what is crowdsourced on Indeed—suggesting that less happy workers are, on average, more likely to respond.[22] However, the key here is not in the levels but rather in the comparisons across groups, including companies, occupations, and industries. The selection biases noted are unlikely to vary significantly across companies and industries, meaning that comparing them remains a fascinating and unprecedented look into the workplaces of the world.[23]

In figure 4-10, we show the distribution of workplace wellbeing responses in the United States.[24] In each case, the mean level is indicated by the dashed vertical line. So, just what does this data demonstrate? All in all, these average responses turn out to be, well, average. When taking all respondents into account, we find that the average working adult tends to report levels of workplace wellbeing that sit between 2.9 and 3.4 on a scale of 1 to 5, depending on which dimension is being considered.

Averages can be misleading, of course. Perhaps more interesting is the distribution. Typically, we would expect to see wellbeing measures with a more normal distribution—the so-called bell curve. However, very disgruntled or happy workers do appear to respond to the survey in disproportionate rates. But taking the data as it is, we can see that more people are likely to report positive work experiences than negative ones. This result carries across all four workplace wellbeing dimensions. In other words, most workers are more likely to report feeling satisfied with their jobs, happy at work, largely stress-free, and engaged

FIGURE 4-10

Individual Responses to Wellbeing Questions in the United States

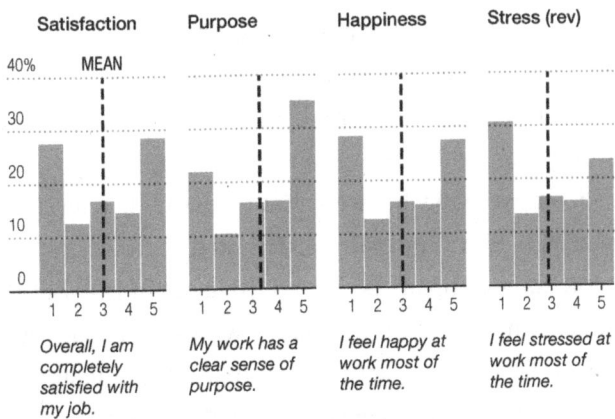

Note: Stress is reversed (1 = high stress, 5 = low stress) for ease of presentation.
Source: Data collected on Indeed, October 2019 to May 2024.

in meaningful pursuits than they are to report extremely negative experiences in all four components. It is concerning, however, that around a quarter of respondents in each case report the lowest level of wellbeing.

A further trade-off in order to gain such large-scale data is that there will inevitably be some responses that provide more noise than signal, particularly if people provide incoherent responses as a result of not paying attention or reading carefully. Respondents are not monitored, as might be the case with, say, a telephone or face-to-face interview (though many national surveys themselves are increasingly done online). Nevertheless, the huge scale of the data makes this less of a general concern, particularly when we aggregate to the level of companies, occupations, industries, and so on.

Wellbeing across Companies

So we've seen that most people have a basic level of satisfaction with their jobs, but don't enjoy being at work. At the same time, stress is growing across the board, and a significant minority are miserable at work. Let's now look a layer deeper at wellbeing across companies and industries using the Indeed data to see if we can detect any patterns. On the website, a company is eligible to have a set of wellbeing scores displayed once it has at least ten surveys, so that the data is meaningful to job seekers. Taking this same threshold, we plot in figure 4-11 the distribution of companies in the United States, across the four components of workplace wellbeing.

Compared to what we saw at the individual level, wellbeing across companies is more normally distributed than across individuals. The mean score for a company is around three out of five. But these averages mask a significant amount of inequality, with some organizations scoring closer to one or five. This is partly to be expected. Companies work in different sectors, doing different jobs and in different locations. But surprisingly, even within tightly defined industries and locations, significant wellbeing gaps exist.

FIGURE 4-11

Company-Level Averages of Workplace Wellbeing in the United States

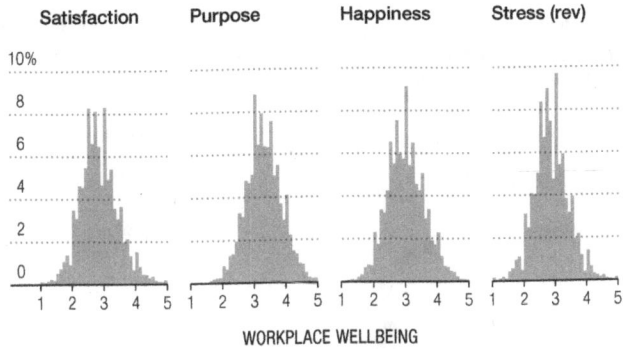

Note: Each observation is a company with 10 or more responses to the individual-level survey question. Happiness = 128,847 companies, Satisfaction = 101,584, Purpose = 125,759, Stress = 86,995. Stress is reversed (1 = high stress, 5 = low stress) for ease of presentation.
Source: Indeed, October 2019–May 2024.

Differences between and among Industries

Let's take four industries—insurance, information technology, restaurants and food services, and retail—and plot firm-level averages and distributions of workplace wellbeing (see figure 4-12). There are differences across industries, as one might expect, but also significant variation within them as well. We do not see, for example, that food service workers are uniformly miserable, while tech workers are uniformly blissful. Rather, some food service companies seem to be doing remarkably well by their employees, in some cases even better than tech companies, while others flounder at the bottom end of the scale.

The US Census Bureau classifies business according to NAICS codes—or the North American Industry Classification System. This code can be at different digits; a two-digit code is fairly general and could refer to manufacturing, education, health care, and so on. But more detailed classification comes with a greater number of digits. The two-digit code 45 refers to

FIGURE 4-12

Wellbeing Differentials between and among Selected Industries

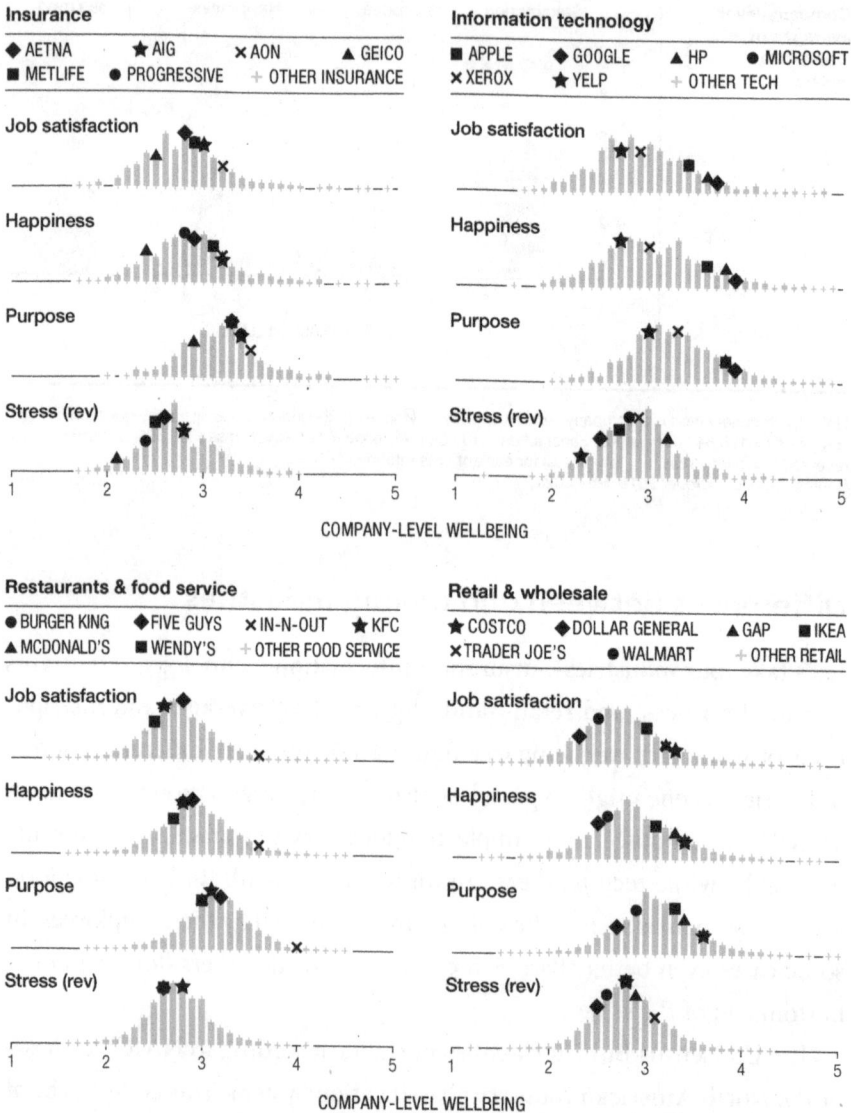

Insurance

◆ AETNA ★ AIG ✕ AON ▲ GEICO ■ METLIFE ● PROGRESSIVE + OTHER INSURANCE

Job satisfaction

Happiness

Purpose

Stress (rev)

Information technology

■ APPLE ◆ GOOGLE ▲ HP ● MICROSOFT ✕ XEROX ★ YELP + OTHER TECH

Job satisfaction

Happiness

Purpose

Stress (rev)

COMPANY-LEVEL WELLBEING

Restaurants & food service

● BURGER KING ◆ FIVE GUYS ✕ IN-N-OUT ★ KFC ▲ MCDONALD'S ■ WENDY'S + OTHER FOOD SERVICE

Job satisfaction

Happiness

Purpose

Stress (rev)

Retail & wholesale

★ COSTCO ◆ DOLLAR GENERAL ▲ GAP ■ IKEA ✕ TRADER JOE'S ● WALMART + OTHER RETAIL

Job satisfaction

Happiness

Purpose

Stress (rev)

COMPANY-LEVEL WELLBEING

Note: Company-level wellbeing scores are plotted by industry, using firms with 20+ responses. Selected firms are plotted with other symbols, as shown in the legend. Stress is reversed (1 = high stress, 5 = low stress) for ease of presentation.
Source: Indeed, October 2019 to May 2024.

retailers, for example, while the code 4561 narrows down to health and personal care retailers. Narrowing even further, which we can use, given the scope of the Indeed data, the code 45612 is cosmetics, beauty supplies, and perfume retailers; 45611 is pharmacies and drug retailers, and so on. Why bore you with such detail? A study—conducted by one of us—found that even within these narrowly defined groups of companies, we continue to see significant variation in wellbeing.[25] Firms that are in the same business and facing the same environment nevertheless differ greatly in how workers feel at and about their jobs.

Two Key Questions

Ultimately, this variation across companies in all four aspects of workplace wellbeing leads us to two main questions: "Why?" and "So what?"[26]

First, the variation demands explanation. Why are workers in some companies happier than others? The existence of wellbeing gaps within industries and locations implies that wellbeing is a company-level choice—workplace misery doesn't need to be the case. But what do good firms do differently? As we will explore in part II, a great deal can be traced back to differing workplace cultures, management practices, and the way that work is designed and organized.

Second, does it matter? Do happier firms have better outcomes? We turn to this issue in part III, looking in turn at productivity, turnover/retention, recruitment, and ultimately, profitability and firm value. Naturally, there is a strong human case for fostering workplace wellbeing, but—as we will see—there is a strong business case for doing so as well.

Part Two

IMPROVING WORKPLACE WELLBEING

Chapter 5

Measure What You Treasure

I n our discussions with managers over the years, almost all have been interested in and committed to improving the wellbeing of their workers. But many have come to a dead end at some stage when thinking about how to do so effectively. Much of this can come from an unsystematic approach that very quickly becomes overwhelming. Instead, it is useful to break down the issue and think about things more scientifically.

Measure, Understand, Act

We open this part of the book by bringing together a framework to help managers think about how to improve wellbeing in a methodical and evidence-driven way.

1. Measure what you treasure with frequent surveys of wellbeing.

2. Understand what actually drives workplace wellbeing.

3. Act on evidence to roll out interventions that effectively improve the drivers of wellbeing.

The first step is to ask workers how they feel at work and about their work. There is no better person to help redesign and improve a job than the person who spends a third of their waking life doing it. Interestingly, a recent field experiment has shown that even the act of asking employees for their feedback on job conditions and managerial performance, providing the approach is authentic, has been shown to reduce turnover and absenteeism. This holds particularly in situations where workers are dissatisfied.[1] We have already covered parts of the first step earlier in the book, but measurement is always the place to start.

The second step is to analyze drivers, as we will detail in the next chapter. Here, the crucial idea is to get a proper and thorough understanding of the relative importance of different workplace and job facets that are causing the high or low levels of wellbeing found in the first step.

In chapter 6 we present a quantitative driver analysis, essentially using as much data as we can find from worldwide surveys, to provide an initial big-picture look at the determinants of workplace wellbeing. You can start here with getting a sense for what the most important drivers of workplace wellbeing in your firm might well be. But it is also important to run such analyses within any particular context, and to complement such analyses where possible with qualitative data. This means talking to workers, exploring what is going on and, in many cases, what about their jobs is making them feel dissatisfied, unhappy, or stressed.

This approach involves a fundamental change in how many managers seem to be thinking about wellbeing at work. Rather than seeing the task as one of mitigating misery through wellness programs, the real work comes in trying to understand its root causes and thinking about how work is actually designed and managed.

Armed with an understanding of what the most important wellbeing drivers are in a given context—perhaps a lack of belonging, poor relationships between workers and managers, low levels of job security, or something else—the third step is to take action and effectively improve the drivers of workplace wellbeing.

When it comes to interventions, there is a lot to learn from others—in both the academic and business worlds. Together with Indeed and the World Wellbeing Movement, we set out to systematically review the academic literature for the best evidence on how to improve each of the drivers.[2]

In chapter 7, we will dig into this systematic review of over three thousand research studies from over fifty countries, encompassing hundreds of company settings. In doing so, we will look in more depth at some key examples of interventions that effectively improve the drivers of workplace wellbeing, while pointing readers to this expanding resource that we hope will be useful to managers worldwide.

Before we look in more detail into the importance of measurement as the stepping stone to improving workplace wellbeing, we first raise the practical point of who should own the workplace wellbeing agenda within organizations.

Who's Responsible for Workplace Wellbeing?

A frequent comment we hear from skeptical managers and executives is that happiness is a personal issue; it has nothing to do with the company. "If workers are unhappy, it's not our fault," they say. "Besides, even if we wanted to, there's nothing we can do to influence how our workers feel." There is some truth to this criticism. But overall, the strong weight of the evidence suggests it is dangerously misguided. How work is managed and organized matters, and it is within the control of managers and executives. This is a large responsibility, but also an opportunity, available to few, to improve many people's lives.

People's wellbeing—either general or work-specific—is determined by a mixture of largely fixed personal factors (such as traits, genes, and so on), variable personal factors (such as marital problems, frequency of doomscrolling the world news in bed, or even stubbing a toe getting out of bed in the morning), as well as organizational factors.

Can an organization ensure that every single worker is happy all of the time? No. And this probability would not even be desirable anyway. But given that similar firms can have very different levels of workplace wellbeing, it is clear that management and organizational practices play a role.

In a nationally representative sample of around four thousand, we asked people in the United States to do a simple task.[3] We got them to allocate a hundred points according to who has an impact on employees' happiness

FIGURE 5-1

The Whole Firm Has a Responsibility for Workplace Wellbeing

Allocate 100 points across the options according to their impact on employee happiness at work	INDIVIDUALS THEMSELVES 46.9	TOP MANAGEMENT 19.9	HUMAN RESOURCES 13.4	LINE MANAGERS 9.0	THE CEO 8.4	OTHER 2.3

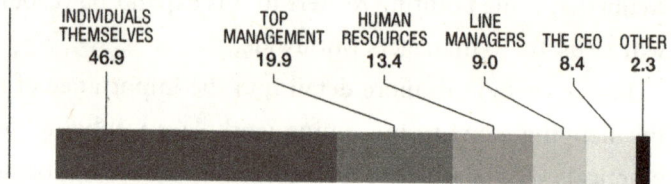

Note: Nationally representative survey of workers in the US, UK, and Canada, carried out in 2023. N = 7,029.

at work. We show the responses in figure 5-1.[4] On average, the largest single number of points goes to individuals themselves. As we've noted, this is fairly intuitive.

But, on average, people allocate over fifty points in total—a slight majority—to organizational factors. Interestingly, human resources—though important in people's minds—is not as significant in determining people's happiness as top management. We think HR professionals do an important job, but it is unfair to make them entirely responsible for workplace wellbeing, as is the case in many firms. In line with what workers themselves seem to recognize and think, workplace wellbeing is a systemwide issue. It relates to how work is designed, managed, and organized and can't be fixed with add-on measures by HR professionals, who have many other important roles within the organization.

Measuring Differences within Organizations

In the previous chapter, we motivated the study of what drives workplace wellbeing by demonstrating clear differences across companies, even within tightly defined industries and locations. In fact, leveraging the richness of the Indeed data, we can go further than this and, in the case of very large firms, even look within them in the same way that organizations should also consider doing internally. In figure 5-2, we take the four largest

FIGURE 5-2

Wellbeing Varies Significantly across States Even within the Same Firm

Each marker represents a state-level average of the company's wellbeing (on a 1–5 scale)

●– STRESS (REV)   ◆– SATISFACTION   ■– HAPPINESS   ▲– PURPOSE

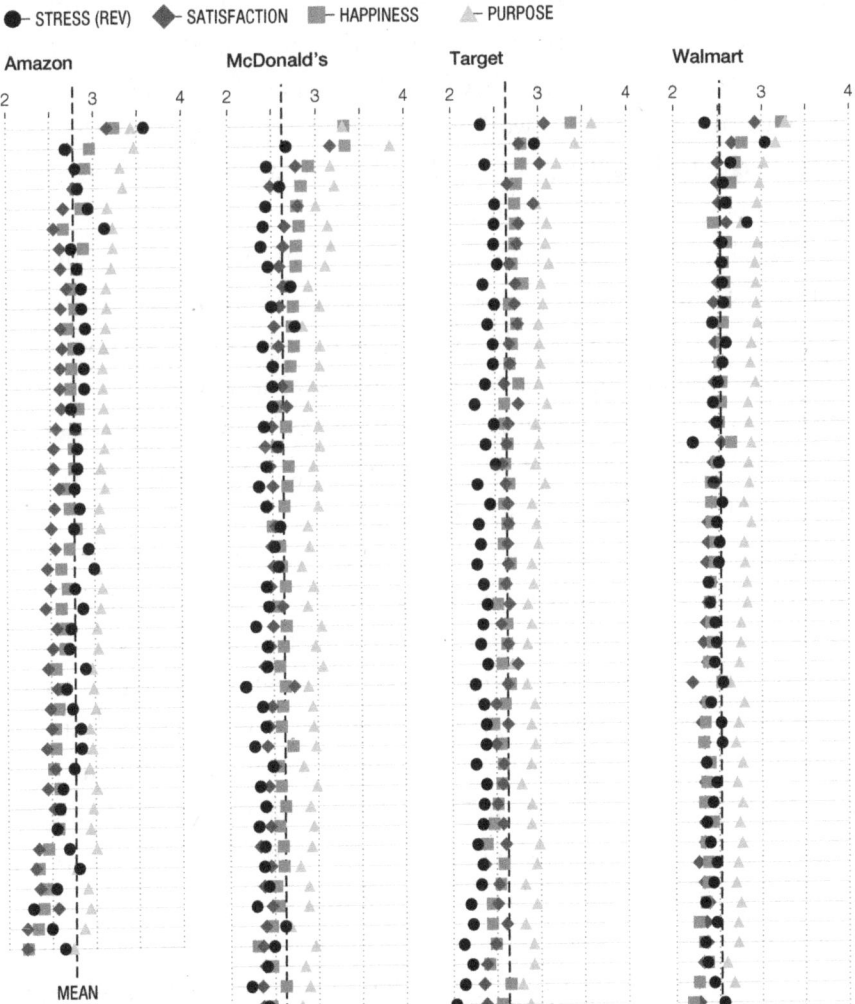

Amazon   McDonald's   Target   Walmart

MEAN

Note: Company-state averages are included in the analysis in cases where the company has 20+ responses in that state. Stress is reversed (1 = high stress, 5 = low stress) for ease of presentation.

Source: Indeed, October 2019 to May 2024.

companies on the platform (in terms of surveys completed by current workers at the time of writing) and plot the average levels of workplace wellbeing across US states.

Looking inside companies, we might expect employees represented in each of the four panels in the figure to be more similar to each other than those in our previous discussions, particularly when comparing across similar or neighboring states. Working in the same company across similar states, we might expect them to have similar levels of education, receive similar levels of income, and live in similar types of communities. If so, any resulting variation in workplace wellbeing between these groups is more likely attributable to differences in both national and local company policies, practices, and procedures.

Instead, what we see in figure 5-2 is significant dispersion in wellbeing within the same company but across state lines. Some of the variation in wellbeing that we observe is likely to come from background conditions, and there are numerous potential explanations for these dynamics. Several surveys of American residents have documented significant variation in subjective wellbeing for residents of different states, for reasons that go well beyond differences in working conditions.[5]

But state differences alone are clearly not the full story. Much of the variation in workplace wellbeing we observe in figure 5-2 crisscrosses state lines in ways that clearly suggest that firms matter. In line with people's intuition, this appears to be evident at both the national and local levels. Overall differences across companies as a whole are more likely to be traceable to national management decisions and policies, many of which can have significant effects on worker wellbeing. The data in figure 5-1 suggests that people attribute around a quarter of the responsibility to either top management or the CEO. That we see wellbeing differences across comparable companies (as we saw in more detail in the previous chapter) suggests that policies and practices implemented at the highest levels of organizations can have important effects on workplace wellbeing.

But the dynamics presented in figure 5-2 also suggest that more local policies and managers can matter just as much, if not even more. Line managers are likely to be particularly important, given the influence they can have on how workers feel. Even within companies, there are significant differences—in ways that cannot be easily attributed to either background state-level factors or to companywide practices. Rather, that different groups of employees working for the same company in different states continue to report such large differences in wellbeing at work indicates that more localized workplace conditions are likely to play a role in explaining such differences.

Measure How Your Company Measures Up

We turn now to the starting point of any evidence-based approach to improving workplace wellbeing—measuring it for your organization. Many firms already do so, in one way or another. Figure 5-3 shows the aspects of wellbeing that employers in the United States most commonly ask about.[6] Around 30 percent ask nothing at all. Those that do most commonly ask about job satisfaction. Some measure purpose, happiness, and stress, though to a lesser extent. So, there is good and bad news here. Many firms are trying to measure wellbeing, but almost all are not getting the full picture.

FIGURE 5-3

Only Half of Employers in the United States Measure Job Satisfaction

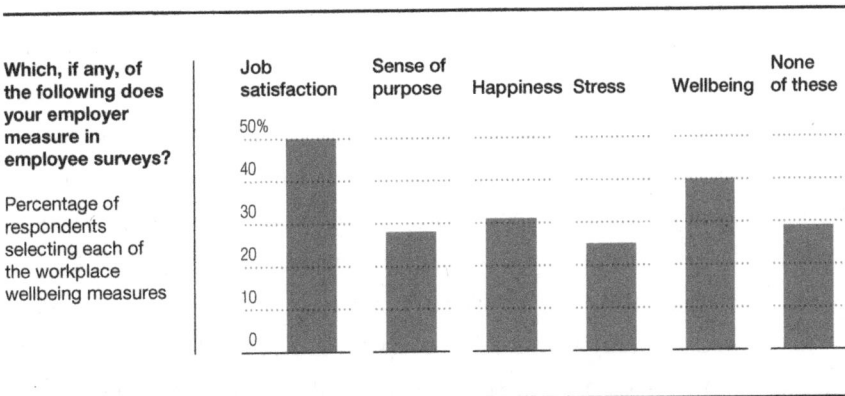

Note: Nationally representative survey of workers in the US, UK, and Canada, carried out in 2022 and 2023.

In chapter 2, we proposed a simple four-question workplace wellbeing survey module, which attempts to measure the full picture of worker wellbeing without burdening respondents. Of course, if there is more capacity to go into greater detail, then it is a good idea to do so, provided that it does not place unreasonable burdens on the employees answering, since they will find this unreasonable and you may be able to collect much less data.[7]

We suggest asking these questions regularly. One interesting comparison is with the Office for National Statistics in the United Kingdom, where the inspiration for our survey module came from. In the early 2010s, it developed a short module of four questions on subjective wellbeing—including life satisfaction, happiness, anxiety, and worthwhileness. The government's next question was where to actually ask these questions. It came up with what we think turned out to be a very good answer: everywhere.

Given that it is a succinct four-question survey that does not take up much time or resources, it might actually be more efficient to have a blanket policy of including the wellbeing items across as many surveys as possible. Over time, the UK government included its wellbeing survey module across the board, from the Annual Population Survey to the Crime Survey for England and Wales, English Housing Survey, Wealth and Assets Survey, and many in between. In total, the module has been included in over thirty different major surveys, even the Civil Service People Survey, which monitors the attitudes and experiences of government workers.

Including wellbeing questions in existing surveys is a good place to start. But there are also other ways to gauge the feelings of workers more regularly, which is particularly relevant for affective measures (such as happiness and stress) as opposed to the more evaluative measures that we might expect to move more slowly over time (such as job satisfaction). We have experimented, for example, with weekly email surveys that place as little burden as possible on workers, to the extent that a simple click from within the email body will register the response. Even for those without email addresses, many workers in occupations across the board typically interact with a screen of some sort during the workday, be it on a cash register or a company tablet out in the field. Such interfaces can be used to gauge employees' opinions simply but effectively.

The major advantage of a light-touch but frequent survey is that it enables company leaders to deal with major issues as they emerge, rather than being hopelessly behind the curve when they gauge wellbeing measures only once a year or even less frequently. After all, by the time senior leaders pick up on a negative trend from infrequent surveys, the problem may have long festered and caused irreparable damage across the organization.

Comparable Statistics

After collecting data, benchmarking is a good way to assess whether you have a problem. One way is to use the ever-more available crowdsourced data from platforms like Indeed, Glassdoor, and others. This can be an easy place to start to compare levels against those of competitors working within the same business sector or geographic area.

Ultimately, we would like to see comparable statistics made available from internal surveys, so that we can get an inside-out look that complements the outside-in view from external sources. This may start happening through voluntary reporting, such as with environmental, social, and corporate governance metrics that are now common for publicly traded firms.

We have, for example, collaborated with S&P Global, a leading ratings agency that collects data from all sorts of sources, including from firms themselves, for its annual Corporate Sustainability Assessment. Its latest handbook—which provides information and guidance for companies on the types of information they should collect and provide it with—follows our lead in suggesting that firms survey their workers on the four aspects that "align with how statistical agencies are measuring general wellbeing, including job satisfaction, purpose, happiness, and stress."[8]

The Importance of Piloting and Evaluation

The beginning of this chapter can be summed up with the direction to "measure, measure, measure." But also important is to "test, test, test" and empirically evaluate the impact any intervention may be having on wellbeing and performance. Whether the approach is a direct intervention on wellbeing or an indirect attempt to improve one of the drivers, it is important to verify it actually works. Whatever change to management and organizational practices is made, you will want to know if it is effective, especially compared to its costs, before rushing to roll it out to the whole company.

It would be nearly impossible to imagine a world in which companies put marketing schemes, research and development plans, and product launches into place without measuring or monitoring the return on their investments. Many will even run experimental A/B tests to decide the best font size and color for their company website. But while much of this testing happens in the context of things like marketing and product development, why not extend it to management practices?

The Power of Randomization

Firms truly interested in identifying the causal effects of their interventions should regularly and routinely run randomized controlled trials (known as RCTs among academics but more often as A/B tests among practitioners). Properly designed trials or pilots, where feasible, will help you understand what works and what does not. It can be challenging to randomize across workers or business units and do the work of measuring the effects. But we think it is far preferable to wasting large amounts of time and money on things that ultimately do not achieve what they set out to do.

When considering a change in a policy or practice in your organization, think about whether it may be possible to randomly divide some subset of employees to experience the change at one point in time, and another group in the future. However, while there is good reason that RCTs are considered the gold standard in assessing evidence and establishing causation, running these sorts of experiments in real-world company settings may not always be feasible. Two important caveats to keep in mind are the potential for ethical concerns and unintended spillovers.

Experimentation in Practice

For an example of an ethical concern, imagine you wish to consider the effects of a pay raise on employee wellbeing. Fully convinced by the arguments and methodologies described in this chapter, you decide to run an RCT. You randomly select one group of employees to receive a 10 percent raise, while another group you have selected as the control does not receive a raise. It seems obvious that this would be an extraordinarily difficult program to implement or justify. Given the importance of social comparisons, depriving one group of an obvious benefit while providing it to another is precisely the kind of thing to avoid if your goal is to improve wellbeing.

Nevertheless, there are plenty of interventions and initiatives where RCTs can and should be employed. Consider, for example, remote work. While many organizations offer remote working opportunities to their employees, few have run rigorous trials to test its effects on employee wellbeing and productivity. Whether or not this policy would have the intended effects in any one organizational context may not be immediately apparent beforehand. As a result, this may be just the kind of initiative that would benefit from an RCT within the company itself without having to contend with the ethical considerations that would accompany randomly assigned pay increases.

To reduce potential ethical concerns further, many companies introduce new policies via a staggered rollout, instead of a standard RCT. This way, the control group can benefit from the intervention if it so chooses, albeit at a later date. And if the first group to get the policy is randomly selected, it is still possible to determine the causal effect of the policy. Alternatively, firms can run initiatives not at the individual level (where social comparisons may arise), but at the business unit or regional level to test for certain effects.

In addition to ethical concerns, another consideration when seeking to implement RCTs in organizational settings is the potential for unintended spillovers. In the case of workers randomly assigned to work from home, remote workers might continue to meet and collaborate with those who remain at the office. As a result, while working from home may have direct effects on the productivity and wellbeing of those asked to do so, it can also have spillover effects on colleagues and coworkers. These sorts of dynamics are difficult to control for entirely, but, as much as possible, it is worth thinking about what the potential (positive or negative) spillovers of a given experiment may be and trying to minimize or at least monitor them throughout the course of the study.[9]

A First Clue: Job Title Differences

Before zooming into specific facets of jobs and workplaces, as we will do in the next chapter, we can start by looking at how wellbeing at work varies across the types of jobs people do. This can give us some initial indication of the types of tasks and work environments that are most significantly associated with workplace wellbeing.

Figure 5-4 shows the different components of wellbeing broken out by the job title that people give when replying to the survey on workplace wellbeing, which we categorize into broad groups. A few things jump out, the first being that wellbeing patterns don't always match up with wages. Among the most satisfied are educational professionals, who are not always the most generously remunerated in the economy. Care jobs also score high on a sense of purpose, along with the arts. Second, stress isn't always bad—military professions score simultaneously very high on purpose and satisfaction while also ranking as the most heavily stressed.

Similarly high-stress jobs are veterinary, pharmacy, and medical practitioners. But who is actually enjoying their jobs? The ones experiencing the most day-to-day happiness are educators and those working in entertainment with jobs in the arts, media, and sport. Agricultural workers too find their jobs enjoyable, on the whole. Manufacturing, warehouse, and transport workers, on the other hand, experience very little happiness in their day-to-day work lives. They are also among the least satisfied, and while these professions were once strongly unionized, union membership has dropped precipitously over the past forty years, particularly (though not only) in the United States.

FIGURE 5-4

Workplace Wellbeing across Types of Job

Average levels
of workplace
wellbeing (on a 1–5
scale) by job type

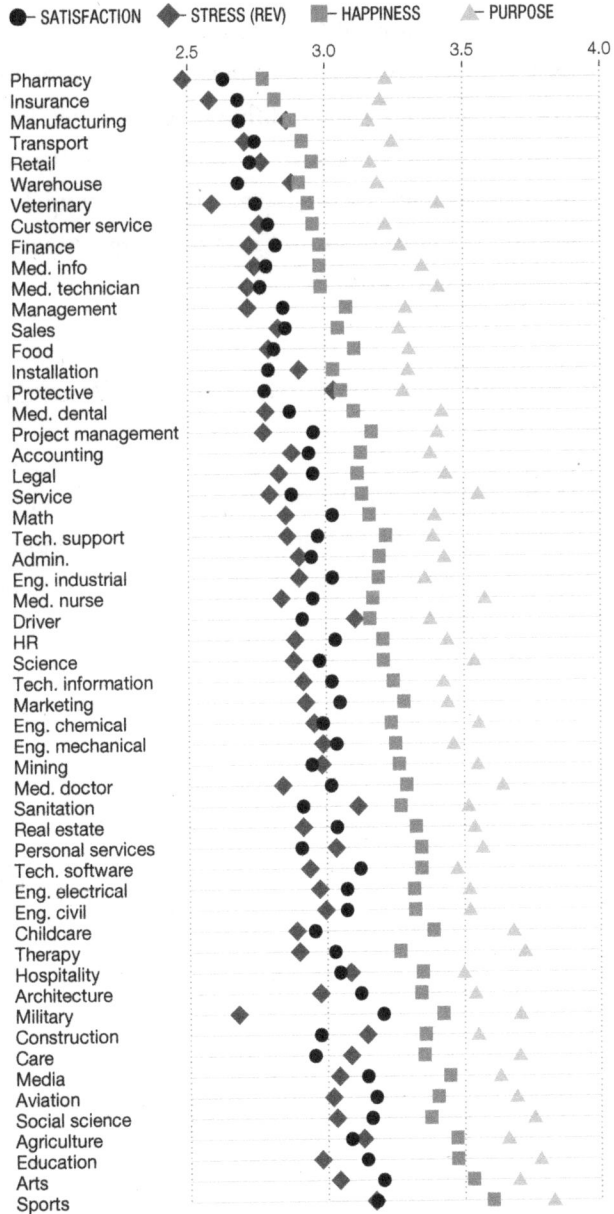

●– SATISFACTION   ◆ STRESS (REV)   ■– HAPPINESS   ▲– PURPOSE

Note: Survey respondents are asked to input a job title, which is then categorized into a broader job type.
Included are all job categories with 500+ responses. N = 9,428,676.
Source: Indeed, using data from October 2019 to May 2024.

It is worth reiterating that even within these job categories, there remains significant inequality in wellbeing, and it is certainly not inevitable that a worker in a certain occupation will be hugely dissatisfied or bereft of purpose.

Thinking about what these jobs involve and imagining why some are happier or more stressed than others can start us off on the journey of discovering what exactly about different jobs and workplaces is conducive to wellbeing—or not. Data such as that shown in figure 5-3 gets us, as academics, immediately theorizing and hypothesizing. But ultimately we need to start breaking things down and thinking systematically about what is going on inside workplaces.

An Evidence-Based Approach to Workplace Wellbeing

We hope that this chapter has inspired the bookish data scientist in all of us, and to ensure that we measure what we treasure. After all, what gets measured tends to get attention in organizations. But once there's action on the ground and interventions are being rolled out, it remains important to continue empirically evaluating the impact on wellbeing and performance measures.

Chapter 6

Understanding What Drives Workplace Wellbeing

A fter looking at how to properly measure workplace wellbeing in the previous chapter, we turn now to the key issue of how to make good sense of the data. After all, the insights derived from the data will set you up for how to best improve workplace wellbeing and help prioritize the interventions that will give the biggest bang for your buck.

Most organizations have all kinds of data on their employees, and this tends to populate a great many reports, memos, and dashboards. However, what's often holding back effective interventions is the lack of a scientific approach to leveraging the data that they have. To derive the insights needed requires conceptual clarity, where you distinguish between the outcome of interest (in this case workplace wellbeing) on the one hand, and what drives or causes it on the other.

In this chapter we will discuss the largest set of global analyses to date designed to figure out what actually drives workplace wellbeing. The "driver" approach, as we'll call it—combined with some basic statistical analysis—will bridge the gap that exists in practice between measurement (of which there's a lot) and evidence-based policies being rolled out to improve wellbeing (of which there's little).

Direct or Indirect Routes to Improvement

Let's assume you have already measured the main components of workplace wellbeing and its primary drivers. Worryingly, you find a concerning amount of unhappiness among many employees. What now? When it comes to trying to improve workplace wellbeing, there are at least two main approaches.

The first is the direct route. This seems to be the most popular and tends, in our experience, to be what immediately comes to people's minds when we begin to discuss the topic of workplace wellbeing. Here the goal is trying to intervene in some way to boost worker wellbeing, while leaving the ways that work is managed and organized otherwise untouched.

The second (which is not mutually exclusive from the first) is somewhat more indirect and is perhaps not immediately intuitive. The goal here is to intervene to change one or more of the key drivers of workplace wellbeing. This can be much more difficult and involves a lot more commitment on the part of the company but, as we will see, is ultimately much more worthwhile.

Wellness Programs

Many people will have at some stage been invited to join a corporate wellness program. These programs have become a major industry, covering many millions of workers worldwide. Though the main goal is usually to improve employee physical health and lower health-care costs, wellness programs are also the prototypical intervention for improving employee wellbeing. The programs involve a range of different components and vary significantly in what they include and how they are implemented. Most involve health screenings and other health-related perks such as free or subsidized gym membership, yoga classes, free lunches, employee assistance programs, and so on.

But do they work? The evidence is unfortunately somewhat mixed. Some studies have found that wellness programs can improve outcomes like health and raise productivity.[1] One study followed 111 employees at an industrial dry-cleaning company, scattered across five laundry plants. Comparing four plants that had access to a wellness program with one that happened not to, the researchers found that participating in the program was associated with improved health and wellbeing.[2]

This makes sense. There is ample evidence that exercise and better health can have a significant positive impact on our wellbeing, including how we feel on a day-to-day basis and how satisfied we are with our lives overall.[3] But as encouraging as this is, the body of evidence has grown to suggest that wellness programs may not be particularly effective overall.

While much of the existing evidence relied on anecdote or before-and-after studies, researchers at Harvard Medical School and the University of Chicago set out to find out using an RCT, the gold standard for causal inference, as we discussed in the last chapter.

They conducted their experiment at BJ's Wholesale Club, a large warehouse retailer with over two hundred worksites across the United States employing over 26,000 people.[4] Twenty randomly chosen worksites were given a wellness program with eight different modules. These included Power Down the Pressure—a stress management course; a series of webinars on the importance of things like nutrition, exercise, and sleep called Nutrition for a Lifetime; and Movin' in May—a month-long program designed to encourage employees to exercise.

Around 35 to 45 percent of workers participated and filled in surveys, and underwent health screenings so the researchers could track their progress. On average, the treated workers completed around one-and-a-half modules. Rates of exercise increased in the treatment group, but the overall results were somewhat disappointing. Ultimately, the wellness program did not have any effect on other outcomes like physical and mental health (either self-reported or gleaned from objective measures like body mass index, blood pressure, and cholesterol), medical spending, or job performance and absenteeism.

In another field experimental study conducted around the same time, economists from the universities of Chicago and Illinois went to impressive lengths to test the effectiveness of wellness programs, by designing and implementing one themselves.[5] Their program, iThrive, ran for two years and included annual biometric health screenings, online health risk assessments, and weekly wellness activities, such as classes on healthy workplace habits, tai chi, and physical fitness.

The organization had around 12,500 eligible employees who were invited to be part of the study. The 5,000 or so who signed up were then randomly assigned either to the treatment group, who had access to the program, or to the control group, who did not. Through a mixture of surveys (including measures of wellbeing), medical data, and administrative company data (including tenure and performance), the researchers were able to estimate the causal effects of the program.

Overall, the experiment provided disappointing results: the program did not have a significant effect on any of the outcomes they studied, including job satisfaction. The major issue here was *selection*.

As it turned out, the 5,000 or so employees who signed up were quite a lot healthier, happier, and more productive to begin with than the 7,500 who did not. They had lower medical expenditures and engaged in healthier behaviors like going to the gym more than the nonparticipants. When comparing the participants with the nonparticipants, as a whole, there does appear to be a strong positive effect, in line with many prior nonexperimental studies. But when comparing the treatment and control employees—that is, among those who were inclined to sign up—there were no discernible differences by the end of the program. In other words, those who decided to participate would have gone to the gym anyway.[6]

In line with this, a recent meta-analysis considered a range of individual-level workplace wellbeing interventions, which included aspects such as mindfulness, lifestyle apps, and resilience training. Using data from across 233 organizations, our colleague William Fleming found that there was little evidence of any wellbeing gains. Interestingly, he did find some evidence of a positive effect for volunteering and charity work—a finding replicated with a recent field experiment within a large Latin American bank.[7] All in all, this important line of research suggests that personal interventions that do not end up addressing or discussing working conditions or organizational practices are unlikely to be a panacea for workplace wellbeing.

Beyond Wellness

None of this is to say that wellness programs cannot work or are a bad idea. Far from it. Given the wide variety of forms they take, making any blanket claims about effectiveness is necessarily problematic. But if wellness programs are to have the intended effects, thinking hard about how to design them is hugely important. Without wanting to sound too glib, you can't yoga your way out of more structural challenges to workplace wellbeing.

And we say this as people who sometimes enjoy yoga, as well as many of the other things that are offered by these kinds of programs. Indeed, there is good individual-level evidence for many of things frequently offered, including physical exercise and anything else that can improve physical or mental health. Efforts to provide increased access to mental health care are especially to be strongly encouraged—particularly in contexts where this not adequately covered by public health-care services—given the strong causal links (which we have ourselves studied in prior work) between conditions like depression and anxiety with many aspects of subjective wellbeing.[8]

One of us (George) once took part in an eight-week mindfulness-based stress reduction (MBSR) class that MIT offered—in the spirit of wellness—while he was still studying for a PhD at the Sloan School of Management. In this small class setting, there was also another economist—a PhD student named Pierre-Luc Vautrey. Shortly afterward, he ended up basing a good deal of his impressive dissertation (investigating the links between mental health and economic outcomes) on a clever experiment that showed the positive effects of providing access to a mindfulness meditation app on wellbeing outcomes.[9] This experiment adds to a growing body of evidence showing the potentially beneficial effects of providing support to people if they use it—particularly in the sphere of mental health.[10]

So we applaud employers who offer people ways to stay healthy, both mentally and physically. But it is crucial to recognize that wellness is not the same thing as workplace wellbeing—the latter of which is a well-fleshed-out and multidimensional concept that includes job satisfaction, positive and negative emotions in the workplace, and a sense of purpose and meaning in work. Unfortunately, the two are often conflated. Even worse, one is sometimes seen as a quick-fix way to improve the other, without really engaging with what are often the root causes for low levels of workplace wellbeing.

Structural and Systems Change

If the direct way to improve workplace wellbeing is limited, what else can be done? Unfortunately, there is often no quick and easy fix. If there were a workshop that could easily solve the problem of an unhappy or unsatisfied workforce, then we would offer it. The uncomfortable truth is that we must think seriously about how work is designed and organized and begin to think about structural issues at work, such as scheduling, wages, hours, flexibility, safety; how managers treat workers on a day-to-day basis; and the ways in which people are hired, among many others. Without addressing the underlying cause, treating the symptoms can only get us so far.

While this may seem daunting, there is also good news. First, there is a growing body of evidence-based interventions for many of the wellbeing drivers. Second, while difficult, improving workplace wellbeing leads to significant gains in terms of productivity, retention, recruitment, and ultimately, financial performance.

The Six Drivers of Workplace Wellbeing

To properly answer the question of what drives wellbeing at work, we need to have a set of potential factors to consider. These attributes need to capture everything relevant about a job—for example, the difference between a carpenter or a financial analyst, and the difference between working at Amazon or Walmart. Characterizing different jobs and workplaces is a difficult task, however. Industries and occupations vary significantly, so that categorizing aspects of a job can be challenging. But if we want to think about what drives workplace wellbeing, we ultimately have to be able to quantify things, even if only to gain an initial big-picture look at the dynamics of workplace wellbeing, before delving into a particular context more deeply.

Wages and benefits are an obvious place to start, of course. Beyond that, there are a number of potentially important factors. A few years ago, one of us (George) investigated—in a book together with colleagues on the general determinants of happiness—the extent to which different workplace characteristics affect wellbeing.[11] To do so, we turned to the European Social Survey, which contains detailed data on life satisfaction and different aspects of the workplace experience, such as wages, hours, security, autonomy, chances for promotion, supportive coworkers and supervisors, time pressure, physical danger, and variety.

In the intervening years, we—along with Christian Krekel, a colleague based at the London School of Economics—have looked instead at the ISSP data we mentioned earlier, where we were able to observe detailed information on pay, working hours, work-life balance, job security, difficulty and danger, opportunities for advancement, interestingness of job, social relationships, and skills match.[12] More recently, the Indeed data has allowed us to revisit the issue, and in this case the data available covers things like pay, flexibility, belonging and inclusion, coworker support, trust, learning, energy, and achievement.[13]

From all this data, we were able to group the drivers into loose clusters. Throughout this chapter and for the remainder of this book, we refer to these as the six DRIVERs (referring to the category initials) of workplace wellbeing:

Development and security

Relationships

Independence and flexibility

Variety and fulfillment

Earnings and benefits

Risk, health, and safety

With these potential drivers, we can now ask which are most important in terms of shaping people's workplace wellbeing. For the purposes of this book, we expanded our previous analyses to incorporate new data from five of the largest-scale data sets available, covering more than 53 countries on 6 continents, 102 individual job characteristics, and working conditions. This surely thus counts as one of the most comprehensive analyses of what drives workplace wellbeing to date.

Driver Analysis Using Worldwide Data

Harmonizing the available data sets is no easy task, however. While all of the data sets include at least a variable for wage (and sometimes also for further aspects of remuneration), making the earnings and benefits category relatively straightforward, the other survey items that the organizers of each survey decided to ask differ somewhat. We examined each of the data sets and conducted a clustering analysis of the key variables that exist within each, so we could start to see the forest from the trees. We then used this to help classify each of the questions in the data sets so that we were able to identify the groups of job and workplace characteristics.

For example, depending on the data set, development and security typically includes the answers to questions about workers' perceived job security, the opportunities they feel they have for advancement, their sense of learning on the job, and access to formal training. Relationships, on the other hand, cover an important range of different workplace phenomena, including the perceived quality of relationships workers have with both colleagues and management. Beyond this, depending on the data set used in each of the analyses, the relationships driver also includes things like organizational trust, a sense of being supported and appreciated, and feelings of belonging and inclusion in the workplace.

The category of independence and flexibility covers aspects of a job or workplace such as working hours and a sense of autonomy at work. But it goes beyond this to consider work-life balance (or, indeed the imbalance and conflict that sometimes exists between the two) and the extent to which workers are able to choose or control where and when they work.

Moreover, it also incorporates whether workers feel they are able to decide how they carry out their work and how much independence they experience.

Variety and fulfillment together capture important aspects of work related to how interesting people find the work that they do, how much of a sense of achievement and learning they get out of the job, the extent to which they feel able to fully use their skills, and the variety of tasks involved in the work. The category of risk, health, and safety incorporates the physical demands of the job, the pace and pressure of work, and the extent to which workers feel their physical and mental health is put at risk by the work that they do.

The Importance of Relative Importance

Very often in academia and elsewhere, we do things study by study. One study says autonomy raises people's happiness, another says wages improve wellbeing, those with better social relationships at work are happier, and so on. In this vein, in chapter 7 we look in greater detail at each of the six groups of workplace wellbeing drivers and assess the best data and evidence from the academic literature in turn. But first we take a step back and consider their *relative* importance.

In figure 6-1, we take the data we have available from Indeed, the European Social Survey (ESS), the International Social Science Survey Program (ISSP), the European Working Conditions Survey (EWCS), and the American Working Conditions Survey (AWCS).[14] We then assess the extent to which each group of drivers predicts job satisfaction, on average. While we find almost no examples in the data where the combined presence of all six drivers does *not* predict high levels of wellbeing at work, serious deficiencies in any one can mean the difference between a happy job and an unhappy one.

But some drivers are more important than others. Almost anywhere in the world we look, similar patterns emerge.[15] While wages are clearly an important factor in terms of determining wellbeing—higher-paid workers have higher wellbeing, on average—it is much less important than social

FIGURE 6-1

Meta-Analysis of the Drivers of Workplace Wellbeing

Impact of various drivers on job satisfaction across five data sources

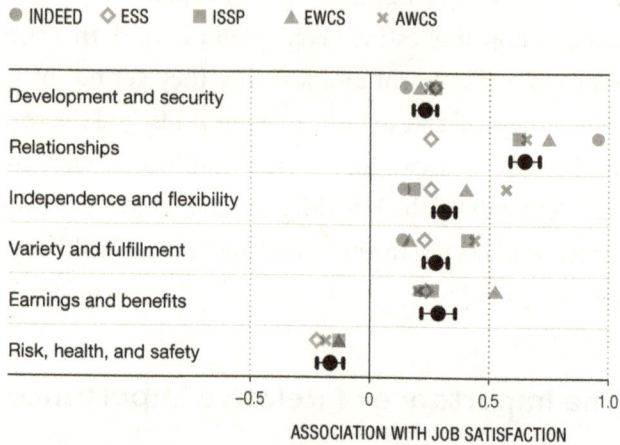

Note: Figure shows the association of various workplace factors with job satisfaction, based on analysis of different data sets. Average association across data sets shown in bold. See text for further detail.
Source: Indeed (N = 7,316,147); ESS (N = 12,047); ISSP (N = 15,658); EWCS (N = 16,973); AWCS (N = 1,684).

factors such as the relationships we have at work with both colleagues and supervisors.

This focus on relative importance is crucial given that organizations are constrained by budgets. Ultimately, decisions have to be made on how to allocate scare resources. Do we increase wages by 5 percent, or do we offer more flexible work arrangements? How much is each going to cost, and what's the likely impact on wellbeing? Only with these numbers in hand can we reasonably start to think about such choices.

Separating Drivers and Outcomes

These analyses highlight again the importance of separating workplace wellbeing from its drivers, both conceptually and in empirical investigation.

A few years ago, the two of us worked on a paper titled "What Makes for a Good Job?," which sounds like a relatively straightforward question. But what exactly is a good job? We all seem to have some innate sense of what this phrase means. Many of us spend considerable amounts of time and energy looking for a good job. That pursuit can inform where we live, how we spend our time, and much else. Yet actually settling on a precise definition can be an elusive task. Any one person's definition seems likely to diverge from another's. So, who gets to decide?

When assessing job quality, there are two main approaches.[16] Jobs have a number of different facets, as we have already seen. One approach is to take the data on all these different aspects of people's jobs and create a summary index of them—including the objective ones like wages, hours, and so on, as well as the subjective ones such as belonging, sense of autonomy, purpose, and satisfaction. In our work with managers and executives—the vast majority of whom are motivated to improve the working lives of their employees—we have encountered this well-meaning approach many times. But it comes with some conceptual confusion. There is considerable difficulty in working out how to weight each of the factors in such an index, and the approach is not ultimately able to tell us much about what managers should focus on.

The second approach is to ask people. As we have highlighted before, this approach is deceptively simple but very powerful and recommended. We see workplace wellbeing as a key outcome measure, which summarizes people's job quality. This more democratic or bottom-up approach allows for the weights about what matters most to workers to be derived from their own responses. We have looked so far at average effects in figure 6-1, but organizations should be collecting data and running these kinds of simple analyses regularly to better understand what lies behind employees' wellbeing or lack of it. This can be a starting point in thinking about where we might look to improve things, which will involve closer analysis, piloting, and experimentation, as we will see in chapter 7.

Cross-Cutting Drivers

The driver analysis provides a powerful way for us to assess what determines workplace wellbeing, to give relative weights to the different factors, and to help us to decide where resources and effort should be targeted if improving wellbeing is the goal. Not everything about a job or a workplace fits neatly into the six categories we noted, however. As we will see in the next chapter, when improving each of the six drivers, some interventions are likely to improve not only one such driver neatly but also others as well.

In some sense, then, it would be appealing to model the workplace characteristics in a more fine-grained manner—perhaps, say, twenty factors or even more. While this may bring more realism, which is good, it very often leads us away from the big picture. After all, at this stage we are examining the overall determinants of wellbeing across all industries and occupations. This may well differ in a range of contexts, and that is why we advocate that firms collect data and run their own driver analyses to get to the bottom of what is driving (un)happiness in the workforce.

Some potential drivers are what we call cross-cutting and do not fit neatly into any one category. These include things like the ability to engage in job crafting, which is a well-studied and effective way for workers to customize their jobs by deciding for themselves a range of aspects such as tasks and interactions with colleagues, customers, and management at work. This sits largely within independence and flexibility, but also has large aspects that are likely to fall within variety and fulfillment.

Worker voice and labor unions are a very important topic that spans multiple driver groups. Though often and unfortunately disparaged, without recourse to the empirical evidence on their effects, by some within the business community, they can have significant beneficial impacts.[17] The traditional focus of unions on collective wage bargaining means they are within the earnings and benefits category, but they—along with other vehicles of workers' voice such as works councils and more informal mechanisms of feedback—also significantly affect various other drivers, such as the relationship between workers and management.

In one sense, one might see the presence of worker voice as detrimental to such relationships. After all, what good could conflict do? But at least some degree of conflict is unavoidable and is indeed, arguably, inherent to the employment relationship.[18] Perfectly aligning worker and management interests is unlikely to ever happen. But conflict need not be pathological. Instead, proper dialogue with mutual respect is far more likely to improve relationships at work in the long run, and to facilitate information sharing in both directions that can also improve productivity.[19]

Both Workers and Managers Are Often Wrong

Isn't this all obvious? Another objection we hear when teaching about these kinds of findings in business schools is that this is just common sense. To put this to the test, we asked employees across the United States, Canada, and the UK what they thought were the most important drivers of well-being at work. Using a large representative sample of employed workers, we collected data on the usual set of workplace wellbeing and driver questions.[20] But we also included something that is more commonly used in the marketing world—a short survey experiment to see what people think are the most important drivers.[21] Using this data, we then compared what people believe drives workplace wellbeing and what actually accounts for the variation in wellbeing we see across those very same people.

What we find—as can be seen in figure 6-2—is that people overwhelmingly *think* compensation and, to a lesser extent, time and location flexibility are the most important. These two dominate the list. Factors like feeling a sense of belonging, having a manager who helps to succeed, and feeling supported and encouraged come a long way down the list.

But when actually analyzing the data—from the same respondents—and running a driver analysis, such as that we conducted to find out what is responsible for explaining workplace wellbeing we find something quite different. A much broader mix of factors helps to explain variation in workplace wellbeing, rather than domination by one or even two factors. Pay and benefits remain a significant predictor of workplace wellbeing, but they are far from being the only or even the most important. Indeed, factors like feelings of belonging ultimately come out at the top of the list, much as when we considered this question with the multitude of other data sets where we were able to find sufficient data.

Executives often get this wrong as well. In a recent survey, 1,073 business executives in the United States were asked what they believe are the top drivers of happiness at work.[22] The results suggest that managers believe

FIGURE 6-2

Determinants of Work Wellbeing: What People Think versus Reality

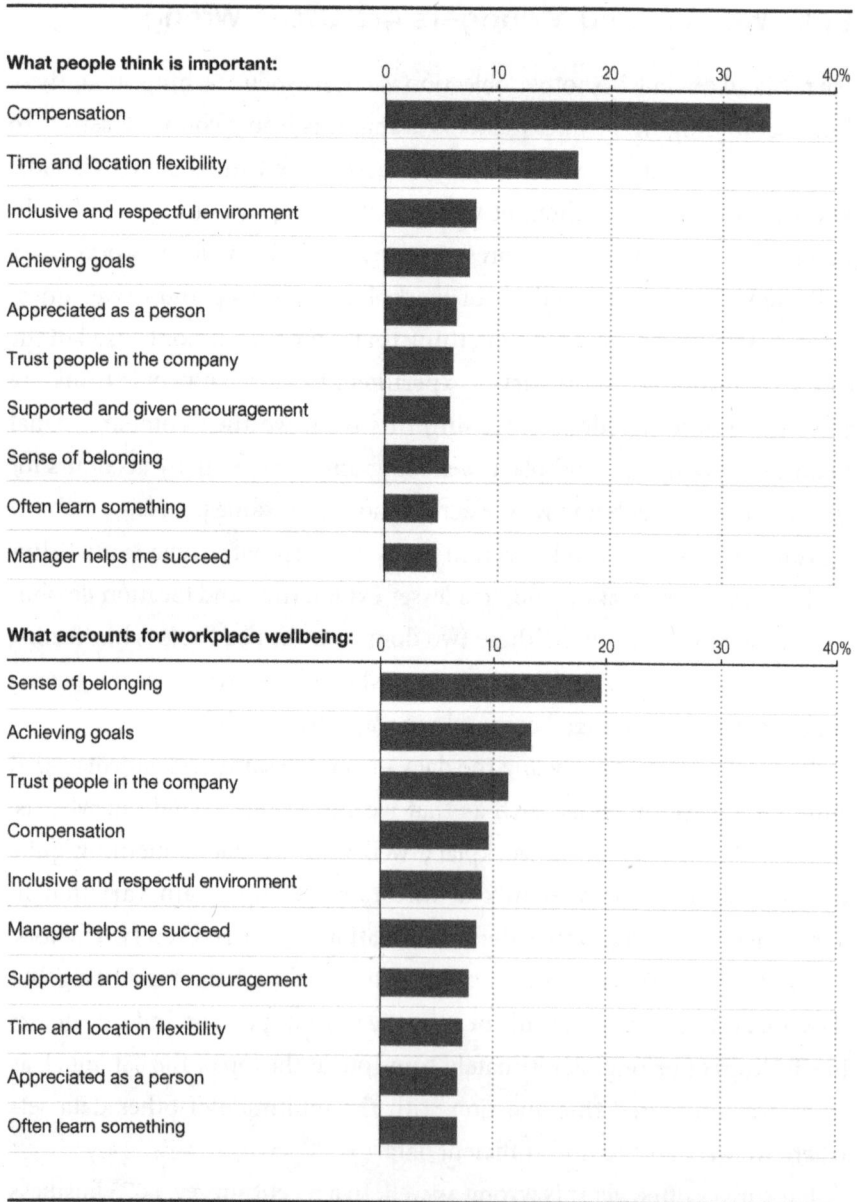

What people think is important:

| | 0 | 10 | 20 | 30 | 40% |

Compensation

Time and location flexibility

Inclusive and respectful environment

Achieving goals

Appreciated as a person

Trust people in the company

Supported and given encouragement

Sense of belonging

Often learn something

Manager helps me succeed

What accounts for workplace wellbeing:

| | 0 | 10 | 20 | 30 | 40% |

Sense of belonging

Achieving goals

Trust people in the company

Compensation

Inclusive and respectful environment

Manager helps me succeed

Supported and given encouragement

Time and location flexibility

Appreciated as a person

Often learn something

Note: Top chart plots the percentage importance from a maxDiff analysis on 5,026 respondents in the US. Bottom chart reports Shapley values from an analysis on the same survey respondents, where the outcome is the mean of satisfaction, purpose, happiness, and (reverse-coded) stress.
Source: Indeed-commissioned survey conducted by Forrester Consulting, 2022.

factors like trust and relationships, with both colleagues and management, are more important determinants of wellbeing than compensation. But they strongly underestimated the potential for employees' sense of belonging and their relationships with managers to shape levels of work happiness.

With neither employees nor managers quite sure, it is no surprise that we see so many well-meaning managers floundering when trying to improve wellbeing. The vast majority of managers see workplace wellbeing as a key source of competitive advantage, recognizing its importance for business success. But only a third report making wellbeing a top priority. And fewer than 20 percent have any sort of wellbeing strategy in place.[23] Workers' expectations surrounding workplace wellbeing are increasing, as we have seen earlier in this book, and they feel their employers are not doing enough.

From our experience speaking to executives and managers in firms both large and small, a growing number are motivated to bring the topic of worker wellbeing to the fore. But to do so, we need to understand better not only what work wellbeing consists of, but also what ultimately shapes it, and in turn, which interventions effectively impact these drivers. That's precisely what the next chapter is all about.

Chapter 7

How to Improve the Drivers of Workplace Wellbeing

After measuring workplace wellbeing and conducting driver analyses, preferably in close collaboration and conversation with workers themselves in order to ascertain the main issues, the natural next step is to improve the drivers. We have argued that it is crucial to go beyond wellness programs and direct interventions to improve wellbeing and instead think about how work is designed and organized. This means intervening on the drivers of wellbeing themselves.

In this chapter, we will go through the six main drivers in turn and consider some of the best existing evidence to effectively improve workplace wellbeing. We do not pretend this is an exhaustive list of things to do, and some will, of course, be more relevant to some organizations than others. As long as they are rigorously tested, new and exciting ideas not yet tried or included here are also possible.

Development and Security

Our first driver encompasses two interrelated and critical components of work—job security and career advancement. We start by considering in more detail the connections between job security and wellbeing, before thinking more practically about how to leverage this driver to increase wellbeing.

Job Security

Controlling for a range of other factors—like age, gender, education, income, and other characteristics of jobs and workplaces—we find, using large-scale data, that employees who feel secure in their positions are not only more satisfied with their jobs, but also with their lives as a whole (see figure 7-1).[1]

It isn't hard to imagine why. For most of us, having a job is critically important to our wellbeing. We spent considerable time earlier in the book explaining the devastating consequences of losing one. For millions of people worldwide, having a job can mean the difference between financial stability and economic insecurity. Anyone who has experienced the misfortune of not knowing how they will pay for rent or food is intimately in touch with the profound toll it can take on mental and physical health.

Not knowing if or when we might become unemployed threatens not only our wallets, but also our sense of self. Some studies have found that feelings of job insecurity degrade wellbeing to an extent that may even surpass unemployment.[2] It may then be unsurprising that most adults around the world report security to be one of the most important characteristics

FIGURE 7-1

The Importance of Feeling Secure in a Job

Note: Regression-adjusted levels of job and life satisfaction are plotted at different levels of perceived job security. Job security is measured by respondents' agreement with the statement "My job is secure," which is coded as High ("very true"), Medium-high ("quite true"), Medium-low ("a little true"), and Low ("not at all true"). N = 11,403 across 26 countries.
Source: European Social Survey (2010–2011).

FIGURE 7-2

What People Say Is Most Important to Them in a Job

How important are the following job features to you?*

Percentage of respondents reporting "very important" or "important"

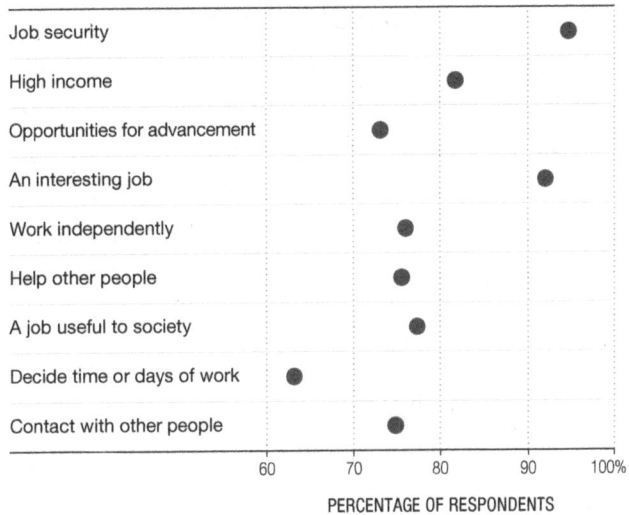

Job security		
High income		
Opportunities for advancement		
An interesting job		
Work independently		
Help other people		
A job useful to society		
Decide time or days of work		
Contact with other people		

60   70   80   90   100%

PERCENTAGE OF RESPONDENTS

*Very important, important, neither important nor unimportant, not important, not important at all.
Note: N = 27,732 across 37 countries. Employed individuals only.
Source: International Social Survey Programme (ISSP).

they look for in a job. In a survey of more than 27,000 individuals in thirty-seven countries, shown in figure 7-2, we find that roughly 95 percent of respondents reported that job security was either important or very important to them, more than any other job feature under consideration.

Job security also varies by individual characteristics and societal conditions.[3] Older and higher-educated workers report higher levels of job security than their younger and less educated counterparts. Those employed in higher-income professions are also generally less concerned about losing their jobs than low-wage workers. Differences also cut across country lines. Levels of job security in the United States—a country where employers can dismiss employees for almost any reason at any time—are generally lower than those in most Western European countries, for example.

A large part of job security has to do with public policy rather than with firms themselves. In our first piece of work together, for example, we demonstrated macroeconomic loss aversion by showing the outsized impact that recessions have on various aspects of subjective wellbeing, as compared to equivalent periods of positive economic growth. But firms can also play a key role.[4]

While it is true that a great deal here can be achieved through public policy—for example, with the implementation of active labor market policies—there are also practical things firms can implement as well. Indeed, the issue of job security presents a clear opportunity to improve wellbeing by leveraging one of the drivers, in this case, providing stable employment to workers so that they can spend more of their time and energy working and enjoying life as opposed to worrying where the next paycheck might come from.

So, what can managers and executives do? Perhaps the most important determinant of job security is the nature of the employment contract itself. Workers on temporary contracts are far more insecure than those on permanent contracts, as we show in figure 7-3. This relationship is so strong that some researchers consider temporary contracts in and of themselves to be indicators of job insecurity.[5] In Europe, workers on permanent contracts are both significantly more secure and satisfied in their jobs. This relation-

FIGURE 7-3

Temporary Contracts Are Associated with Lower Wellbeing

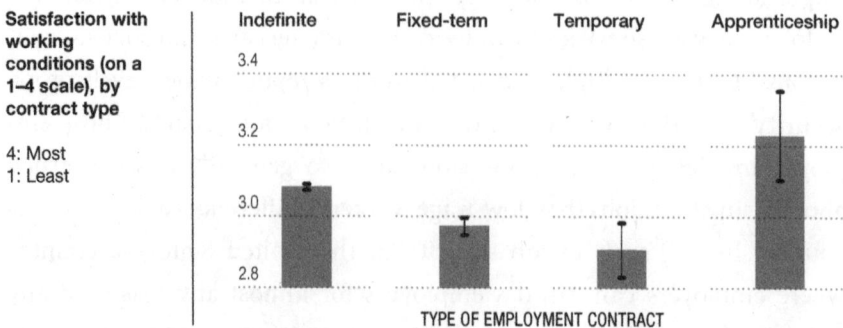

Note: N = 30,206 across 35 countries. Employed respondents, 21–24 years old.
Source: European Working Conditions Survey.

ship is important to pay attention to. In the United States, temporary employment has been increasing by roughly 1 million jobs per year since the Great Recession.[6] Today, roughly 10 percent of European workers are on temporary contracts. In some countries, the rate climbs to upward of 25 percent.[7]

In addition to the importance of contracts, the advancement of worker voice—whether through labor unions or other mechanisms—can also play a crucial role here as well as in many other areas, as we will see later. While the link between employee voice and job security may not be immediately obvious, a raft of research has demonstrated that one of the most fundamental reasons workers feel insecure about their working arrangements is a sense that they lack control over their work lives and responsibilities.[8]

One careful analysis investigated the effects of a policy reform in Finland in 1991 that made worker representation on company boards mandatory. The researchers cleverly exploited the fact that the policy was only mandatory for firms with more than 150 workers and looked at subsequent differences in employee wellbeing following the policy change for firms just above and below this cutoff. The study found that the policy led to improvements in workers' sense of job security and subjective job quality.[9] And contrary to common expectations, the reform increased labor productivity rather than providing a drag on firms.[10] While American firms, and particularly American lawmakers, tend to remain highly skeptical of these sorts of arrangements, an emerging contingent of companies including Gore-Tex, Semco, and Freys Hotel have recently implemented "workplace democracy" structures where employees have opportunities to directly vote on and contribute to organizational initiatives and decisions, suggesting that benefits are becoming more widely acknowledged.

Finally, another important practical element for firms is communication. Not knowing where the organization is headed, what the institutional or organizational goals are, or what the intentions or objectives of supervisors may be can all be key predictors of job insecurity. Businesses can improve feelings of job security by ensuring that leaders—CEOs, managers, supervisors, or human resource managers—also try to keep employees sufficiently informed, not only about their own roles and responsibilities, but also about organizational challenges, objectives, and directions.

One analysis looking at more than 3,800 European employees across twenty organizations found significant links between low levels of organizational communication and high levels of job insecurity.[11] Another study of faculty members at an American university found that workers who reported having sufficient and accurate information about the challenges facing the organization subsequently reported lower levels of job insecurity.[12] In fact, higher feelings of job security stemming in part from insufficient communication predicted lower levels of job satisfaction and organizational commitment, as well as higher levels of withdrawal behaviors.

Other researchers have employed more experimental methods to test these relationships. For example, a team of researchers developed and tested an internal communication program during a merger between two firms. Employees were divided into treatment and control groups, with the former receiving a series of detailed communications from higher-ups about the nature and potential consequences of the merger. The study found that workers who received these communications were significantly less likely to report high levels of insecurity than counterparts who did not.[13]

Career Advancement

Most workers express strong preferences to advance in their careers. In a recent analysis by Glassdoor, not having access to career development opportunities was one of the most important predictors of turnover in the United States.[14] Unfortunately, career development opportunities are not equally available to everyone. Relative to those without university-level educations, workers with graduate degrees are more than twice as likely to report having good prospects for advancement. Older workers are generally more pessimistic about their ability to progress in their careers than younger counterparts. Gender gaps are also apparent. In Europe, men consistently report having greater access to advancement opportunities than women, though this gap appears to be shrinking.[15]

On-the-job training is a key mechanism through which firms can provide workers with a greater sense of possible career advancement. Unfortunately, those who stand to benefit most from job training programs are also often those with the most limited access to them. In Europe, half of the top 20 percent of earners report undergoing training programs in the last year, compared to only one-fifth of the bottom 20 percent.[16] Full-time and permanent workers are significantly more likely to receive job training than part-time and temporary workers.[17] One study using longitudinal data in Canada found that job training had no significant effects at all on the wages of high-income workers, but led to significant earnings improvements among low-wage workers.[18]

One of the most common ways to provide on-the-job training is to offer subsidized training or tuition replacement as part of workers' benefit packages. In 2012, Amazon introduced the "Career Choice" program, which provides up to $12,000 in tuition replacement for any employees seeking to pursue an academic degree while working at the company. More than 110,000 employees have taken advantage of the initiative to pursue advanced degrees, as well as GED and ESL certifications.[19] Other firms including Adobe have since followed suit, offering up to $10,000 per employee for those seeking professional development opportunities through its own learning fund. Google also offers tuition reimbursement and 50 percent refunds on all college-level courses employees wish to pursue, even if they have nothing at all to do with workers' professional responsibilities.

Apprenticeship programs funded by companies themselves have also shown positive results. In the United States, for example, many of the most successful companies already offer apprenticeship programs to early-career workers. Accenture provides a twelve-month program combining classroom and on-the-job training in more than thirty cities around the country.[20] Airbnb offers a six-month coding apprenticeship to undergraduates where participants receive full-time salaries and benefits and are offered mentorship opportunities, coding courses, and ultimately placement in working groups at the company in the later stages of the program.[21] Google, IBM, LinkedIn, Microsoft, and many more have hopped on board with similar initiatives.[22]

Other interventions to consider for career advancement are mentoring programs, which have been shown to be a significant contributor to both skill development and workplace wellbeing.[23] These depend fundamentally on interpersonal relationships within the organization, which are hugely important in shaping workplace wellbeing.

Relationships

The late professor Chris Peterson, an early voice in positive psychology, used to say that much of the research on happiness can be summed up in three words: "Other people matter."[24] People with strong relationships are more satisfied with their lives, feel more frequent and stronger positive emotions, experience fewer negative emotions, and perceive their lives to be more meaningful.[25] They are less likely to experience mental health issues, more likely to be physically healthy, and generally live longer.[26]

The critical importance of social relationships carries over into workplace settings too. Simply having personal contact with others at work is not in itself predictive of workplace wellbeing, though. Rather it is the quality of relationships with both managers and coworkers that can make a profound difference to wellbeing. In figure 7-4, we plot average quality of working relationships from workers in thirty-seven countries around the world.[27] Across the board, relationships with coworkers are stronger than with bosses, with some countries such as France and Japan faring particularly poorly when it comes to the ways in which management and workers interact with each other. This has the potential to be ruinous for workplace wellbeing.

Among the various aspects of workplace relationships that are strongly associated with wellbeing, a sense of belonging typically comes very near or at the top of the list, regardless of which data set we look at. What do we mean about a sense of belonging? In a survey run by our colleagues at Indeed, workers were asked what would make them feel like they "belong."[28] What came out of this deep dive is that employees want to feel "like my company cares about me as a person," that they have friends at work, and that they understand how they impact other people and teams in the

FIGURE 7-4

Quality of Workplace Relationships Varies Significantly across the World

Average reported levels of workplace relations (on a 1–5 scale), by country	How would you describe relations at your workplace between . . .?	
5: Very good 1: Very bad	**Management and employees**	**Workmates and colleagues**

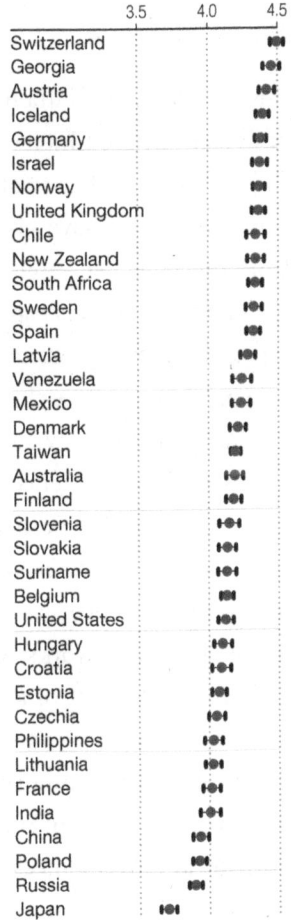

	Management and employees	Workmates and colleagues
	3.5 4.0 4.5	3.5 4.0 4.5
	Georgia	Switzerland
	Austria	Georgia
	Venezuela	Austria
	Switzerland	Iceland
	Israel	Germany
	Germany	Israel
	South Africa	Norway
	Mexico	United Kingdom
	Taiwan	Chile
	Latvia	New Zealand
	Iceland	South Africa
	New Zealand	Sweden
	Spain	Spain
	Chile	Latvia
	India	Venezuela
	Philippines	Mexico
	United States	Denmark
	United Kingdom	Taiwan
	Suriname	Australia
	Slovakia	Finland
	Hungary	Slovenia
	Estonia	Slovakia
	Finland	Suriname
	Croatia	Belgium
	Lithuania	United States
	Norway	Hungary
	Australia	Croatia
	Sweden	Estonia
	Czechia	Czechia
	China	Philippines
	Denmark	Lithuania
	Russia	France
	Belgium	India
	Slovenia	China
	Poland	Poland
	France	Russia
	Japan	Japan

Note: N = 25,655 across 37 countries. Employed individuals only, 21–64 years old.
Source: International Social Survey Programme (ISSP).

organization. Also indicative of belonging were conversations with cowork-ers about things not related to work and invitations to informal social events outside of working hours, and, of course, invitations to important internal meetings. Somewhat related to a sense of belonging is also feeling that the workplace environment is inclusive and respectful, which typically features heavily in regard to quality relations as well.

Mentorship

But despite its fundamental importance as a driver of wellbeing, the body of evidence-based interventions designed to improve workplace relation-ships is small relative to other drivers considered in this chapter. One prom-ising avenue we have noted is mentoring programs. Mentees can benefit from the expertise, attention, and support they receive from higher-ups in the company. This is especially true if they are new or come from under-represented backgrounds. At the same time, mentoring relationships can also produce positive changes in mentors themselves.

One systematic review of twenty-six studies found that mentoring pro-grams proved to be effective strategies to increase workplace wellbeing as well as measurable positive organizational outcomes.[29] Another carefully conducted quasi-experimental study of mentoring programs implemented in a software company in China found that the program produced stronger social ties and networks among women—an effect that was particularly no-table in the context of a workplace environment generally dominated by men.[30] Yet another randomized control trial of mentoring programs for underrepresented minority workers in an academic medical center found significant short-term increases in psychological wellbeing and need ful-fillment among mentees (though no long-term organizational or career outcomes were measured).[31] Once seen as a novelty or luxury, these sorts of initiatives have become increasingly commonplace in the modern world of work. More than 70 percent of *Fortune* 500 companies now offer some form of mentoring for employees, some of which have been rigorously tested with strongly positive effects on worker wellbeing, development, and retention.[32]

DEI Training

Along with mentoring, one obvious intervention is a training program on diversity, equity, and inclusion (DEI). Well-meaning as these programs often are, the evidence on their effectiveness is not wholly encouraging—though, of course, the content and way in which they are designed matters a great deal.[33] In one of the most carefully conducted studies to date, an all-star team of researchers who work on these and similar issues ran a large-scale field experiment in the actual workplace settings of a large international corporation. In multiple locations, the researchers asked randomly selected subsets of employees to complete an online diversity training course. They found only minor and short-lived effects of the training on employee attitudes, and almost no effect on actual behavior, compared to the control group. Ultimately, they concluded that "one-off diversity trainings that are commonplace in organizations are unlikely to be stand-alone solutions for promoting equality in the workplace, particularly given their limited efficacy among those groups whose behaviors policymakers are most eager to influence."[34]

In many ways, the issue here is similar to that of the wellness programs we discussed earlier. Individual-level training programs for employees can miss the point, and in some cases even backfire.[35] Instead, firms need structural and systematic change to the ways in which they hire and treat their workforce. The topic of hiring and diversity is beyond the scope of this book, but a lively research field has pointed toward several practices—none of which is a panacea—including studies on practices like blind hiring, special hiring, and joint evaluation.[36] When it comes to fostering relationships within the organization, mentoring programs show some promise, while employee training programs generally do not. Training for managers may be more effective, however.

Taking a close look at data from more than eight hundred companies over a three-decade period, researchers have also found that employee training on the related topic of sexual harassment (an important issue we will return to later) reduces the number of women who ultimately become managers.[37] Training for managers, on the other hand—which generally serves to teach managers to recognize signs of harassment and equip them with tools to intervene and stop it—seems to be more effective and leads, ultimately, to a greater number of women managers in their sample.

Relational Atmosphere and Managerial People Skills

Managers matter, in other words. And an organization's relational culture is something that leaders can influence and shape.[38] The importance of social skills in the labor market as a whole has been shown to be rising in recent years.[39] This is particularly the case for managers. Indeed, social skills are strongly associated with better team performance in general.[40]

Using data from a large tech firm, for example, a careful analysis shows that people management skills measured within surveys are strongly related to employee turnover, a finding that remains even when looking at what happens when managers move around the firm.[41]

Running a large-scale field experiment including over three thousand employees across twenty large corporations in Turkey, researchers tested the effects of an intervention they called "Transforming the Relational Atmosphere in Firms," designed to increase prosocial behavior, trust, and cooperation.[42] The program was administered at all levels of the organization but was particularly focused on leaders' behavior and the interactions between supervisors and subordinates. It emphasized effective and peaceful communication, prosociality, and professional support. The program also involved an eight-week follow-up exercise in which participants develop and propose to top management projects designed to improve prosocial interactions.

The program ultimately led to increased levels of job satisfaction—achieved, as we have stressed throughout the book, by an improvement in one of the key drivers of workplace wellbeing. In improving this particular driver, the treatment lowered toxic competition, raised levels of reciprocity, and generally fostered a more collegial atmosphere within the firms. Much of this impressive effect came through the improvement of relationships between managers and their subordinates. For their part, workers were more likely to see their supervisors with more empathy and consider them more supportive.[43]

Another impressively designed intervention is the STAR program (an acronym for support, transform, achieve, results), which has been tested rigorously in an experimental setting by an interdisciplinary team of researchers led by Erin Kelly, a professor at MIT, together with Phyllis Moen, a professor at the University of Minnesota.[44] The multifaceted intervention took place in a *Fortune* 500 firm and was designed to increase supervisor and coworker support as well as employees' control over their working time. Taking fifty-six work groups within the IT division, they randomly assigned half to go through the STAR program, which was a form of "dual agenda work redesign"—in other words, it attempted to change the organization in ways that benefit both employees and the firm more generally.

Independence and Flexibility

One aspect of the STAR program tackles the relationships driver by encouraging managers to increase their communication of professional and personal support to their subordinates. But the other main aspect tackles the next main driver group—independence and flexibility. In workshops, teams together with their managers were encouraged to consider questions about how they worked, where they worked, and what it might look like if each employee were allowed to craft their own workweek. The program did not proscribe anything specific but instead encouraged teams to think creatively about how to effectively work together, not ruling anything out.

The results were impressive. The intervention increased levels of workplace wellbeing, including evaluative measures of job satisfaction, and reduced the affective measures of stress and psychological distress. Again, this is an example of increasing workplace wellbeing not by intervening directly in how people feel, but rather by changing the way that work is organized and managed. It is not necessarily easy, but it takes seriously the process of work and job redesign in ways that improve people's work lives while also boosting organizational performance.

One consequence of the intervention was an increase in remote work, a topic ever more salient since the global pandemic. Underlining the importance of flexibility, companies implementing return-to-office policies see lower job satisfaction with no effect on performance.[45] We will return to the issue of working from home later in the book, when discussing issues surrounding technology and the future of work. But in this example, an increase in the ability to choose to work more flexibly led to increased wellbeing—that is, it was not necessarily a blanket policy of one flexible working arrangement compared to another, but rather a greater ability for employees to decide themselves how and where to carry out their work. In other words, the issues of flexibility and independence are fundamentally interdependent, and focusing on one without the other leaves both unlikely to be effective strategies to improve the quality of work.

Whose Flexibility?

In addition to where work gets carried out, there is the question of when it gets done. Scheduling may not seem like the most exciting of workplace practices, but it turns out to be particularly important for wellbeing. One experiment found that, on average, workers would be willing to sacrifice 20 percent of their overall salaries to avoid schedules that employers set on short notice.[46]

One remarkably detailed analysis of data for hourly service-sector workers in the United States found that exposure to employer-driven schedule instability predicted higher levels of psychological distress, poor sleep, and lower levels of happiness.[47] Particularly detrimental were canceled shifts, last-minute on-call shifts, and the receipt of timetables less than two days in advance. Schedules are often flexible in this context, but the flexibility lies almost entirely with the employer. Indeed, the negative results were almost entirely driven by the unpredictability around scheduling interfering with workers' abilities to plan and allocate their time to pursuits and relationships outside of work.

Employer-driven scheduling practices remain the norm in many workplace settings worldwide, particularly in the health sector, often with negative effect. Relatively simple practices like providing workers with plenty of prior notice about their schedules can go a long way to improving workplace wellbeing. Clearly this is not always possible, although many firms have seen success with policies such as collaborative or "self-rostering" scheduling where workers collaborate as a group to decide which schedules are most suitable to their needs and the needs of the organizations they work for.[48] For example, one randomized control trial of twenty-eight Danish companies in the health-care sector found that, after a self-rostering system was introduced, employees subsequently reported higher levels of wellbeing overall and lower levels of work-family conflict, with no negative effects on productivity or performance.

The Dark Side of Flexibility

Figure 7-5 shows the importance of flexibility and independence for wellbeing, with strong positive impacts—over and above a range of other factors

FIGURE 7-5

Work-Life Balance Has a Substantial Impact on Wellbeing

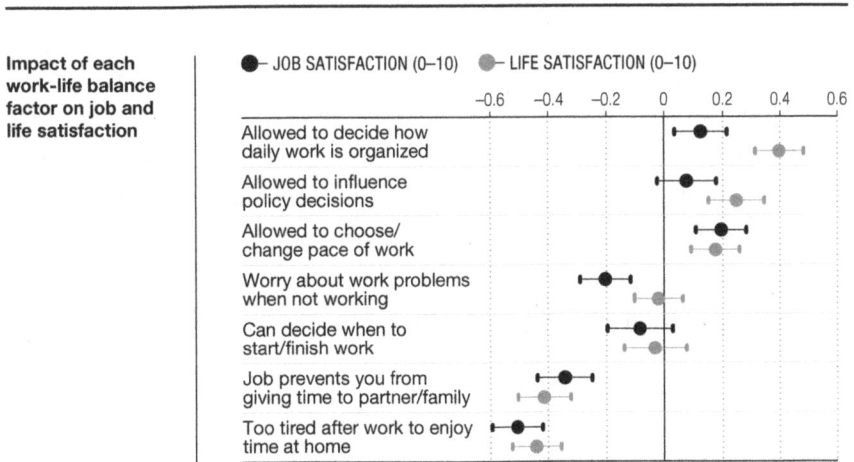

Note: Plotted are coefficients from two multivariate regression analyses with outcome job/life satisfaction. N = 11,406 across 26 countries. Employed individuals only, 21–64 years old.
Source: European Social Survey (2010–2011).

that are accounted for in the analysis, such as age, income, education, age, and so on—of the ability to decide how daily work is organized and the negative implications of work interfering with the functioning of family life.[49] But while flexibility can increase worker wellbeing, it can also in some cases undermine it.

One major issue is the extent to which it can lead to a blurring of the lines between work and personal lives. Being available at all times of the day and night, not to mention reachable by colleagues and bosses through various forms of technology, leads people to become overwhelmed and overloaded.[50]

No set of interventions is likely to be universally beneficial for all groups of workers all the time. In this case, several studies have highlighted important risks in introducing flexible scheduling in real-world organizational settings. One experiment found, for example, that flexible working arrangements lead to employees working longer hours than may be necessary, productive, or enjoyable.[51] As the authors of the study put it, "pursuing work activities outside the traditional Monday-Friday, 9-to-5 work week undermines employees' desire to engage in work out of interest, enjoyment, and meaningfulness."

Associated with figures as diverse as Henry Ford, Dolly Parton, Robert Owen, Frances Perkins, and Sheena Easton, the standard nine-to-five workday has become an inescapable hallmark of how work gets done around the world. But given the ever-increasing, changing demands of work, it may not be with us forever. Yet, what exactly will replace this system is likely to be a myriad of policies and practices that may look entirely different depending on the organizational context or workers who they are intended to target. There is bound to be a period of experimentation and trial and error to find the proper arrangement for different workers and firms in the coming years.

Working Hours

Along with where and when to work, there is the thorny issue of how much to work. One strand of research investigating this question has examined the effects of national policy reforms. In Japan, South Korea, France, and Portugal, a series of policy reforms have limited the number of hours workers can log per week. After reforms in Japan and South Korea limited workweeks to forty hours (from forty-eight hours and forty-four hours, respectively), the life satisfaction of workers and their spouses in both countries appeared to improve.[52] Similar policy reforms were introduced in France and Portugal in the 1990s, shifting the maximum number of work hours per week allowed by law from thirty-nine to thirty-five hours in France and from forty-four to forty hours in Portugal. In both cases, workers affected by the policy change experienced subsequent improvements in both job satisfaction and work-life balance.[53] In France, another analysis revealed the positive effects of shorter workweeks on workers' mental and physical health.[54]

But while workers who work fewer hours tend to report higher levels of workplace wellbeing, the differences are not always as significant as we might expect. The data suggests, for example, that the overall difference in job satisfaction between employees working fewer than ten hours and more than seventy hours is only about 0.1 points on a scale from 0 to 10.[55] Ultimately, the relationship between total hours worked and employee wellbeing turns fundamentally on the extent to which workers can work the number of hours they want or need to. When workers are not able to decide for themselves how many hours they work, the effects of too many or too few work hours on wellbeing can be significant.

Autonomy

Many of the practices we have discussed so far are characterized by an approach to management that allows workers to decide for themselves how best to complete their assignments and fulfill their essential duties. They involve an orientation toward results rather than requirements. This reflects a basic desire among humans for autonomy. Zooming out from a specific workplace, for example, we show in a global sample, in figure 7-6, the strong relationship between the ability to choose what type of work you

FIGURE 7-6

Work Autonomy Drives Wellbeing Both in and outside of Work

| Do you, personally, have many choices in regard to the type of work you can do in your life? Work enjoyment and life satisfaction by autonomy with regard to work | % Enjoy work | Life satisfaction |

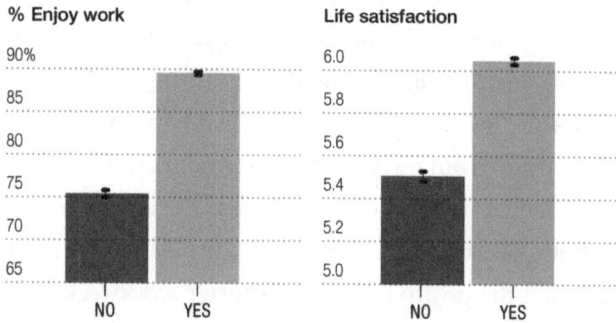

Note: Nationally representative global survey of full- and part-time workers (aged 21–64). N = 132,281.
Source: Gallup World Poll, 2020–2021.

can do in your life and the extent to which that work is either enjoyable or satisfying.

A growing contingent has begun to codify this approach as a "results-only work environment," or ROWE, which focuses on results rather than looking at the amount of time people spend at work. The idea itself was pioneered by two employees of Best Buy and Erin Kelly and Phyllis Moen, together with colleagues, assessed whether ROWE was able to shift key worker and organizational outcomes.

The researchers found that the intervention increased employees' perceived control of their schedule while also improving work-life balance.[56] Moreover, using company personnel records from eight months later, they were able to show that it reduced employee turnover.[57] This approach may not be suitable in all contexts, of course, particularly in situations where the products of work are not easily visible or measurable. Nevertheless, a host of companies have implemented similar initiatives, including GitHub, Toggl, and Trello, with many employees testifying to their positive effects on wellbeing, productivity, and overall work-life balance.

Variety and Fulfillment

Much of our discussion of independence and flexibility has revolved around when we work, where we work, and how we pace our work. But what about the actual content of the work itself? Is it valuable, interesting, or useful? Variety and fulfillment are conceptually distinct from meaning or purpose, one of the main workplace wellbeing components. Simply put, the latter is an outcome of the former. In other words, we are not just interested in the extent to which employees find purpose in their work, but also in what makes work feel purposeful.

Pursuing valuable work consistently emerges as a top priority for employees and job seekers. As we saw earlier in this chapter (in figure 7-2), more than 75 percent say that it is important or very important to them to have a job where they can contribute meaningfully to society, and over 90 percent want to do work that they find interesting. Turning back to the Gallup World Poll and a recent series of questions added to the survey, thanks to the Wellbeing for Planet Earth Foundation and Persol Holdings, we can see in figure 7-7 that having a job that improves the lives of others is much more enjoyable. Moreover, having a job we feel passionate or enthusiastic about is significantly associated with being more likely to find work fun and interesting.[58]

A variety of practices can improve this particular driver, including rotating jobs, considering how tasks are divided between jobs so that each does not become too monotonous, thinking about how tasks are framed, and introducing employees to the beneficiaries of their work. One recent study took a more direct approach. A team of economists conducted a field experiment with three thousand white-collar employees at a large consumer goods multinational firm to test the effects of a "Discover Your Purpose" intervention. The workshop encouraged workers to reflect on meaningful life experiences and align them with their work. As a result, employees reported higher levels of meaning, job satisfaction, and life satisfaction.[59]

FIGURE 7-7

Meaningful Work Is Usually Enjoyable Work

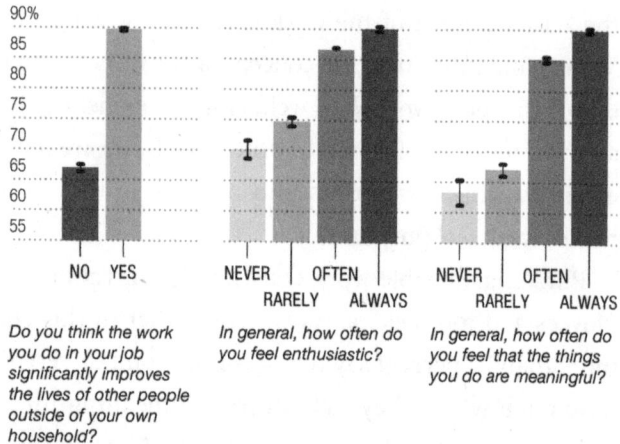

Percentage of respondents who say they enjoy work by various measures of meaning at work

Do you think the work you do in your job significantly improves the lives of other people outside of your own household?

In general, how often do you feel enthusiastic?

In general, how often do you feel that the things you do are meaningful?

Note: Nationally representative global survey of full- and part-time workers (aged 21–64).
Source: Gallup World Poll, 2021.

Contributing to Society and Improving the Lives of Others

In two separate field experiments, job seekers were willing to give up 12 percent and 44 percent of their wages to work at companies with stronger commitments to social responsibility.[60] Another experiment found that job postings with an explicit social mission attracted 26 percent more applicants than nearly identical job posts without one.[61] Workers not only prioritize purpose at work, but are also generally better at their jobs if they perceive the work they are doing to be meaningful. In one aptly titled paper—"Man's Search for Meaning: The Case of Legos"—researchers describe a series of experiments in which students were asked to build robots out of Legos.[62] Participants were split into two groups and paid diminishing amounts for each robot they built—$2 for the first one, $1.89 for the second, and so on. In one group, finished robots were neatly arranged on a desk in front of their builders as they went. In the other, research assistants dismantled each robot as soon as the students were done building them.

Participants in the first group ended up building significantly more robots than those in the second group.

In three field experiments, organizational psychologist Adam Grant examined the effect of interventions designed to stimulate purpose at work for fundraising callers.[63] In the first experiment, fundraisers were divided into three groups. The first group read stories about how the work of former callers directly benefited the lives of scholarship recipients. The second group read stories about how their work could benefit their own lives, while the third group received no treatment at all. In the second and third group, fundraisers made just as many calls and raised just as much money as they had at baseline. However, callers in the first group raised more than twice as much money as they had before.[64]

In data from the International Social Survey Program (ISSP), employees who feel as though their work is useful to society and those who feel their work helps others are on average 2.2 points more satisfied with their jobs (on a scale from 1 to 10) than counterparts.[65] In table 7-1, using data from 432 unique professions in thirty-seven countries, we present the top- and bottom-ranking occupations along each dimension.[66] If we look closely at the low-usefulness jobs on this list, many are not actually inherently useless at all. Manufacturing laborers, metalworkers, food producers, precision-instrument makers, and computer technicians are by no means unimportant to society. They fulfill crucial and necessary functions. And while management and organizational practices might be able to go some way to reframing tasks and connecting them to the bigger picture, as we will discuss in more detail later, there is also a role for society to play in more strongly respecting the work of what during the pandemic were all-too-briefly referred to as key workers.

Reframing of Tasks

Workers who find more fulfillment in their jobs tend to make more money. That difference is not insignificant, but it also does not seem determinative. In fact, the richest workers in table 7-1, financial professionals, are some of the least likely to feel useful to society, while community health workers

TABLE 7-1

Most and Least Meaningful Jobs According to Workers Themselves

Top and bottom professions by workplace eudaimonia	In my job I can help people	My job is useful to society
	Top 10	
	Traditional and complementary medicinal associate professionals	Ambulance workers
	Nursing and midwifery associate professionals	Audiologists and speech therapists
	Traditional and complementary medicinal professionals	Religious professionals
	Religious professionals	Midwifery professionals
	Psychologists	Community health workers
	Audiologists and speech therapists	Traditional and complementary medicinal associate professionals
	Midwifery professionals	Special needs teachers
	Medical and pharmaceutical technicians	Paramedical practitoners
	Paramedical practitioners	Childcare services managers
	Physiotherapists	Nursing associate professionals
	Bottom 10	
	Food processing and related trades workers	Street and market salespersons
	Packing, bottling, and labeling machine operators	Food preparation assistants
	Manufacturing laborers	Bartenders
	Sales and purchasing agents and brokers	Woodworking-machine tool sellers and operators
	Street and market salespersons	Precision-instrument makers and repairers
	Metal-finishing, plating, and coating-machine operators	Sales and purchasing agents and brokers
	Printers	Computer network and systems technicians
	Keyboard operators	Advertising and marketing professionals
	Mixed crop and animal producers	Financial and mathematical associate professionals
	Metal working machine tool sellers and operators	Information and communications technology user support technician

Note: Highest and lowest of 432 unique professions in 37 countries are shown according to responses to the extent to which they feel their job helps others and is useful to society.
Source: International Social Survey Programme (ISSP).

place in the top ten.[67] Nevertheless, low-wage work can often involve boring and unfulfilling tasks. One way to improve this is by reframing such tasks to make them more interesting.

In two studies of motivation and workplace performance, participants recruited to label medical images were significantly more productive if they were told the work they were doing was helping to identify cancer cells, as were subjects recruited to perform data entry tasks if they were told their efforts were helping to advance important research projects.[68] Connecting tasks to the bigger picture in this way—superordinate framing, to use the fancy name—can improve how enjoyable those tasks are. The key caveat is, however, that such attempts at reframing are authentic. Indeed, constantly hearing messages about meaning can backfire, particularly if the workplace promises significant impact but these ideals clash with the monotony of employees' daily tasks.[69]

Contact with Beneficiaries

A series of experiments, both in the laboratory and in real-world employment settings, have studied the effects of providing workers with opportunities to meet consumers, customers, and end users. Going back to the example of fundraising callers, Adam Grant again found positive effects of stimulating meaning, but this time by having treated workers receive personalized expressions of gratitude from scholarship beneficiaries, which increased subsequent levels of productivity and improved subjective feelings of social worth.[70]

Another more recent study also looked at the relationship between beneficiary contact, productivity, and performance.[71] In this case, the researchers randomly allocated employees of a federal regulatory agency into a control group or a treatment group, which was introduced to those who had directly benefited from the agency's efforts. Treated workers subsequently reported significantly higher levels of social worth as indicated by subjective assessments of feeling appreciated and valued by others.[72]

Even without direct beneficiary contact, highlighting and emphasizing the prosocial, positive elements of work can go a long way. Wharton School professor Andrew Carton, for example, analyzed archival evidence of John F. Kennedy's leadership strategy in the space race throughout the 1960s.[73] He concluded that Kennedy implemented four "sense-giving steps," each of which helped to frame and contextualize the efforts of NASA employees and researchers. The goal was not simply to come to work and receive a paycheck, but rather to contribute to scientific progress and expand the human imagination. In one interesting interaction, Carton tells the story of an encounter between Kennedy and a custodian during a late-night tour of the NASA headquarters. When Kennedy asked why he was working so late, he responded, "Because I'm not mopping the floors, I'm putting a man on the moon."

Finally, there is some evidence that participation in volunteering can also improve employee motivation and retention. One field experiment conducted at a large firm in Latin America explored the effects of short-term corporate social impact activities on employee behavior. Newly hired employees were randomly assigned to participate in a daylong social impact activity during their onboarding process. The researchers found that those who participated had significantly lower turnover nearly a year later.[74]

It is again worth noting the importance of authenticity. Such interventions may backfire if workers perceive them to be disingenuous or manipulative. If the goal of these interventions is to remind workers of the value of their work and efforts, they can have positive effects on motivation and wellbeing. However, when workers see the motives as more self-serving—for example, to contribute to a firm's image, brand, or bottom line—the interventions can backfire and evoke negative emotional responses from the employees they intend to benefit.

Earnings and Benefits

With regard to pay and subjective wellbeing, we often hear two viewpoints. One is that money cannot buy happiness—that there is little if any relationship between how much people are paid and how they feel or think about their lives and jobs. The other is more common among economists—

that money is the most important thing determining people's wellbeing, and the former can perhaps even be used a good proxy for the latter.

Money Matters

The relationship between money and wellbeing is one of the most widely studied in the scientific literature on subjective wellbeing, and the truth ends up somewhere in the middle. Money does matter, but not as much as you might think. Perhaps one of the most frequently cited studies in this area is by two Nobel laureates, Daniel Kahneman and Angus Deaton.[75] The number that seems to stick impressively in people's minds— whether friends, family, taxi drivers, or anyone else—is $75,000. Above that, the number makes no difference. This is true, but with some important caveats that sometimes get lost along the way. One is that the study was in 2010, so the figure is likely higher now. The cumulative rate of inflation in the United States from 2010 to 2024 suggests that it would now be just over $105,000.

But perhaps more importantly, this applies only to affective measures of wellbeing—that is, how happy we feel on a day-to-day basis. When it came to life satisfaction, however, the plateauing appears to happen only at a much higher level, if at all. Another study, later in 2018, expanded on these results by looking at data from 1.7 million people in 164 countries.[76] In that study, income ceased to predict life satisfaction past a threshold of $95,000 per year, while emotional (i.e., affective) wellbeing became untethered from income past a threshold $70,000 per year.

Diminishing Returns

Whether or not there is an optimal income threshold for wellbeing may be an interesting question for academics to tussle over, but it is a red herring. Every study finds diminishing marginal returns of income. Even in the original study that showed little or no plateau for life satisfaction, the relationship in question was between the natural logarithm of income and evaluative wellbeing. This is perhaps easier to see graphically. In our own analysis of cross-country data in Europe, figure 7-8 shows that the gradient of the relationship gets less steep as we get higher up in the income distribution.[77] This is true for both job satisfaction as well as life satisfaction more generally.

In other words, moving from $15,000 to $30,000, from $60,000 to $120,000, and from $240,000 to $480,000 is likely to predict similar gains in life satisfaction.[78] If you are an employer, this study suggests that for the amount of money it would take to improve the life satisfaction of someone earning $240,000 a year, you could instead improve the life satisfaction of sixteen other people earning $15,000 per year to exactly the same degree.

Raising wages is likely to raise wellbeing, but consider the cost of doing so compared to other potential interventions. It is likely to be quite a cost-effective way of increasing the wellbeing of low-wage workers. Working for low wages and living in a state of financial precarity is particularly detrimental to subjective wellbeing, and in the process typically also has an

FIGURE 7-8

Income Is Important, Up to a Point

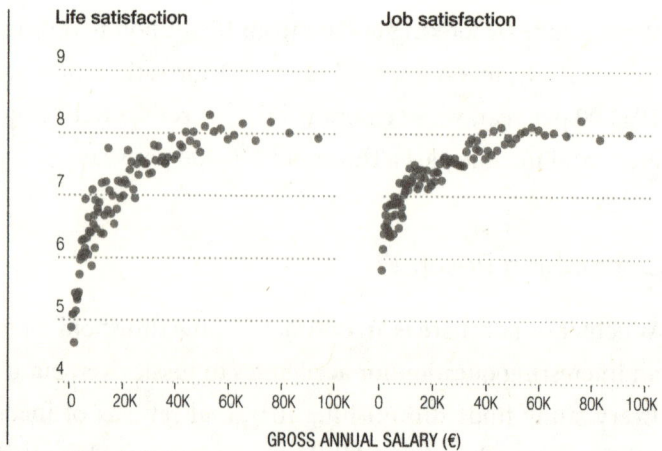

Levels of life and job satisfaction (on a 0–10 scale), by 100 percentiles of income

Life satisfaction

Job satisfaction

GROSS ANNUAL SALARY (€)

Note: N = 15,565 across 27 European countries.
Source: European Social Survey (ESS).

adverse impact on organizational outcomes like productivity.[79] So paying living wages is a must.

But the cost-effectiveness, in terms of raising wellbeing, gets smaller as we go higher up in the income distribution, and focusing on other ways to improve wellbeing may be more prudent. For workers with already high salaries, improving work-life balance, increasing flexibility, or offering skills training can be much more cost-effective and impactful strategies to promote wellbeing at work.

Fairness Concerns

It is not just the level of income people receive that matters for wellbeing, but also how it compares to a reference point. This comparator level of income is often what colleagues and friends are receiving, but it could equally be a more abstract concept such as what the employee feels is fair. In this sense, think of wages and benefits not only as an objective workplace factor to include in any driver analyses of wellbeing but also a subjective one as well. Questions in surveys can get closer to understanding people's feelings about income, which can matter a great deal.

David Card, a recent Nobel Prize winner and professor of economics at UC Berkeley, happened to notice, some years ago, something many had not.[80] Following a court decision, the income of all his colleagues at the University of California was made publicly available. A local newspaper had even created a website where the salaries of all university employees were easily searchable. Working together with colleagues, he decided to split employees into randomly allocated treatment and control groups and email the treated workers to let them know about the site's existence, wait a while, and see what happened. As it turned out, workers whose salaries fell below the median for their occupation and were told about it reported significantly lower job satisfaction than those who were not alerted to it. Those who fell above the median did not report any significant differences in job satisfaction, however. In other words, upward pay comparisons proved to have significantly negative effects on wellbeing, while downward pay comparisons had no effect.[81]

In a more recent field experiment in a large corporation in Southeast Asia, Zoë Cullen and Ricardo Perez-Truglia again found strong evidence that perceptions matter. Finding out that their manager earned more than they had originally thought did not lead to any significant changes in job satisfaction. But finding out that their peers made more did lead to strong declines in how satisfied people were with their jobs overall.[82] One explanation for this is that the effect was driven largely by reference groups so that peer salaries were much more salient. But another reason is that fairness concerns matter a great deal, and horizontal differences in pay are likely to be seen as non-meritocratic. When there are clear meritocratic reasons for pay differentials, effects are likely to be smaller in that case.

In a field experiment with manufacturing workers in India, run by Emily Breza, Supreet Kaur, and Yogita Shamdasani, employees were randomized to receive a flat daily wage or differential wages based on productivity. In cases where productivity was difficult for everyone to observe, the pay inequality led to significant declines in morale. But when the differentials were clearer and it was obvious that the more highly paid were in fact more productive, the inequality did not have any effect on morale.[83]

In addition to the amount that people get paid for their work, there is also the issue of how they get paid. One popular way is to compensate workers based on their individual performance, an arrangement that has become prevalent in sales. In two of the studies looking at the relationship between job satisfaction and performance pay discussed earlier, the positive effects of the latter on the former were only observable in cases of group-based performance pay schemes.[84] Individual-performance pay was found to have no relationship with job satisfaction. Other studies have revealed much more concerning dynamics. One analysis of 27,793 workers in South Korea found that individual-performance pay predicted significantly elevated risks of anxiety and depression, with risks falling disproportionately on vulnerable workers.[85] Another study of 318,717 full-time employees at 1,309 Danish firms between 1995 and 2006 found that individualized performance pay schemes predicted higher levels of mental illness and use of prescription drugs, controlling for other factors.[86]

Shared Capitalism

A growing number of firms have experimented with alternative forms of compensation. These initiatives have increasingly come to be referred to as "shared capitalism." The array of workplace policies and programs that fall under this heading are as various and diverse as the organizations that are associated with them, and we are unable to do justice to the large amount of scholarship on the topic, which stretches back decades.[87]

However, we can categorize these approaches to include arrangements such as employee ownership, stock options, profit sharing, and gain sharing. In the case of employee ownership, workers collectively own minority or majority stakes in the organization, an arrangement that is often accompanied by workers' seats on company boards. Stock options have become popular, particularly in industries like technology, and refer to employees being offered shares in the firms they work for as part of their compensation. In profit sharing, employees receive rewards at least partly in proportion to the success of the company, while in gain sharing, workers are compensated in proportion to the performance of their working group within the organization.

These arrangements are by no means mutually exclusive, nor are they necessarily substitutes for more standard forms of financial compensation. Numerous small companies around the world, as well as major organizations including Publix, Gore, and Procter & Gamble, are now at least partially if not majority-owned by workers. Other international firms including Ford, Delta, and Southwest offer profit-sharing schemes to employees. One analysis in the United States even found that about half of private-sector employees participate in at least one of the four primary forms of the shared capitalist arrangements we detailed earlier.[88] Overall, more than a hundred studies conducted across a wide variety of contexts, companies, cultures, and countries have examined the relationship between employee ownership, profit sharing, gain sharing, and stock options. Meta-analyses of this body of work have consistently found significant positive associations between shared capitalism and firm performance.[89]

Taken together, this research implies that shared capitalism is not only unlikely to be antithetical to business success, but rather directly contributes to it. Far from being free riders, workers belonging to organizations in which they are offered opportunities for shared ownership prove to be even more likely than counterparts to be motivated in their work. And the research shows that they are more satisfied too.[90]

Risk, Health, and Safety

While we noted earlier that living wages are a nonnegotiable base for workplace wellbeing, so too is the freedom from severe risk. Indeed, health and safety on the job can reasonably be thought of not only as part of wellbeing, but rather as a prerequisite for it. It is then perhaps unsurprising that workplace safety and security has been one of the most fundamental goals and focus areas of public and private institutions going back decades.

As we can see in figure 7-9, workers who feel safe are more likely to be satisfied with their jobs, an association that remains strong when account-

FIGURE 7-9

The Psychological Dangers of Dangerous Work

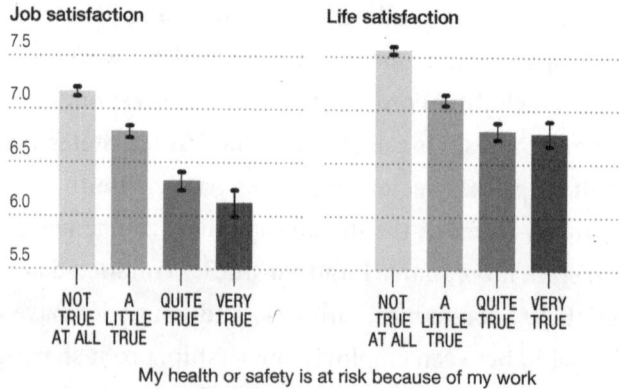

Levels of life and job satisfaction (on a 0–10 scale), plotted separately by perceived level of health risk at work

Job satisfaction

Life satisfaction

My health or safety is at risk because of my work

Note: N = 19,552 across 27 countries. Employed individuals only, 21–64 years old.
Source: European Social Survey (ESS), 2010–2011.

ing for a range of other personal and workplace factors.[91] But despite its importance and encouraging signs of progress, not all workers are entirely free from threats to their physical safety and security. Even in high-income countries with considerable legal protections in place, significant portions of the labor force continue to face persistent threats to their health and safety at work. Every day in the United States, more than fourteen employees who leave for work in the morning do not make it back home, amounting to more than five thousand fatal workplace accidents per year.[92] An additional 7,500 workers per day are moderately or severely injured, leading to more than 2.8 million cases of reported workplace injuries in 2022.

Safety Culture

Health and safety training programs—particularly those with strong management support, broad-based employee commitment, and hands-on active engagement—are largely successful in reducing workplace accidents and promoting worker wellbeing. A long line of research points toward the benefits of adequate training for health and safety outcomes.[93]

Facilitating healthy work environments requires buy-in and contributions from employees, managers, and business leaders alike. Creating a culture that prevents adverse events from occurring in the first place is largely a collective undertaking. As we already saw in the context of interventions to promote positive relationships at work, introducing effective measures to promote health, safety, and security is often best accomplished by implementing changes to institutional cultures and processes, rather than seeking to change the hearts or minds of individual employees.

In an early review of the antecedents of workplace safety, one influential meta-analysis found that, when it came to reducing rates of workplace accidents and injuries, "group safety climate" was the strongest single predictor of safe and secure working environments.[94] Another more recent, large-scale systemic review of safety interventions to reduce workplace accidents and injuries published in 2022 considered over a hundred randomized controlled trials, and encompassed a sample population of more than 31 million workers. The authors concluded that "strong evidence supports greater effects being achieved with safety interventions directed toward the group or organization level rather than individual behavior change."[95]

A remarkable field experiment examining the effects of introducing occupational safety and health committees in eighty-four garment factories, supported by twenty-nine multinational apparel buyers in Bangladesh, showed promising results in terms of effects both on workers and on factories. The intervention, which included training and intensive monitoring over nearly a year, led to increased compliance and improved safety practices without increasing costs for the firms or depressing wages for their workers. The most significant benefits were seen in well-managed factories, highlighting the need for both strong external enforcement and robust internal management to ensure effective workplace safety regulations.[96]

The Importance of Mental Health

Much of the existing discussion focuses, for the very good reasons we have outlined, on physical safety and health. But worker mental health, though sometimes overlooked, is equally important. Previous research has shown that mental health significantly influences and is influenced by different aspects of wellbeing; in fact, over a third of those with the lowest life satisfaction are in treatment for a mental health condition, illustrating the strong link between these factors.[97]

One promising workplace approach is Mental Health First Aid (MHFA), a training program developed in Australia in 2000. MHFA equips individuals with the skills to provide initial support to someone experiencing a mental health crisis. This initiative has grown significantly in popularity. However, the evidence supporting MHFA's effectiveness remains limited. Recent meta-analyses found that while first-aiders showed small to moderate improvements in their confidence and knowledge, the actual improvements in help given were small or nonexistent according to self-reports.

Moreover, there is a lack of data on the recipients of MHFA to determine its actual impact. More experimental research is needed to robustly test the extent to which MHFA programs are effective, but the intuition behind these programs is promising. The idea that people inside the organization can spot, help, and care for people in need suggests a culture that prioritizes wellbeing and comes together when needed. Of course, it is vital to stress that none of this is a substitute for access to evidence-based mental health care, but the hope is that such initiatives may help facilitate hand-offs to outside professional help for mental health support when needed.

Some of the most significant threats to mental health at work come from intimidation, harassment, and other severe forms of interpersonal conflict and misconduct. This is not to say that long working hours or job insecurity cannot and do not pose threats to mental health at work—they do.[98] Rather, we emphasize that when considering risks to mental health, it is first worth focusing on the most severe forms of interpersonal misconduct.

Studies looking into sexual harassment in contemporary workplaces continue to reveal deeply concerning dynamics. One analysis found that more than one in three women report experiencing sexual harassment at work, with one in seven actively seeking new job opportunities as a result.[99] Others have estimated that 60 percent of women experience unwanted sexual attention, coercion, or crude conduct in the workplace at some point in their careers.[100] And over 70 percent of sexual harassment cases are never reported.[101]

Figure 7-10 uses data from the American Working Conditions Survey and reports the percentage of workers experiencing verbal abuse, unwanted sexual attention, threats, and humiliating behavior in the past month.[102] Unfortunately, the sample size is not such that we can easily break down the analyses into more specific and meaningful racial and ethnic categories (and we thus look instead at non-Hispanic white workers on the one hand and everyone else on the other). As can be seen, a disproportionate amount of the exposure is to people of color.

Unfortunately, as we noted in relation to DEI, the effectiveness of individualized employee training programs on issues surrounding harassment is

FIGURE 7-10

Unequal Exposure to Adverse Behavior in the US Workplace

Over the last month, during the course of your work have you been subjected to:

Percent responding "Yes"

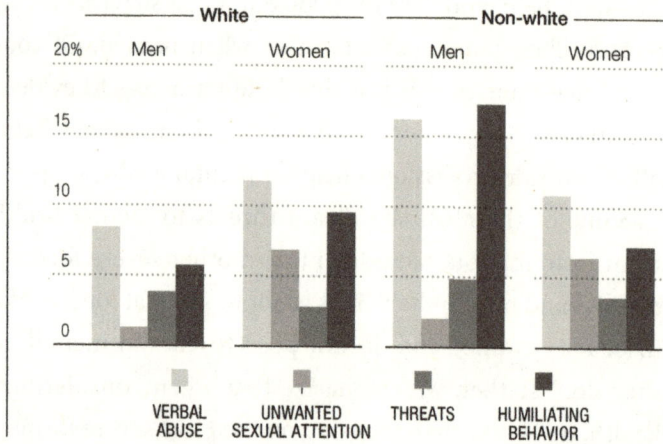

Note: N = 2,051.
Source: American Working Conditions Survey (AWCS); Nicole Maestas et al., "The Value of Working Conditions in the United States and Implications for the Structure of Wages," *American Economic Review* 113, no. 7 (2023): 2007–47.

disappointing.[103] More promising are programs aimed at training managers and executives as well as those that seek to promote positive bystander behaviors.[104] Both of these approaches aim to equip managers and others with the tools to recognize harassment and intervene to prevent it.

Clearly, however, new and creative solutions are needed to address and reduce workplace harassment and unfair treatment of minority workers in the modern workplace. These issues remain unsolved and are sure to benefit from continued attention and experimentation. Nevertheless, the results of the existing research suggest that, at least with training programs, those that frame participants as the solution rather than the problem are likely to be the most effective in producing positive workplace outcomes.

Systems of Grievance

One final mechanism by which organizations have long sought to combat, address, and reduce instances of harassment at work is through systems of grievance and accountability. These can take many forms but are generally characterized by formal processes in which workers who experience harassment or intimidation and those who witness such events are encouraged to (confidentially) report the incident to a predetermined office or individual. This typically kicks off a chain of protocols and procedures to gather information, redress harms, and distribute consequences to those responsible. While grievance systems have become standard practice across industries, countries, and cultural contexts, the evidence for their effectiveness is often mixed.

In many cases, victims distrust grievance procedures—a belief that may be well founded given that they rarely lead to the removal of perpetrators.[105] At the same time, women who do file complaints often find themselves facing some form of retaliation.[106] Perhaps as a result, grievance systems not only seem to be unhelpful and unsupportive for victims but may even cause harm. Several studies have shown that, even among women who experience some form of harassment, those who go on to report it suffer worse mental health and career outcomes as a result.[107]

While most grievance systems are implemented within the organizational structure of the firm itself—typically through human resource departments—many institutions have begun to introduce independent, third-party organizations and individuals to handle complaints and resolve conflicts. Generally classified under the heading of "ombuds" offices, these bodies tend to sit outside the typical organizational chains of command. While these arrangements have become particularly commonplace in academia, they have also begun to proliferate in other sectors including public institutions, media organizations, and law firms. Major companies including Nike, Chevron, and American Express have now introduced ombuds offices in their organizational structures. Unfortunately, most of the existing evidence regarding their effectiveness tends to be largely anecdotal.[108] Examining whether these initiatives truly help reduce rates of harassment and interpersonal conflict in organizations will be a central task of organizational researchers and business leaders in the years ahead.

Improving Wellbeing at Work

In this chapter we have considered a number of evidence-based interventions to improve the drivers of workplace wellbeing. However, the discussion has been far from exhaustive. Together with colleagues at Oxford and the World Wellbeing Movement, and the support of Indeed, we have put together a much longer list of potential interventions, after conducting a major systematic review of over three thousand research articles, and we invite interested readers to look in more depth at the results, which we have made freely available online as the Work Wellbeing Playbook.[109]

Moreover, while we have separated the drivers into six groups, neatly doing so is impossible. Indeed, many interventions improve multiple drivers, so it is a mistake to think about these drivers—or even aspects within them—in isolation. The workplace is a system with a range of interdependent parts. When thinking about the drivers and how to improve them, it makes sense to focus on the areas that are causing the most misery. But, in doing so, we recognize that many aspects of the workplace depend on others, and thus thinking about how work is managed and organized as a whole is crucial.

Part Three

THE BENEFITS OF WORKPLACE WELLBEING

Chapter 8

Productivity

W hat do we really know about the link between employee well-being and firm performance? Do investments in employee wellbeing pay off? Are managers and executives justified in dedicating time, energy, and resources to trying to raise worker wellbeing? Ultimately, is there a business case for happiness? Wellbeing is desirable for its own sake, but there is also mounting evidence showing its importance for performance.

Pathways to Firm Performance

In the next three chapters, we sift through the best existing evidence and contribute to it with new analyses, looking closely at both the individual and firm levels. Beginning at the individual level, there are essentially three main questions. First, do happier workers perform better in their jobs? Second, are happier workers less likely to quit? Third, does a happier workforce make it easier to attract talented workers in the first place?

These three issues—productivity, retention, recruitment—are the focus of this and the next chapter. We consider these as the *pathways to performance*. Each one of these pathways will have its own time horizon for positively impacting the bottom line of organizations. From our own research—which we describe in more detail in this chapter—we know that changes in how workers feel will have a relatively immediate effect on their productivity, for example. On the other hand, the effects of workplace wellbeing that work their way through the retention and recruitment pathways will likely take a longer time to show up in the financial reports.

What studies on each of the channels do not necessarily tell us, however, is whether there ultimately is a business case for prioritizing and investing in the wellbeing of the workforce. That is an organizational question that requires us to focus the analysis at the level of firms or possibly business units within them. The reason why is the key issue of costs. Even if it may be beneficial to improve the happiness of workers, given the productivity gains, the overall effect on the bottom line depends very much on what costs are associated with the organizational and management changes that bring about the improvement. To understand whether there actually is a financial return on investment—beyond the obvious human case for investing in worker wellbeing—we will look in chapter 10 at whether company-level happiness predicts the subsequent financial performance of the firm, using measures of profitability and company value.

Early Explorations of the Happy Productive Worker Thesis

One of the most widely studied aspects of workplace wellbeing is its relationship to productivity. In fact, this work stretches back nearly a century. Some researchers have even referred to the wellbeing-performance link as the "holy grail" of organizational research.[1] While that may be a little over the top, the reason for such enduring levels of interest is that the relationship has profound implications for the way in which firms treat their workers and the extent to which employees should be thought of and discussed as labor costs or, rather, as a key intangible asset that can play a central role in shaping a firm's competitive advantage.

So, what does the literature tell us about the relationship between wellbeing and productivity? As it turns out, the empirical study of these relationships has a long history. In the 1930s, as part of an early wave of research, the sociologist George Elton Mayo began to argue against prevailing Taylorist understandings of workers as mere economic inputs and instead as complex human beings with psychological wants and needs—an apparently radical concept at the time. His efforts eventually contributed to the rise of what became known as the human relations movement, which gave psychological models of motivation and attitudes a central role to play in organizational research.

This led to some of the first scientific experiments on worker wellbeing and productivity at the Hawthorne plant of the Western Electric Company in the 1930s.[2] The experiments sought to examine the productivity effects of improving physical working conditions, such as introducing softer lighting into workspaces. The apparent success and early notoriety of these studies—spurred on by the endorsements and related initiatives of powerful business magnates including Henry Ford, George F. Johnson, and Henry Bradford Endicott—led to a lot of enthusiasm. The idea that companies and managers ought to provide for employees' wellbeing, not only as a matter of principle, but also as a matter of good business, began to take root.

But despite the enthusiasm, early research produced decidedly mixed results. Two influential reviews of the early literature found the relationship between job satisfaction and job performance to be mostly negligible and irrelevant for practical purposes.[3] One study even concluded that job satisfaction and job performance were only "slightly related to each other" and suggested that the relationship boiled down to little more than "an illusory correlation."[4] The Hawthorne studies themselves were eventually discredited as a classic example of observer bias—employees likely worked harder because they knew they were being monitored by researchers, and not because of changing lighting conditions.

Following this wave of critical analysis, academic study of the relationship between wellbeing, productivity, and performance largely fell out of fashion. To many, the relationship between happiness and productivity was best consigned to the general category of "management mythology."

Determining Cause and Effect

There were a number of important limitations of these early studies, many of which have been overcome with the advent of newer statistical techniques as well as access to (a lot) more data over time.[5] One issue was that many of the earlier studies tended to rely on relatively small and unrepresentative samples. But more importantly, they typically struggled to separate correlation from causation, a notoriously tricky problem. Employee wellbeing and productivity can relate to each other in any number of ways, many of which are not necessarily mutually exclusive. Happier workers may become more successful workers, but more successful firms may also make workers happier. Or—even more likely—these two channels may be mutually reinforcing. Much of the initial research tended to focus on raw associations and correlations between all three variables, making it somewhat difficult to arrive at any firm conclusions about what exactly was causing what.

At the same time, background variables could also be responsible for driving any observed relationships. There are numerous factors capable of influencing both employee wellbeing and performance. On a societal level, these could include national labor protections, general living standards, community ties, or social networks. On an individual level, workers' age, gender, marital status, or background could influence their wellbeing, which could in turn influence job performance, and vice versa. Without sufficiently accounting and controlling for these types of influences, it can again be difficult to arrive at a reliable understanding of how employee wellbeing, productivity, and performance truly relate to each other.

Worker wellbeing itself was often poorly defined in early research. Some studies used an affective indicator—such as happiness or stress—while others used an evaluative measure like job satisfaction. Even within these categories, there was often considerable variation. Early understandings of job satisfaction referred variously to happiness, motivation, energy, pride, commitment, engagement, and a number of related positive attitudes. Considering these domains as interchangeable constructs creates not only conceptual headaches, but also practical difficulties. Even before looking at the data, it would be remarkable if all favorable dispositions toward one's job affected productivity and performance in precisely the same way. Without considering them separately and individually, resulting assessments of the relationship between each construct can become muddled and hard to interpret.

Accounting for these limitations remains a central challenge to con-temporary organizational research. But recent studies have made con-siderable strides in developing and implementing careful research designs to uncover robust relationships between wellbeing, productivity, and performance.

A Reassessment of the Evidence

In an assessment of more recent evidence, using modern analytical tech-niques, one large-scale meta-analysis improved and expanded on the meth-odology of previous reviews by looking at 254 studies, comprising 312 unique samples with more than 54,000 unique observations.[6] Controlling for background characteristics, the authors estimated the overall correla-tion between job satisfaction and job performance to be around 0.3.

Across contexts, employee wellbeing does appear to influence and improve productivity and performance. One analysis surveyed numer-ous studies looking at the impact of job satisfaction and organizational commitment on employee performance.[7] The researchers considered both task performance (within job requirements) as well as contextual perfor-mance (beyond job requirements—e.g., helping colleagues). Most of the sixteen studies included in the analysis assessed each domain using some combination of self-reports, peer reports, supervisor reports, and objec-tive indicators. Overall, the authors found that both job satisfaction and organizational commitment predicted increases in employee performance across domains.

Following the Same People over Time

Longitudinal studies carried out in workplace settings have also uncovered links between employee wellbeing and job performance. Here researchers follow the same individual over time and assess how workplace wellbeing predicts their subsequent performance.

One study looked at call-center workers in two locations of a large in-surance company and evaluated the impact of morning moods on the productivity and performance of the workers.[8] The researchers surveyed employees' happiness and other indicators of positive affect at the start of each workday and then tracked subsequent differences in productivity and performance throughout the day. Employees who were in better moods handled calls more efficiently—measured in terms of independently resolving issues without a supervisor and having more time available to customers—than colleagues performing the same work who were in worse moods at the start of the day.

Another longitudinal study of a large and representative sample of adults living in the United States conducted by one of us (Jan) in collaboration with Andrew Oswald—one of the most influential economists to use wellbeing data—found that higher levels of self-reported wellbeing in people's teens predicted average earnings once they neared age thirty.[9] This remained true even when comparing siblings, effectively holding constant a range of factors that may contribute to both wellbeing and earnings. Some of the higher earnings were due to having a job, but much was also due to the greater likelihood of getting promoted, an indicator of higher employee performance.

Experimenting with Happiness

Another stream of research has looked at the effect of happiness on productivity in laboratory experiments. Originating with the pioneering work of the late psychologist Alice Isen, who put together a series of laboratory studies on affective states and individual behavior, these experiments generally try to induce positive affect in participants—often with funny or uplifting videos, music, or expressions of praise and gratitude—and then compare their performance on particular tasks to a control group.[10]

Now a sizable literature, most results point in the same direction.[11] Overall, inducing positive affect is generally found to improve productivity, as well as other outcomes of interest to employers such as prosocial behavior, negotiating skills, and organizational citizen behaviors.[12]

One of the most widely cited pieces of evidence comes from a team of economists led by Andrew Oswald.[13] In a series of three experiments, participants were exposed to happiness-inducing treatments (including watching ten-minute comedy videos). Control groups were shown placebo clips of neutral footage or nothing at all. Both groups then were asked to perform moderately complex tasks—like adding up five two-digit numbers under time pressure—and were paid per task completed. In the treatment group, the authors found that the comedy videos increased happiness, which then, in turn, increased productivity. The happier people were, the more productive they became. They attempted more of the additions and also got more of them correct (see figure 8-1).[14] On the other hand, participants in control groups did not become happier or more productive. Increases in happiness were associated with a sizable 12 percent increase in productivity, demonstrating a causal effect of positive mood on worker performance.

This type of experimental research is generally considered to be the gold standard in identifying causal relationships. But it has one potential drawback: generalizability. Lab settings often look very different from real-world

FIGURE 8-1

Happier Workers Are More Productive Workers in the Lab

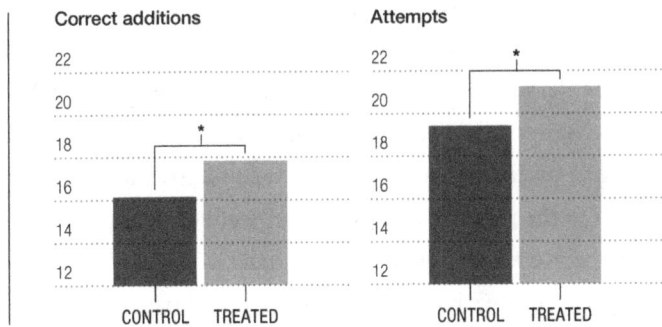

Performance on an incentivized productivity task according to whether the person saw a comedy clip beforehand (treatment group) or a neutral clip (control group)

*Difference between the two groups was significant at the 5% level. N = 276.
Note: Left-hand side shows the number of correct additions of 5 two-digit numbers, according to whether the participant was randomly chosen to first watch a comedy clip (or a neutral video in the control group).
Right-hand side shows the number of additions that were attempted by the participants in each group, regardless of getting the mathematics correct or not.
Source: Andrew J. Oswald, Eugenio Proto, and Daniel Sgroi, "Happiness and Productivity," *Journal of Labor Economics* 33, no. 4 (2015): 789–822.

settings. A causal effect identified in a controlled experiment may not necessarily be indicative of an analogous causal effect in the field. For this, we need field experiments.

Effects in the Field

A series of experiments in the field point in the direction of happiness influencing productivity, even if they do not pin down the exact line of causality. For example, an impressive field experiment at Virgin Atlantic involved randomly assigning airline captains to either treatment or control groups, and then implementing changes to management practices for treated workers. This included things like targets, performance monitoring, and prosocial incentives. The treated captains not only increased their productivity (for example, using less fuel) but also became more satisfied with their jobs.

In a similar vein, a team of researchers led by Nicholas Bloom of Stanford University found that randomly assigning Chinese call-center employees to work from home led to a 13 percent increase in productivity among the treated group, as well as higher levels of job satisfaction.[15] Equally, another study found that promoting family supportive behaviors in a *Fortune* 500 company improved job satisfaction and reduced employee turnover.[16]

All of these studies demonstrate complementary relationships between employee wellbeing, productivity, and performance. However, because most of the interventions targeted job tasks and workplace behaviors, rather than wellbeing specifically, it can be difficult to infer causal pathways from wellbeing to performance from their results. An ideal experiment would be to combine the random assignment of wellbeing in the laboratory setting with a real-world employment context. This is impossible to do practically, but in our own work we have looked for so-called natural experiments.

A Natural Experiment

We began studying call-center workers at British Telecom (BT) some years ago and, in doing so, stumbled on an ideal research setting, one that gave us a quasi-experiment in which to examine the effects of employee wellbeing on productivity.[17] Together with a third colleague, Clément Bellet—now a professor at the Erasmus School of Economics, Rotterdam—we started thinking about how to design a study that could meaningfully add to the existing mountain of research on happiness and productivity.

Tracking productivity and performance was not a problem. Many workplace behaviors and outcomes are routinely tracked in call-center settings, such as time taken per call, number of calls converted to sales, adherence to workflow scheduling, attendance, breaks taken, and so on. But we still had to measure how workers felt. We considered a number of ways to do that to ensure reliable and valid data without having to impose too much on workers during their workdays.

We developed a simple pulse survey on worker happiness that we sent out to employees once a week by email asking them how happy they felt that week.[18] Using this data, we found a strong relationship between happiness and sales performance within the same individuals over time. As can be seen in figure 8-2, the average difference in weekly sales we observed when someone felt very happy versus very unhappy from one week to another was just over 13 percent.[19]

FIGURE 8-2

Happier Workers Are More Productive Workers

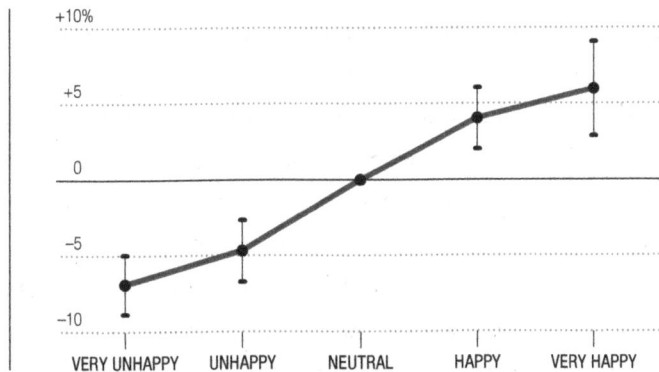

Effect of worker happiness on sales performance

Note: N = 1,793 workers, followed weekly over a 6-month period. Figure shows the relationship between self-reported happiness and productivity among telesales workers in call centers at a large UK employer.
Source: Clément Bellet, Jan-Emmanuel De Neve, and George Ward, "Does Employee Happiness Have an Impact on Productivity?," *Management Science* 70, no. 3 (2023): 1656–79.

As with the existing longitudinal studies, this evidence is consistent with a causal relationship but does not prove it. After all, doing well on the job feeds back positively into how you feel more generally, especially if that means dealing with more satisfied customers on the phone. Instead, we had to get a bit more creative in terms of study design.

In an ideal world, as in randomized control trials, we would randomly induce some BT workers to be happy and others to be sad, and then examine the effects on productivity throughout the day. Needless to say, neither the management team nor the union reps we were meeting with would likely be too thrilled with that kind of plan, even if it were feasible or in any way ethical. Instead, we set out to find some sort of random variation in wellbeing that we could observe in the real world—a sort of natural experiment. This being the United Kingdom, our minds immediately went to one place—the weather.

When integrating weather data into our analyses, we found that workers were more productive on sunny days. Since the day's weather isn't influenced by the goings-on at BT, then we can think of this as being as good as randomly allocated—a bit like a lab experiment. This strongly hints at a causal link between good weather and higher productivity. But two potential issues remained.

First, it could be customer mood, not worker mood, that is driven by the weather. Might it be that any effect on sales is just due to happier customers? One of the dubious benefits of living in the UK is that the weather is not only frequently bad but also notoriously variable. It can be sunny in one place but cloudy in another on the same day. Fortunately, the call centers are spread across the UK and workers stay in one place, but they receive calls from everywhere, depending on who is available. So, even after accounting for national trends each week, we could still pinpoint the impact of local weather on each worker's sales performance.

Second, there's the possibility that the weather affects productivity in other ways, for example, snow causing traffic delays on the way to work. Here's where our field visits (something that economists, unfortunately, do not do nearly often enough) provided an unexpected insight. The architecture of the call centers varies a lot from one place to another. Some are in glass towers where workers are surrounded by windows; others are more like windowless warehouses. This difference allowed us to test the hypothesis that weather affects productivity solely via mood. Remarkably, we found no effect of gloomy weather on happiness or sales in places where workers had no access to windows. However, when workers were near windows, the effect was significant.

Taken together, the results show a strong causal relationship between happiness and productivity. Interestingly, we also found that the effect depended a lot on the type of tasks done by the call-center employees. Tasks that demanded high levels of emotional and social intelligence were particularly sensitive to the employees' mood. Dealing with a disgruntled customer, for example, and trying to keep their business requires a lot of emotional effort. If you're not in a good place to begin with, it's tough to emotionally connect with others' issues.

Why Might Happiness Improve Performance?

Taken together, the evidence discussed in this chapter—from longitudinal studies, laboratory experiments, field experiments, and quasi-experiments—strongly suggests a causal effect of happiness on individual productivity and performance. Yet at this point, it is perhaps worth asking just one more question—why? Why should happier workers be better at their jobs? We have already hinted at a variety of potential mechanisms by which these relationships can operate. Next, we briefly comment on three in particular: (1) health, (2) positive working relationships, and (3) creativity.

Happy and Healthy

The relationship between health and wellbeing is one of strongest and most robust associations documented in the literature. Life satisfaction, positive affect, negative affect, and eudaimonic wellbeing have all been linked to an array of health indicators and behaviors, and the relationship is generally found to be reciprocal. It may be unsurprising that people are happier when they are in better health, but the causal arrow cuts in both directions.

Happier people tend to live longer, experience less pain, and have better cardiovascular health, lower blood pressure, lower body mass index, and improved immune functioning.[20] Wellbeing is predictive of lower rates of smoking, lower rates of drinking, higher rates of exercise, better diet, and better sleep.[21] At the same time, almost by definition, wellbeing is also inversely related to a variety of indicators of poor mental health, including lower levels of burnout, depression, distress, and anxiety.[22]

All of these dynamics can have profoundly important implications in workplace settings. Poor physical and mental health have been linked to reduced work performance.[23] Two important pathways are absenteeism (missed days of work) and presenteeism (working while sick). In the former case, employees with low job satisfaction have been found to be more likely to leave work early, arrive at work late, and miss days of work entirely.[24] These dynamics can have substantial effects on individual- and organizational-level performance. One analysis of a large high-tech manufacturing firm found that low evaluative wellbeing at work accounted for 11 percent of voluntary absenteeism at the company, amounting to an annual loss of $92 million.[25] Longitudinal studies have also found that employees with low wellbeing are more likely to be absent from work.[26]

Recent scholarship has also paid increased attention to presenteeism, or as one researcher described it, "being at work, but out of it."[27] Presenteeism has been linked to a host of wellbeing indicators, including low levels of positive affect, poor wellbeing at work, and increased negative affect.[28] One analysis of 2,264 employees in a large American firm found that feelings of stress and low emotional fulfillment were the leading predictors of productivity loss due to presenteeism.[29] However, the relationship between presenteeism and wellbeing is not necessarily straightforward. Other studies have found that high rates of job satisfaction, motivation, and self-efficacy can actually lead to overcommitment and therefore increased rates of presenteeism.[30] One recent study—one that hit particularly close to home—interviewed 6,874 academics in the United Kingdom and found that almost nine out of ten reported occasionally working while sick. Within this group, those with higher levels of work engagement, dedication, and vigor reported the highest rates of doing so overall.[31]

Social Skills and Relationships

Almost as important as the link between wellbeing and health is the link between wellbeing and social relationships. A vast literature has identified positive feedback loops between happiness, satisfaction, and social relationships.[32] Happier people are more likely to attract and maintain strong social relationships, while social relationships themselves also make us happier. These dynamics can also have a number of positive implications in organizational contexts. Happier employees have been shown to (1) develop more supportive relationships with colleagues and supervisors, (2) demonstrate higher capacities for cooperation and collaboration, (3) have more satisfied and loyal customers, and (4) even prove to be better negotiators.[33]

This evidence again cuts across correlational, longitudinal, and experimental contexts and is very much in line with our own field work with the BT call-center workers. Alongside correlational evidence that happier employees receive more supportive performance reviews from colleagues, longitudinal analyses have also shown that employees who report feeling frequent positive emotions at work are more likely to receive supervisors' praise of good work and personal interest over a year later.[34] In the customer service sector, several studies have found that customers of happier employees are more likely to become happy themselves, provide more favorable reviews of service quality, and express greater intentions to return for repeat business.[35]

Experimental studies have also revealed that participants induced to experience positive moods were more likely to reach compromises with counterparts considered to be mutually beneficial.[36] Even just perceiving positive emotions in others can promote cooperative behavior. In one experiment, participants exposed to happy faces generally considered social situations to be more cooperative, whereas angry faces promoted feelings of competition.[37]

Creativity

A large body of related research has also demonstrated the important role that wellbeing can play in promoting creativity, generally defined as the production of novel and useful ideas. Theoretical accounts of positive emotions suggest that happier people have greater mental flexibility and broader awareness, thereby enabling them to make sparse connections and generate original ideas.[38] These theories have been put to the test in a number of contexts, with broadly confirmatory results.[39]

In one of the most widely cited studies on this relationship, a team of researchers monitored daily wellbeing levels of 222 employees working in seven different companies across three industries over the course of several months.[40] The authors then asked colleagues and supervisors to evaluate their creative output—defined as the production of novel and useful ideas. After analyzing a resulting data set of 11,471 daily reports from employees and colleagues, the researchers were able to significantly predict subsequent increases in creativity depending on happiness levels up to two days earlier.

A handful of related studies have observed similar dynamics.[41] In laboratory settings, an array of experiments have also found that inducing positive mood enhances creative thinking.[42] In a series of early studies conducted by Alice Isen and colleagues, research participants who were made to feel happier were subsequently more creative on various problem-solving tasks, including word associations and grouping exercises.[43] A more recent meta-analysis looking at the results of sixty-two experimental studies found broadly significant effects of positive affect on creative performance, although the size and strength of the relationship varied depending on the task participants were asked to perform.[44] One experiment found that groups of participants randomly assigned to positive-mood-inducing treatments were more creative than controls, suggesting that happiness can enhance group creativity as well as individual creativity.[45]

Happier Workers Work Better

As we have seen, there is good evidence for happier workers being healthier, taking less time off, forming better social relationships, and being more creative. These mechanisms are not isolated; they often intersect and reinforce one another. Whatever the underlying mechanisms, the academic consensus is clear: improving employee wellbeing typically leads to enhanced productivity and performance at the individual level.

Chapter 9

Recruitment and Retention

ttracting and retaining high-quality workers is vital for any organization to function properly. But to what extent is workplace wellbeing a key ingredient for improving recruitment and retention? In a recent survey of executives and managers in the United States, 87 percent agreed that raising workforce happiness could give their companies a competitive advantage.[1] As Alan Jope, then CEO of Unilever, noted at the Wellbeing Research & Policy Conference that we organized in 2022, "To be effective, companies need to attract and retain the very best people. And good luck doing that if you're not putting their wellbeing at the center of what you do."

The main reason managers and executives themselves believe that workplace wellbeing can boost performance is due to the dual channels of retention and recruitment. Figure 9-1 shows that 94 percent believe creating happier places to work would make it easier to attract talent, and an even larger fraction felt it would help them to retain workers. Another survey found that seven out of ten senior human resource managers considered employee wellbeing and mental health to be a top priority in their organizations.[2]

FIGURE 9-1

Managers See Recruitment and Retention as the Main Wellbeing Dividend

Survey of US-based managers on the effects of wellbeing at work	Percentage of US executives who believe . . .			
	. . . a happier place to work would make it easier to attract talent	. . . that a happier place to work would make it easier to retain workers	. . . that unhappiness among their workforce is hurting productivity	. . . workforce wellbeing can give their company a competitive advantage
	94%	96%	79%	87%

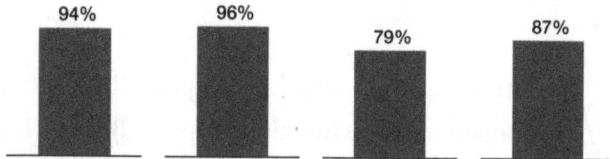

Note: N = 1,073 drawn from US-based HBR audience of business executives across a range of organization sizes and sectors, 76% of whom are managers.
Source: HBR Analytics, "Cultivating Workforce Well-Being to Drive Business Value" survey, collected 2020.

Workplace Wellbeing and Employee Turnover

While not all turnover is necessarily bad for organizations, it is typically a significant cost for businesses and detrimental to metrics of future financial performance such as profitability.[3] Much as with productivity, research on the link between workplace wellbeing and turnover stretches back many decades and has caught the attention of both academic researchers and business practitioners.[4]

In 1958, Herbert Simon and James March wrote the book *Organizations*, a classic in management research in the decades ever since. While remembered today largely for its remarkable discussions of bounded rationality and cognition, the book also laid much of the theoretical groundwork for an enduring literature on the determinants of employee turnover.

While people had studied turnover prior to the book, a great deal of it had been done without much recourse to theory. According to Simon and

March, the decision to leave hinges on two factors: the ease of movement (How good are the alternatives?) and the desirability of movement (How satisfied am I in the current job?). Much theorizing has happened since, of course, but the fundamental idea that dissatisfied or unhappy employees are likely to leave has stayed the course and has been demonstrated empirically in a great many contexts.[5]

Early reviews of correlational and longitudinal studies found sizable and significant negative effects of happiness and job satisfaction on both intentions to leave work and objective data on quitting.[6] Two separate German longitudinal studies from 1985 to 2003 also found that workers who reported high levels of job satisfaction were significantly less likely to quit than less satisfied counterparts.[7] With extensive longitudinal data from Germany, the UK, and Australia, more recent evidence strongly indicates that job satisfaction significantly predicts subsequent quitting.[8]

In a related analysis of Gallup data covering over 140,000 respondents, positive evaluations of work predicted higher levels of employee retention the following year, while another study identified significant links between feelings of depression, anxiety, and job satisfaction and subsequent quitting behavior in a sample of British adults.[9] Job satisfaction proved to have the most significant effects on quit behavior overall.

Another longitudinal study of managers at a large American company found that workers reporting high levels job satisfaction in an initial assessment were less likely to leave the company over the next two years.[10] Yet another study of *Fortune* magazine's "Best Companies to Work For" list also noted that employees of highly rated companies (particularly those with group incentive pay schemes) were less likely to express intentions to leave than counterparts.[11]

An array of experimental studies also suggests strong links between employee wellbeing and turnover. Several related studies have shown that introducing workplace interventions to encourage family-supportive behaviors and manager support decreased turnover intentions and objective rates of quitting, while increasing various measures of employee wellbeing.[12] Other studies have shown that providing employees with opportunities to give organizational feedback and receive management support can improve wellbeing, lower turnover intentions, and reduce rates of quitting.[13]

Evidence from Millions of Workers

One key issue with much of the existing evidence on wellbeing and turnover is that it is necessarily focused on individual firms where researchers have been able to gain access to employer surveys and personnel data in order to assess the extent to which the former predicts subsequent turnover in the latter. We can go beyond this, however, using data from Indeed, which gives us an unprecedented look at the wellbeing of millions of workers and the aggregate levels of workplace wellbeing at their places of work.

One natural place to start is to think about the people answering the survey on the platform. Since we began asking the wellbeing questions back in 2019, there have been over 20 million workers leaving a response, and one of us (George) has looked extensively at how these surveys relate to turnover decisions.[14]

Figure 9-2 looks at people leaving a review for their current employer and subsequent job applications made on Indeed over the next seven days.[15]

FIGURE 9-2

Your Unhappy Workers Are Already Looking for a New Job

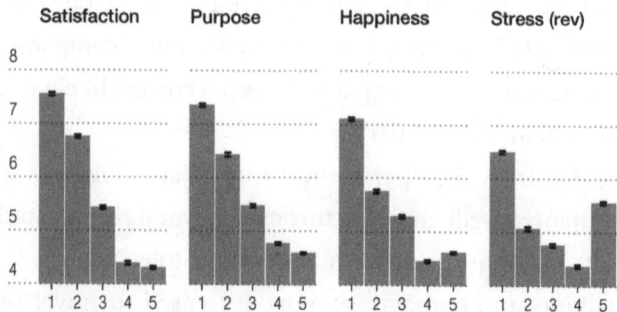

Note: Stress is reversed (1 = high stress, 5 = low stress) for ease of presentation.
Source: Indeed data, collected between October 2019 and May 2024; George Ward, "Workplace Wellbeing and Employee Turnover," University of Oxford Working Paper, 2024.

What we find is that unhappy workers—across all four key components of workplace wellbeing—apply for more jobs. For example, very unsatisfied workers make over 60 percent more job applications than very satisfied workers.

This helps cement the case that happier workers are more likely to stay. Along with job search behavior, we can compare externally measured employee turnover metrics at the company level with our crowdsourced measures of workplace wellbeing (see figure 9-3).[16] We see that happier

FIGURE 9-3

Workplace Wellbeing and Lower Employee Turnover

Voluntary employee turnover rate, by company wellbeing score (on a 1–5 scale)

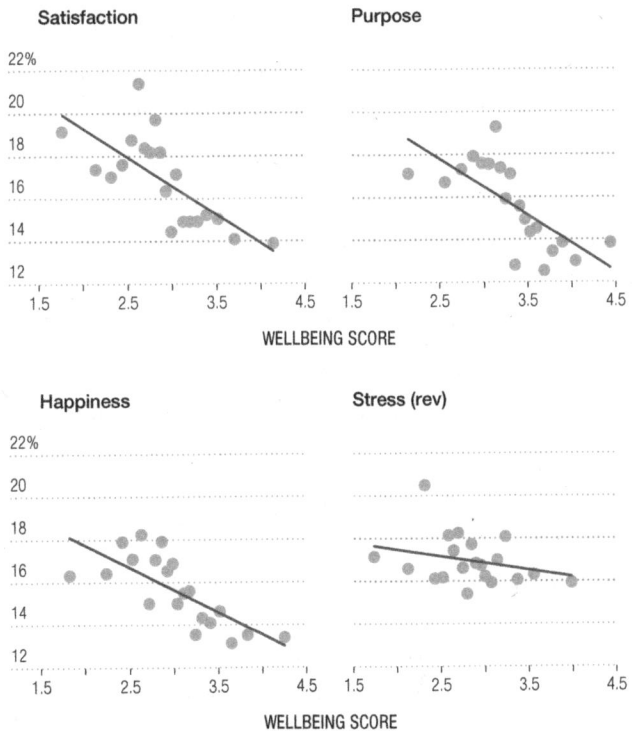

Satisfaction

Purpose

Happiness

Stress (rev)

WELLBEING SCORE

Note: Binned scatterplots shown where mean levels of wellbeing are calculated per company-year for publicly traded companies and matched to data on voluntary turnover. N = 3,983 company-years; 1,745 companies. Stress is reversed (1 = high stress, 5 = low stress) for ease of presentation.
Source: Indeed data, collected between October 2019 and May 2024; turnover data from DiversIQ; George Ward, "Workplace Wellbeing and Employee Turnover," University of Oxford Working Paper, 2024.

companies have lower voluntary employee turnover.[17] In fact, companies with an average job satisfaction of, say, about four (out of five) instead of three would typically have about a quarter less employee turnover from year to year. That is a very meaningful difference that will have effects that percolate throughout the organization and, ultimately, shape the bottom line in a number of ways.

Recruiting Talent in the First Place

In addition to the productivity and retention effects documented so far, another important mechanism through which wellbeing can affect the bottom line is by improving a firm's ability to attract talented workers. Much scholarship has demonstrated that employees are attracted to jobs for more than just income.[18] Correlational, longitudinal, and experimental evidence has found that workers are often willing to trade some level of financial compensation for a variety of work amenities, including autonomy, job security, flexibility, and organizational purpose.[19]

In two field experiments on online job marketplaces, Vanessa Burbano found that randomly exposing job seekers to information about a firm's commitments to corporate social responsibility reduced their proposed wage requirements.[20] Among high-performing candidates, job seekers were willing to entirely give up the wage premium they would have otherwise demanded relative to less desirable candidates. These dynamics could suggest that eudaimonic wellbeing is a driver of job search behavior. Alternatively, job seekers may view corporate social responsibility commitments as a signal that firms are more likely to treat their workers well, and thus job seekers may imagine themselves being happier there.

Do Workers Actually Care about Happiness?

As a key part of the PhD thesis at MIT, one of us (George) examined the effects of a firm's happiness on attracting talent.[21] As interesting as it is for us to have an unprecedented view of the wellbeing of workers across companies around the world, it is also vital information for job seekers themselves to have. With data collection well underway by early 2020, Indeed began using the crowdsourced data to help job seekers find out more about the companies they might consider applying to. Wellbeing metrics are now shown prominently at the top of each firm's page on the site, giving millions of job seekers a deeper insight into what life is like working there (see figure 9-4).

This presented an exciting opportunity for an experiment. Indeed introduced the score to the website, but agreed to stagger its availability so that only a randomly selected subgroup of users could initially see it. Compar-

FIGURE 9-4

Everyone Can Now Easily Find Information on Workplace Wellbeing

Screenshot of the employer page of Indeed on the Indeed platform

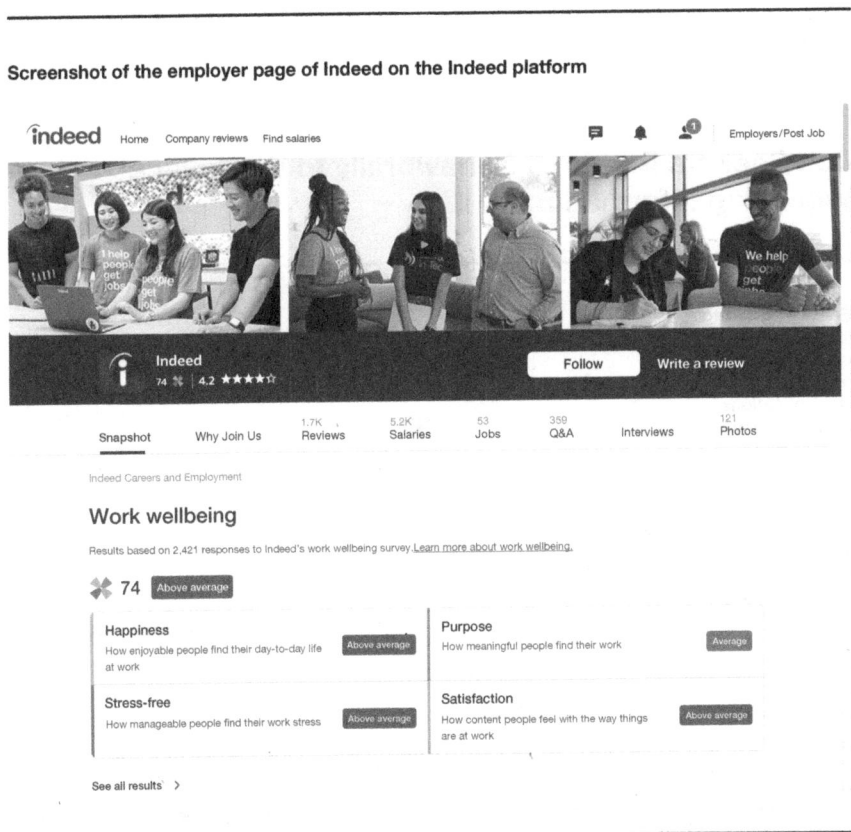

ing these two groups, we had an experiment including no less than 23 million job seekers in the United States looking at real companies and making consequential life decisions.

In the control group, visitors to the site saw company information as usual, including detailed crowdsourced information on salaries and other aspects of jobs. But the treatment group also saw prominent information about how happy people are at the company. This addition led to notable behavioral shifts. As shown in figure 9-5, job seekers in the treatment group tended to avoid companies with low happiness scores and preferred those with higher scores, effectively filtering out less happy workplaces from their searches.[22]

The information treatment led to an overall slight decline in the number of applications, suggesting that job seekers became more selective or picky in where they applied. They particularly discarded companies at the lower

FIGURE 9-5

Job Seekers Respond Behaviorally to Workplace Wellbeing Information

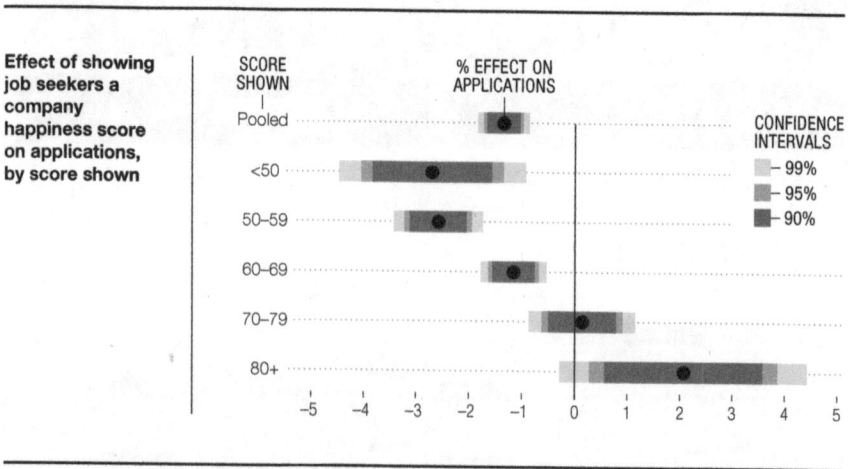

Note: Users were randomized into the control group and saw all company pages as normal, or the treatment group where they saw company pages with added information about workplace happiness. Experiment ran for 10 months beginning in May 2020. N = 23,376,519 job seekers.
Source: Data from Indeed; George Ward, "Workplace Happiness and Job Search Behavior: Evidence from a Field Experiment," MIT Sloan Working Paper 6607-22, 2022.

end of the happiness distributions, meaning they used it largely as a screening tool. For companies with scores below sixty, which are labeled as "below average" in the happiness score widget on the site, applications went down by nearly 3 percent. There was a positive effect of showing higher happiness scores, but the size of the effect—around 2 percent—was less strong than that of revealing how miserable people were at certain workplaces.

The experiment estimated the effects of showing the information versus not showing it. But over the ten-month duration of the experiment, we also monitored changes in companies' scores. We discovered that companies improving their scores saw an increase in job applications, highlighting the significant role employee wellbeing plays in attracting talent. This finding is particularly relevant in today's labor market, where transparency about workplace conditions is increasing. People are getting savvier, and it is increasingly untenable to preside successfully over a workforce that is unhappy if you want to attract the best and brightest.

Wellbeing and Income Trade-Offs

It's not unsurprising that people are attracted to companies with a happier workforce. But are they willing to pay for it? Another of the PhD thesis's chapters looked at whether people would trade off salary for a happier company or to avoid having to work in a miserable company.[23]

Using a large nationally representative survey of workers in the United States, Canada, and the UK, we asked people to make hypothetical choices between jobs. In each case, they had a choice between position A and position B. Position A stayed the same and involved a company with a happiness score of sixty-five out of a hundred and the same wage as their current job. But position B differed across the respondents and across the multiple times they were asked: either offering higher levels of happiness and lower wages (to measure people's so-called willingness to pay) or lower levels of happiness but higher pay (to measure people's willingness to accept). Overall, the findings suggest that workers do value happiness at work and are willing to sacrifice salary for it.

FIGURE 9-6

Workers Say They Would Trade Off Income for More Workplace Wellbeing

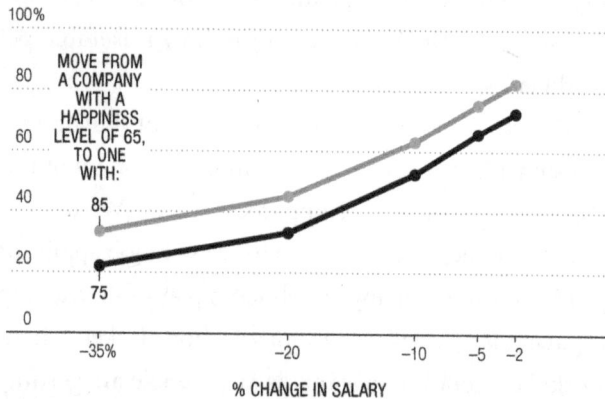

Note: Nationally representative sample in the US. Respondents are asked to imagine two positions at companies where the job description and companies are the same other than for pay and happiness levels. N = 4,033.
Source: George Ward, "Workplace Happiness and Job Search Behavior: Evidence from a Field Experiment," MIT Sloan Working Paper 6607-22, 2022.

Figure 9-6 shows the cumulative share of respondents choosing position B when they are asked how much salary they would be willing to give up (or "pay") to work at a happier firm.[24] What we found is that people do value happiness. But while a significant majority highly values workplace wellbeing, there's still a notable minority—about 20 percent—who wouldn't switch to a happier company even for a 2 percent salary decrease.

In the United States, to work at a company with a happiness score of seventy-five (compared to sixty-five), respondents would, *on average*, accept a 13 percent reduction in their current salary. For a company scoring eighty-five, they'd accept a 16.5 percent cut. This suggests diminishing returns as the happiness score increases. Ultimately, this study indicates that job seekers consider workplace wellbeing (when available) alongside salary and are willing to pay significant amounts for it.

Democratization of Information: A New Challenge (and Opportunity) for Firms

Workplace wellbeing information is increasingly accessible to job seekers. The labor market has changed substantially in recent years, with a shift toward online job search. Previously, it was only possible to know what it was like to work somewhere by working there yourself or by hearing the stories of friends and family. Now, such information is readily available to anyone with a computer or phone through websites like Glassdoor, Indeed, and other online forums.

This rise in the flow of information—from incumbent to prospective workers—has occurred when workers' expectations surrounding workplace wellbeing have also increased. Together, the two developments place a strong onus on employers to prioritize workplace wellbeing if they want to keep their workers or be able to attract them in the first place.

Chapter 10

Profitability and Firm Financial Performance

I n the previous two chapters, we outlined how workplace wellbeing can improve productivity, recruitment, and retention. But do these pathways to performance actually translate to company success? The key question is whether or not prioritizing employee wellbeing is best seen as a luxury, accessible only to elite companies with ample resources, or if it actually leads to better firm performance. While there is not necessarily a need for a business case for investing in workplace wellbeing, given that there is already a strong human case for doing so, in this chapter we assess the extent to which the data suggests there is one anyway.

The Importance of Factoring in Costs

One concern is that experimental studies may simply not translate to the complex realities of the workplace. What we observe in a laboratory setting may not actually play out in a real-world place of work, for example. Or it may be that any boost from experimentally induced happiness is somewhat short-lived and unlikely to make a difference to anything overall.

Another concern is that the time it might take for productivity gains, and especially recruitment and retention improvements, to make their way to the bottom line is an open question. While feeling happier may have an immediate impact on individual performance, the organizational impact of becoming a better and more attractive workplace might take months—if not years—to feed its way into hard financial performance metrics.

But perhaps most importantly, raising workforce wellbeing usually costs money. Even if happier workers are more productive, as we and others have shown, it is possible that the benefits do not outweigh the costs. So, any discussion about improving workplace wellbeing must factor in costs, even if the evidence on the effects of workplace wellbeing on productivity, retention, and recruitment makes it tempting to jump to the conclusion that the business case is clear. One way to assess the business case for workplace wellbeing is to look not at individual-level processes like productivity but at the firm as a whole. Are firms with a happier workforce at large generally more profitable?

Evidence across Business Units

To begin answering this question, we first looked at the correlation between employee wellbeing and performance at the level of firms or business units. Together with our colleague Christian Krekel at the London School of Economics, we were able to analyze some of the treasure trove of data that Gallup has accumulated over the years while working with different companies.[1] As part of its regular data collection while advising companies, Gallup has frequently included a survey question on job satisfaction, meaning that we can compare across companies and across business units within them, and also link such comparisons to objective data on performance.

Our analysis covered anonymized data from Gallup's client database, encompassing 339 independent research studies in 230 organizations across 49 industries and 73 countries. This comprehensive data set contained job satisfaction and performance data from 1,882,131 employees and 82,248 business units, mainly from the United States but also from various other countries as well.

For each business unit, we calculated the correlation between employee wellbeing and various firm performance outcomes. Our focus was on employees' satisfaction with their organization as a place to work—an evaluative measure of workplace wellbeing.[2] We were able to link this to a number of different organizational outcomes, including pathways such as productivity, turnover, and the ultimate outcome of profitability.

As we can see in figure 10-1, happier workplaces have substantially higher customer loyalty and productivity as well as much lower levels of employee turnover. This matches what we discussed in previous chapters. Importantly, however, this is also reflected in higher profitability—a finding that holds regardless of the geographic context or industry we study.

These findings are in line with other studies in different contexts. For example, using data on manufacturing plants in Finland, one study found a strong link between job satisfaction and value added per hours worked.[3] In the UK, job satisfaction and performance outcomes are linked at the establishment level, including financial performance, labor productivity, and

FIGURE 10-1

Wellbeing and Performance Are Correlated across Business Units

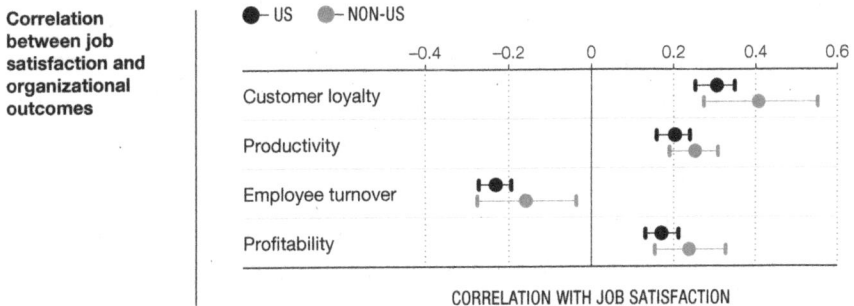

Note: Adjusted average correlation coefficients shown calculated using data from Gallup (1994–2015). N = 1,882,131 employees, 82,248 business units. 95% confidence intervals shown.
Source: Christian Krekel, George Ward, and Jan-Emmanuel De Neve, "Employee Well-Being, Productivity, and Firm Performance: Evidence and Case Studies," Saïd Business School Working Paper 4, 2019.

quality of product or service.[4] Importantly, in this latter study, changes in job satisfaction from 2004 to 2011 predicted shifts in performance outcomes over the same period, suggesting it is satisfaction that leads to performance and not the other way around.

Lists of Best Places to Work

Another way to see the relationship between firm-level wellbeing and performance is to use proxy measures for wellbeing like inclusion on *Fortune* magazine's 100 Best Companies to Work For list. Alex Edmans, a colleague and prominent finance professor at London Business School, conducted one of the first studies to take this approach.[5]

Seeing an opportunity to answer a question that is, as we have already argued, of fundamental importance in terms of how firms ought to treat their workers, he was able to obtain the winning firms' data and estimate the extent to which they subsequently outperformed their peers in the stock market in the years after being included. Ultimately, he found that they had 2.3 percent to 3.8 percent higher annual stock returns. In a later study using an expanded sample of companies featured on Best Places to Work lists in fourteen other countries, similar dynamics were observable.[6]

In a pair of related studies, researchers examined the stock returns of American companies selected for Glassdoor's Best Places to Work lists. In this case, the ranking was based on employee star ratings. The authors found that highly rated companies outperformed the market by 115.6 percent from 2009 to 2014, and by 57 percent from 2009 to 2019.[7] For context, a $1,000 investment in these top-rated companies in 2009 would have grown to $6,529 by 2019, a total return of 553 percent. The same investment in an S&P index fund would have grown to $3,580.[8] Moreover, the announcement effect was notable—companies' stock value increased by 0.75 percent within ten days of being named to Glassdoor's Best Places to Work list.[9] This echoed an earlier study that identified a 1.03 percent stock market bump for companies selected to *Fortune*'s list in the days following the announcement.[10]

Company Star Ratings

Along with looking at inclusion in Glassdoor's Best Places to Work list, another approach is to use its star ratings directly. A series of papers have used such ratings—which are collected from a prompt that asks for an overall rating and provides a set of five potential stars—as a measure of job satisfaction. As we will discuss later, this is a fairly loose proxy but is nevertheless a good place to start.

One analysis looked at the financial performance of 993 large American firms and 100,000 employee surveys from 2008 and 2012. The study found that improvements in Glassdoor ratings are predictive of improvements in Tobin's q (market valuation relative to assets) and return on assets (net income to assets) ratios in the following quarter.[11] More recent analyses have also arrived at similar results, using this kind of data.[12] Again using Glassdoor star ratings as a proxy for employee wellbeing, the studies once more considered links between company ratings and firm value, sales growth, profitability, and earnings announcements. In general, all studies continued to find positive and significant relationships between company ratings and firm performance.[13]

What can we take away from these studies? At the very least, employee wellbeing does not appear to be at odds with organizational performance. This suggests that whatever investments are necessary to raise employees' wellbeing do not detract from firms' bottom line. In firm-level studies, these costs are factored into the equation.

That we do not see negative returns for companies that are more supportive of wellbeing suggests that investing in employee wellbeing may be both prudent and sustainable. In fact, happier companies appear to be even more successful than their counterparts. In this way, far from being antithetical to business success, the results reported in this section suggest that employee wellbeing directly contributes to it. Even after controlling for a wide variety of firm characteristics, companies with higher levels of employee wellbeing have higher valuations, stock market returns, greater sales growth, stronger earnings to asset ratios, and more frequent earnings surprises.

At the same time, the market often undervalues employee wellbeing. For example, companies with high employee star ratings—much like those appearing on magazines' Best Places to Work lists—are more likely to report earnings surprises and outperform analyst expectations, which points toward an untapped potential of wellbeing investments. In an efficient market, publicly available information from employee reviews would be quickly factored into stock prices and investment decision-making. Instead, the evidence suggests that the market does not sufficiently (or at least expeditiously) recognize the financial value of employee wellbeing. This may change as more information on firm-level wellbeing becomes available to investors in the future.

The Need to Measure Wellbeing

Encouraging as these initial studies have been, there are also important limitations to this body of work. Studies based on the highest-rated companies may be unreliable since they do not study a representative set of firms. In Best Places to Work lists, we are looking exclusively at the winners rather than comparing the full distribution of firms. Moreover, companies often opt in and apply to be on such lists, meaning that employers that frequently take the low road when it comes to employment relations may not even be in these analyses.

Perhaps even more importantly, almost all existing studies use rough and potentially unreliable proxies for the key concept that they purport to be studying, namely, employee wellbeing. Company rankings, ratings, and reviews are likely to be a mix of all forms of positive organizational culture, behavior, and possibly also financial performance. As a result, even when including control variables, it can be difficult to isolate causal pathways from evaluative, affective, and eudaimonic wellbeing to financial returns.

A Big Data Approach

One of the many benefits of the Indeed data that we have helped collect since 2019 is that it enables us an unprecedented look at wellbeing across the full distribution of companies, from the very worst to the very best and everything in between—as opposed to standard surveys that take a relatively small cross section of the whole workforce, making it impossible to determine differences between organizations. This feat is made possible thanks to the more than 20 million respondents (and counting) who have shared with Indeed how they feel at their workplaces—making this data set the world's largest focused on workplace wellbeing.

The survey is also designed with the aim of directly measuring the main aspects of employee wellbeing. It does so along the lines of the most up-to-date academic understanding of the concept. The data gives us firm-level measures of job satisfaction, purpose, stress, and happiness for a large cross section of firms in the economy and allows us to look at how these also vary over time. For publicly traded companies, at least, we can link this to various aspects of financial performance.

Together with a colleague, Micah Kaats, we were able to match wellbeing measures to financial data from around 1,800 public companies listed on the US stock exchanges. Our goal was to see if and to what extent employee wellbeing predicts company success. As it turns out, we found strong evidence that it does.[14]

Wellbeing and Profitability

While the lowest-rated companies in each domain score between 1 and 1.9 out of 5, the highest-rated companies score between 4.7 and 5. Responses to all four items are at the company level, largely normally distributed. The fact that we included such a broad cross section of company wellbeing levels in our sample represents an important extension of previous results and allowed us to make broader claims about both the benefits of high levels of employee wellbeing for firm performance and the potential consequences of low levels of wellbeing.

To evaluate firm performance, we relied first on return on assets, a measure of profitability.[15] Following the literature, we calculated this as net income over lagged asset value, providing a snapshot of profitability.[16] We aggregated our workplace wellbeing measures to the company level for each

FIGURE 10-2

Workplace Wellbeing and Greater Firm Profitability

Return on assets
(ROA), by wellbeing
score (on a 1–5
scale)

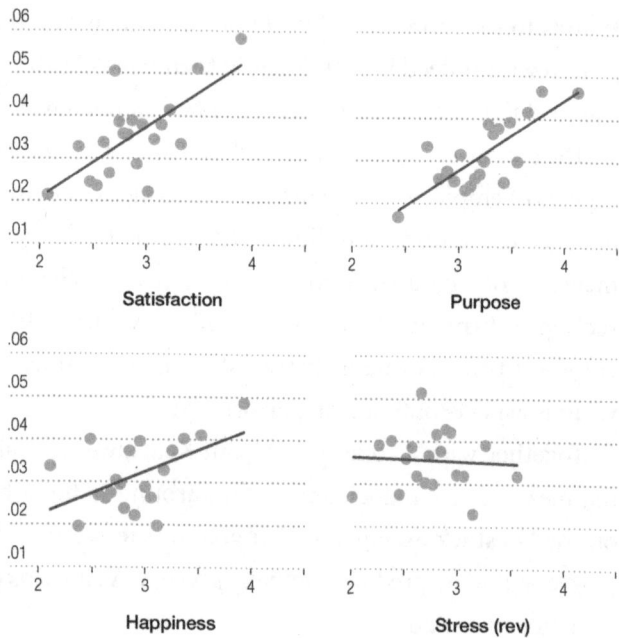

Note: Annual data for wellbeing sourced from Indeed, 2020–2023, using responses from current employees only. Financial data sourced from Compustat. Binned scatterplots shown, with controls included for number of employees, logged assets (lagged 1 year), time-fixed effects, and industry-fixed effects. N = 4,770. Stress is reversed (1 = high stress, 5 = low stress) for ease of presentation.
Source: Jan-Emmanuel De Neve, Micah Kaats, and George Ward, "Workplace Wellbeing and Firm Performance," University of Oxford Wellbeing Research Centre Working Paper 2304, 2024.

year and assessed their relationship with financial performance.[17] Our findings align with previous results, but in a larger context. Figure 10-2 represents these regression models—which include an analysis of over 1,600 firms—graphically by grouping the wellbeing scores into ten deciles (adjusting for a range of other factors that you may worry are affecting the relationship) and looking at their firm performance in terms of profitability. We find strong relationships with satisfaction, purpose, and happiness, but no association with stress.[18]

Wellbeing and Firm Value

We can also assess the relationship between wellbeing and the value of firms. Here we use the widely studied Tobin's q as our main measure. Tobin's q, or the Q ratio, is the market value of a company divided by the replacement cost of its assets. Originally introduced by the economist Nicholas Kaldor and later popularized by James Tobin, it is widely used as forward-looking measure of firm value.[19]

In figure 10-3 we show a strong correlation between company wellbeing and firm value. Breaking down the analysis by wellbeing measure, we found strong relationships with satisfaction, purpose, and happiness, but perceived stress was less clearly associated with firm value.

Longitudinal Evidence

These analyses are, of course, only capable of reflecting cross-sectional and contemporaneous relationships. In most of our analyses here, empirical relationships are estimated within a one-year period—comparing a company's wellbeing and performance in, say, 2021. What we found is that, even within the same industry, companies with higher employee wellbeing generally outperform their competitors. But while these results are consistent with an interpretation that suggests employee wellbeing leads to gains in firm performance, they could also be consistent with the reverse interpretation—firm performance may itself lead to higher levels of employee wellbeing.

We also looked at the association of company happiness in one period and then firm performance in the next. To do so, we split the wellbeing data so that we could analyze the predictive power of pre–Covid-19 happiness on post-Covid financial performance. We calculate average happiness levels for all companies in our sample from October 2019 to February 2020 inclusive— the pre-Covid period. We then use these averages to predict firm performance in the post-Covid period, up to the end of 2020 and beyond.[20]

Overall, we find positive relationships between pre-Covid happiness levels and post-Covid performance for all three indicators of performance we have looked at so far. These results indicate that company happiness levels are at least as predictive of future firm performance as they are of contemporaneous firm performance.[21]

Abnormal Stock Returns

Another way of looking at firm performance is to consider stock market returns. Along these lines, we have already looked in detail at firm value. But

FIGURE 10-3

Workplace Wellbeing and Higher Firm Value

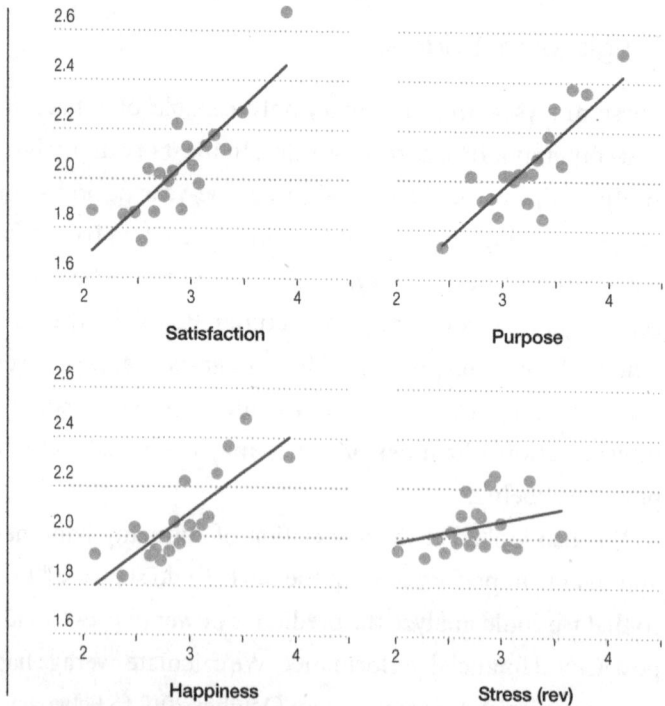

Note: Annual data for wellbeing sourced from Indeed, 2020–2023, using responses from current employees only. Financial data sourced from Compustat. Binned scatterplots shown, with controls included for number of employees, logged assets (lagged 1 year), time-fixed effects, and industry-fixed effects. N = 4,727. Stress is reversed (1 = high stress, 5 = low stress) for ease of presentation.
Source: Jan-Emmanuel De Neve, Micah Kaats, and George Ward, "Workplace Wellbeing and Firm Performance," University of Oxford Wellbeing Research Centre Working Paper 2304, 2024.

we can extend this by conducting an arguably easier-to-understand simulation or "back test" where we see what happens if we invest in companies based on their happiness data collected on Indeed.

To simulate how an investor might use information about worker happiness, we create "Happiest Place to Work" lists on an annual basis—in the way that a platform like Indeed might do using its extensive data on various aspects of worker wellbeing—by ranking the firms each year. We then created the Wellbeing 100, a list that takes the top one hundred companies in terms of their wellbeing (measured as a composite score of job satisfaction, purpose, happiness, and lack of stress).

We then tracked stocks from the first trading day of the year until the final trading day, when we rebalanced.[22] To make things simple, we ignored dividends and taxes.[23] As a benchmark, we compared these stock returns to the S&P 500 index, which is a widely recognized proxy for overall market performance.[24] We put together our first portfolio of companies based on the 2020 data—the first complete year of our Indeed crowdsourced data set—and invested in it at the start of January 2021. For the following year, we then used the 2021 data to recompile the list of best workplaces and reinvested the money on the first trading day of 2022, and so on. So, how did the companies with the highest levels of wellbeing fare?

The wellbeing-focus portfolio does not outperform the market in every period. But, in line with our findings on firm value, we do find from this very simple exercise, over the course of the nearly four years we are able to track so far, that companies with high wellbeing ratings perform more strongly in the stock market (see figure 10-4). Using an aggregated measure of subjective wellbeing that combines happiness, stress, satisfaction, and purpose, investing in high-wellbeing firms provides a greater return over the period that we studied.

Given the relatively short time frame, this exercise is only able to provide initial evidence. It will be important to continue to track and monitor this data over time and, perhaps one day, it might even underpin an index tracker or exchange-traded fund that people can invest in. As we collect more and more information about the lived experience of workers across

FIGURE 10-4

Investing in Wellbeing Pays Off

Value of $1,000 initial investment

Wellbeing 100 portfolio was constructed each year by taking the top 100 public companies with the highest average wellbeing

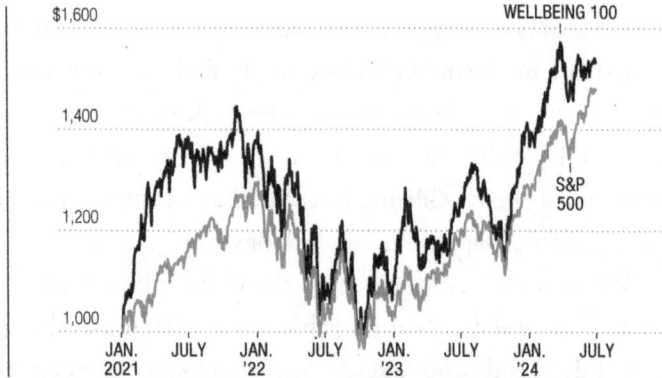

Note: The chart simulates an investment strategy that annually invests equally in the top 100 companies based on the previous year's wellbeing data (across all 4 dimensions), holding the stocks for one year before rebalancing. Includes only companies with at least 100 individual-level responses in that year.
Source: Wellbeing data drawn from Indeed; daily stock return data drawn from Compustat.

firms, we will be able to gain an even clearer picture by putting together a fuller analysis that has more time periods and the ability to factor in a range of other factors that may be associated with both wellbeing and stock returns, such as industry, firm size, and so on, as we did in the more formal analysis of the relationship between wellbeing and firm value as measured by Tobin's q. However, this simple initial simulation provides promising evidence of the power of wellbeing to predict future returns.

Raising Capital: A Future Pathway to Performance?

In earlier chapters, we explored three main pathways by which wellbeing leads to better company performance: productivity, retention, and recruitment. But there may be an emerging fourth factor: the ability to raise capital. There is not much research on this yet but, considering the superior stock market performance of high-wellbeing companies, along with the growing transparency in wellbeing information, it's possible that this data will start guiding investors' decisions on where to allocate their money.

Business leaders and investors have already begun incorporating non-financial measures of company performance into decision-making procedures. Chief among these are the so-called environmental, social, and governance (ESG) indicators.[25] The significance of the growing movement toward sustainable investing is perhaps best captured by a 2019 statement released by the Business Roundtable, a nonprofit organization whose members include executives of Amazon, Apple, and General Motors. In a statement signed by 181 CEOs, the group committed to redefine and redirect the purpose of their organizations from generating profit to "creating value for all stakeholders, including customers, employees, suppliers, communities and shareholders."[26]

If true, this would represent a significant shift from the corporate thinking that dominated the second half of the twentieth century. It reflects not only changes in what investors say they value, but also changes in what firms are expected to provide as evidence of positive impact. In the coming years, the ability of firms to demonstrate social value (the "S" in ESG) is set to become an even more important driver of investment decisions. It is here that workplace wellbeing is likely to become an important indicator for social impact and, in turn, emerge as a potential pathway to superior firm performance.

As we noted earlier in the book, after long discussions with the influential ratings company S&P Global, workplace wellbeing—measured according to satisfaction, purpose, happiness, and stress—is now included in its corporate sustainability assessment (CSA), which surveys most of the world's major public firms and ultimately feeds into their ESG scores. There is indeed now a whole section in the CSA on trends in wellbeing, where companies are asked to report on employee wellbeing. Having a workforce with high levels of wellbeing is thus likely to become a key aspect of a firm's reputation that will help it to raise capital.

One particularly interesting prospect in years to come will be to cross-check the inside-out data that companies report to S&P Global with the outside-in data crowdsourced through the Indeed platform.[27] As more information on organizational wellbeing becomes available to investors and consumers, a fundamental issue will likely be to ensure that companies prioritize and support their employees' wellbeing. Companies that fail to do so may face the increased scrutiny of investors and lenders and thus have a greater cost of capital or less access to it in the future.

Part Four

THE FUTURE OF WORK AND WELLBEING

Chapter 11

Technology and Workplace Wellbeing

W ill robots take all the jobs? This question is at the core of a heated debate surrounding technology and the labor market. For years, the conversation has centered on the potential for massive job loss and a future where work as we know it might become obsolete. Questions about large-scale technological unemployment, the risk of job automation, and the possibility of job creation versus job destruction have dominated discussions in public, private, and academic spheres. Might automation lead to large-scale technological unemployment? Who is most at risk of having their job automated? Will job destruction make way for even more job creation? Seemingly ever-expanding academic literature, newspaper column inches, and television segments chart the potential automatability of jobs in colorful and creative detail.

This is a conversation, above all, about the *quantity* of jobs. In this chapter, we want to shift the focus away from how many jobs technology might replace to the question of how technology might transform the nature of work. This is not just a matter of counting jobs lost or gained, but instead one of understanding how technological advancements could reshape the ways in which work is designed, organized, and managed and, ultimately, have an impact on worker wellbeing. The key conversation we need to have is about the *quality* of jobs.

Predictions about the Future of Work (or Lack of It)

In 2013, colleagues at the University of Oxford, Carl Benedikt Frey and Michael Osborne, published a paper with the title "The Future of Employment: How Susceptible Are Jobs to Computerisation?"[1] In it, they tried to estimate what percent of existing jobs could, at least theoretically, computers do in the coming years. By matching detailed data on job roles and responsibilities for 702 occupations with expert ratings and reviews about the likelihood of computerization, they found that 47 percent of US jobs were at risk of being automated. The *New York Times*, the *Economist*, the *Wall Street Journal*, and just about every other major news publication covered the paper's findings at the time. Their striking claim set the tone for much of the subsequent debate, fueling speculation about a future dominated by machines, where job scarcity could become a new norm. But these estimates have been subject to significant debate. A pivotal shift in this discussion has been the move from a job-based to a task-based analysis of automation.

While in common conversation, we are generally used to referring to occupations by their titles—like manager, painter, plumber, and so on—it is much more useful to think of jobs as bundles of tasks. Whereas some tasks within a job may be automatable, others may not be—and the bundle can change within a job over time. Studies taking this view find that very few, if any, occupations are made up of tasks that can all be automated.[2] Following this approach, estimates of automatability suggest a more modest figure, with around 9 percent of jobs at risk of being fully automatable in the coming years.[3]

If we look at automation over the last thirty years, the evidence is mixed. Some studies find that more robots mean fewer jobs and lower wages. Others find little or no effect. Encouragingly, more-recent studies using firm-level data (mostly from factories) even suggest an increase in employment following the adoption of automation.[4] However, robots in factories are one thing, but technologies like generative AI, popularized with remarkable success by ChatGPT, are quite another. The differing and evolving types of automation technologies make it challenging to draw broad, one-size-fits-all conclusions about the future of work.

To make matters even more complicated, the very nature of technological progress is such that it is in constant flux. When thinking about standard academic timelines, 2013 may not seem like such a long time ago. But considered in the context of technological progress, papers published ten years ago can start to look like relics of history. This can make it exceedingly difficult to arrive at reliable predictions of the extent to which incoming waves of technological progress may or may not supplant large swaths of the labor force.

Finally, while automation is likely to make some tasks and occupations redundant, it is almost guaranteed to create others. Previous waves of technological progress have tended to produce at least as many jobs as they have destroyed, which is largely why historical trends in overall unemployment have tended to remain flat.[5] For example, a team of researchers led by a noted labor economist at MIT, David Autor, found that roughly 60 percent of the jobs done in 2018 had not even been invented in 1940.[6] This can render any overall estimate of future job losses due to automation particularly difficult to pin down.

Refocusing the Conversation from Quantity to Quality

The debate surrounding the future of work and technology needs a critical shift: from the quantity of jobs to their quality. While much attention has been given to the number of jobs at risk from automation, a more significant aspect is often overlooked—how technology transforms the nature of work and how that impacts worker wellbeing.

Automation, in its various forms ranging from robotics to AI, reshapes job roles by augmenting, creating, and sometimes replacing tasks.[7] The move from thinking mainly about jobs as a whole to thinking more in terms of tasks (and jobs as bundles of tasks) has been a key step forward.[8] When firms ultimately adopt and implement new technologies, the constellation and nature of tasks that workers do are typically changed. So the ways in which technology actually alters those tasks and how these changes are likely to affect the nature of work is a hugely important question—and one that we need to grapple with more properly as a society.

The impact of these technologies on the workplace is not predestined. Technology is not deterministic. That is not to deny that technology plays a hugely important role in shaping society. It does, but it does not evolve and develop out of nowhere and according to its own logic. It is developed by humans, who face choices and make decisions. Do they make decisions about technology development that are human-centered—an important idea that goes back at least to the 1950s—or not? Do we design technology to maximize efficiency? Or do we design it to best augment the existing skills of workers and improve the experience of work?

Ultimately, the impact that technology will have on jobs hinges on multiple factors, including the nature of the technology itself and how it was designed, organizational strategies and practices, and how these technologies are integrated into the workplace. For instance, the introduction of AI into a job has the potential to either augment human skills, likely enhancing wellbeing in the process, or lead to a reduction in autonomy and an increase in monotony, with negative impacts on workplace wellbeing.

The more we worry about whether we will have any jobs in the future, the less we focus on how to create the jobs we actually want to have. We need to start thinking about job quality. And the most natural way to think about job quality is to consider systematically how technology might influence workplace wellbeing.

Technology and the Nature of Work

Thinking about the impact of technology on job quality requires that we shift our focus from jobs that new technologies may destroy to those that will be affected by the technologies. Just how many workers fall into this category remains an active area of debate. Nevertheless, there seems to be no doubt that they represent a significant portion of the labor force. For most of us, automation seems just as unlikely to eradicate our jobs entirely as it does to leave them entirely untouched. The most likely event seems to be that new technologies will change the way we work, not whether or not we work at all.

After all, in many ways, this is already happening and has been for some time. One hundred years ago, writers spent their days plugging away on typewriters. One hundred years before that, they wrote books by hand. Today, we are writing this book on a computer rather than using a quill. Waves of innovation have not made writers obsolete—at least not yet. They have simply changed how we do our work. And we are not alone. Emails, calculators, personal computers, smartphones, and robots have already dramatically reshaped the dynamics of work for millions of employees worldwide. Whether or not these trends will continue is not really up for debate. However, the rate, pace, and scope of these changes—and even more importantly, their effects on job quality—is another matter. The crucial question is therefore not how many workers will be displaced by automation, but rather how their experience of work will change.

Where discussions about the nature of work have entered mainstream consciousness, they tend to focus heavily on productivity. If the most important question in the minds of academics, policy makers, and business leaders has been how many workers will lose their jobs, the second most important question has been how automation will affect the productivity of those who remain employed.[9] In general, these studies seek to estimate the extent to which impending waves of automation are likely to promote, diminish, or otherwise affect the amount of output that we can produce per worker.

But whether new technologies may or may not make workers more or less productive tells us little about their likely effects on wellbeing at work. Whether or not new technologies will make our jobs better or worse in the future remains a much more open question.

Technological Change and the Drivers

The driver setup we have used throughout the book provides a simple but systematic framework to explore the potential impacts of technology on key dimensions of jobs and the workplace. We will go through each of the six main driver groups and consider the extent to which technological advancements—whether robots, algorithms, AI, or otherwise—are likely to improve or degrade jobs.

Development and Security

Technological advancements can be a catalyst for professional growth. By automating routine and mundane tasks, technology can enable workers to focus on more complex and intellectually rewarding activities. This shift away from routine tasks often then necessitates continuous learning, lifelong skill development, and the ability to adapt. New technologies like AI can themselves also be used to help train people and develop new skills.

Integrating AI into various job roles, for example, has the potential to transform them from monotonous tasks to roles requiring strategic thinking and decision-making. Workers in this scenario are not replaced but are instead required to upskill—adapting to oversee and collaborate with these newer technologies. This shift can lead to the creation of new job roles, offering fresh career pathways and learning opportunities.

But as promising as this all sounds, the introduction of new technology in the workplace also brings challenges to the domain of development and security. Technological advances have the ability to put people out of work, as we have discussed, but even the threat of this happening can have significant impacts on people's wellbeing at work. New technologies can give workers a sense of uncertainty and insecurity, primarily due to fears of job loss but also because of the potential erosion to the quality of their current roles.[10] The rapid pace of technological change can render certain existing skills redundant, for example, leading to concerns about obsolescence and the devaluation of established skill sets.[11]

Moreover, while robotization may be able to take away more mundane tasks, advances in technology—such as the development of generative AI (think ChatGPT)—mean that more complex or creative tasks may be automatable. This brings with it the risk of deskilling for a broader set of workers. The simplification of job roles, where workers are left monitoring or supervising automated processes rather than doing them directly themselves, can lead to a reduction in the breadth of skills used on the job.

While it is true that technology often creates new jobs, even if it leaves others obsolete, this does not necessarily benefit all workers, or even the ones initially displaced. These emerging roles often require a different set of skills, leading to a gap where workers whose roles have been automated find themselves unprepared for the new jobs. This mismatch can result in a workforce polarized between those who possess the new, in-demand skills and those who do not.

Relationships

The integration of technology can have a significant impact on relationships among colleagues, shaping the way we interact and collaborate in the workplace. Technology has revolutionized workplace communication and collaboration, particularly in environments where remote work is common. Digital communication tools and platforms enable teams spread across different locations to work together effectively, breaking down geographical barriers. This evolution in communication can also foster a more inclusive and connected workforce, one that allows for flexible network structures within organizations. The boundaries between different departments and teams can become more fluid, encouraging collaboration and information sharing.

Developments in technology can also facilitate more democratic and inclusive interactions. By providing platforms for shared communication and decision-making, technology allows voices from different parts and even levels of the organization to be heard, potentially flattening traditional hierarchies. This can lead to a more egalitarian workplace where contributions from all employees are valued and considered. However, technologically mediated communication, while efficient, often lacks the emotional depth and nuances of face-to-face interactions, which are crucial for building strong, meaningful connections. The shift to digital platforms has the potential to disrupt the established social dynamics within a workplace, leading to a more isolated and less engaged workforce.

Changes to the physical setup of the workplace, necessitated by the introduction and adoption of new technologies, have the ability to fragment existing social structures and leave workers isolated. Moreover, workers might perceive the replacement of human-led tasks with automated processes as undervaluing the human element in work. Much ultimately depends also on which sorts of tasks firms try to automate. Replacing tasks that involve interaction with customers and colleagues will reduce the quality of relationships—and, ultimately, wellbeing.

A major concern is the rise of so-called algorithmic management, where workers are managed by algorithms rather than people.[12] In this case, responsibilities like scheduling and performance tracking are automated and overseen by an algorithm, so that work becomes highly impersonal. In this case, the quality and quantity of human interactions are likely to decrease sharply, leading to disconnection and isolation on the part of affected workers.

Independence and Flexibility

Technology has in some ways already reshaped the concept of workplace autonomy. Remote work—facilitated by new and old digital tools such as email, video conferencing, instant access to files and data, and more—allows many employees to work from anywhere, offering a level of flexibility previously unimaginable. This flexibility can in theory enable employees to balance work with personal life more effectively.

If automation takes away some of the more mundane or routine tasks from a job, it can enable workers to spend more of their time on tasks that increase their sense of autonomy. Moreover, wider and easier access to detailed information and analytics tools can also allow for more local and decentralized decision-making—something that can empower employees and increase a sense of autonomy. Workers can take ownership of their tasks, harnessing technology to make informed decisions and manage their workflow more independently.

However, this increased flexibility and autonomy can come with drawbacks, some of which we have already begun to see in the past few years.

Remote work can blur the boundaries between personal and professional life, leading to situations where employees feel like they are always "on" and, as a result, are often unable to fully disengage from work. The ability to be reached instantly can also lead managers to expect access to their employees at all hours of the day and night. All of this contributes to what has been described as a growing prevalence of *overload*—even in supposedly good jobs where wages are relatively high.[13]

The autonomy afforded by remote work can also be a double-edged sword. In theory, it offers freedom, but in practice, it can lead to increased expectations for availability and responsiveness. Beyond this, technology that dictates work schedules and tasks—sometimes or even often with little room for human discretion—can place severe limits on workers' creativity and personal input. In such environments, employees might find their roles becoming more rigid—with technology-driven protocols dictating their workday, leaving little room for job crafting or personal initiative.

The rise of algorithmic management—particularly in more gig-style employment like working for delivery or driving apps and in other remote-work settings—can further diminish workers' sense of autonomy. Employees may find themselves closely monitored, with technology tracking their productivity and work patterns. This surveillance can create a sense of being constantly watched, undermining the autonomy that remote work is supposed to offer.

Such surveillance is not limited to remote work, however. There is a strong danger that firms will very closely monitor every move of their workers in places like factories and warehouses, to the extent that workers' autonomy is thoroughly undermined, not to mention obvious and important issues surrounding people's right to privacy.

Variety and Fulfillment

The potential for technologies like robotics and AI to augment job variety and fulfillment is significant.[14] By automating routine and repetitive tasks, technology can free employees to focus on more engaging and meaningful work. This shift can lead to a broadening of job roles, allowing workers to explore a diverse array of tasks and challenges.

Beyond this, technologies such as AI can help people to make more of their skills—that is, they can navigate new and interesting challenges where they are able to apply their skills to new domains and problems. In doing so, work becomes meaningful and fulfilling.

However, there's also a significant risk of work intensification and fragmentation. As technology streamlines and accelerates work processes, employees may face increased demands to perform a higher volume of tasks in the same amount of time.[15] We have seen this over the past few decades with research showing that work intensity is clearly on the rise despite rapid technological advancements that could have moved things in the opposite direction.[16]

Technology-driven standardization of tasks could also lead to a loss of variety in work. When tasks are broken down into smaller, more standardized components, some of which are automated, the remaining work for humans can become monotonous and less fulfilling. This standardization can detract from the richness and diversity of job roles, making them less engaging and more routine.

While much of the existing discussion has surrounded the potential for robotics to automate routine or unfulfilling tasks, as technology evolves, there is a risk that even more complex and interesting tasks may become automatable. Generative AI, for example, has begun to take away writing tasks, advanced data tasks, analytics, and so on. Though still early days, we are already beginning to see large language models used in a variety of new and interesting contexts. This advancement could challenge the sense of meaning and fulfillment employees derive from their work, particularly for those who see machines taking over their core skills and tasks.

As technology becomes more advanced, there is also a danger that the work left to humans in actively managing or passively monitoring the machine—preferably the former rather than the latter, in terms of possible wellbeing effects—is done without fully understanding how the technology works.[17] Not fully grasping how key tasks are carried out risks alienating employees and undermining their sense of mastery.

Navigating these challenges requires a deliberate approach to incorporating technology in the workplace. Key, as ever, is ensuring that the automation of tasks does not lead to a reduction in job variety or an intensification of work. The goal is to use technology to enhance the richness and diversity of job roles, fostering an environment where employees can find fulfillment and satisfaction in their work. This approach involves balancing the efficiency gains from technology with the need to maintain meaningful and varied work for employees, ensuring that technological advancements contribute positively to the overall work experience.

Earnings and Benefits

While the bulk of the existing discussion on technology and the future of work has focused on job quantity, quality is brought into the debate most commonly through discussion of wages.[18] Technological advancement can be a catalyst for wage growth—particularly in sectors that require high-skilled labor to complement prevalent technology. Workers with the expertise to manage, develop, or work alongside advanced technologies often see an increase in their earnings.[19] However, this benefit is typically not uniformly distributed across the economy and can polarize wages further.

Technology can exacerbate wage inequality by suppressing the wages of middle- and low-skilled workers whose jobs may be more susceptible to automation. Research by professors Daron Acemoglu and Pascual Restrepo has shown, for example, that increases in robotization between 1990 and 2007 have corresponded with declines in wages (as well as employment) across cities in the United States, a finding that has also been borne out in other studies using other US data.[20]

The rise of the gig economy, facilitated by digital platforms, has also created new job opportunities, offering flexibility and independence for many workers. Yet, these roles often lack traditional employment benefits. The absence of health insurance, pension plans, and job security in many gig economy roles raises concerns about the long-term financial and social security of these workers.

Risk, Health, and Safety

One of the most significant benefits of technological innovations is their ability to reduce physical risks in the workplace. Automation and robotics, for example, can take over hazardous, dirty, or physically demanding tasks, and in doing so, decrease the risk of accidents and injuries. This shift is particularly impactful in industries like manufacturing or logistics, where the introduction of robotic systems has made work environments safer.

In addition to taking away inherently dangerous tasks from humans, technology like AI also has the potential to better analyze risks for the tasks that remain in human hands, helping workers more easily avoid accidents and injury. Moreover, such analysis can even potentially happen in real time and be fed back into work systems so that they can anticipate and avoid dangers to physical health.

Nevertheless, the increasing reliance on technology, especially in office environments, introduces new health concerns. Prolonged computer use, for example, can lead to poor posture, repetitive strain injuries, and other physical health problems associated with sedentary work. By taking away more routine aspects of work, humans may be left with only the most challenging aspects—potentially leading to a danger of cognitive overload.[21]

As we've noted, evidence from the past couple of decades suggests that technology has brought about work intensification.[22] This can place extra physical strain on workers, but it can also induce greater stress and contribute to other mental health issues. This has the potential to be compounded in environments where electronic performance monitoring and other forms of algorithmic management are prevalent, adding to the psychological pressure on employees.

Far from technology increasing safety, recent quantitative analyses—as well as a mounting series of more qualitative accounts—of workers at Amazon warehouses (and other similar work contexts) suggests that large percentages of workers feel great pressure to work faster and that physical injury, pain, and burnout are commonplace.[23]

Worker Beliefs about the Impact of Automation

After assessing the theory behind the potential impacts of new technologies using the driver framework, we can come at it from another angle. A different approach is to ask workers themselves. We were able to add questions on the impact of one particular technology, AI, on the drivers of wellbeing to a recent cross-country survey.[24] Figure 11-1 suggests that people are generally cautiously optimistic, though not across the board. Areas where people are most concerned are in job security, relationships, and earnings. As for flexibility and the nature of the tasks themselves, people are somewhat more optimistic, believing that AI has the potential to improve those particular drivers.

Asking what people think will be the overall effects on the four main aspects of workplace wellbeing, there is again some cautious optimism, but

FIGURE 11-1

Worker Beliefs on AI's Impact on Wellbeing Drivers

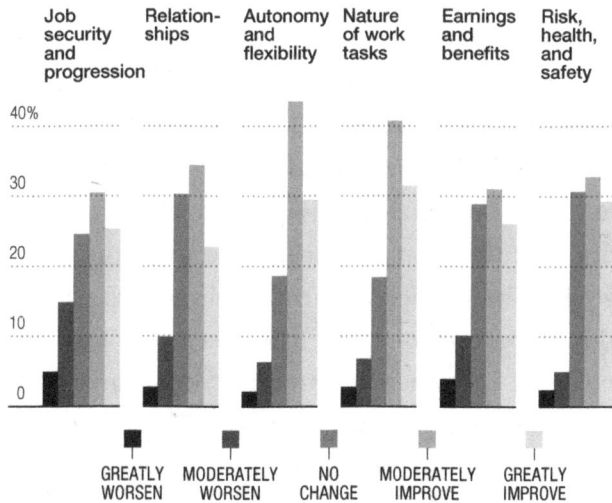

To what extent do you think the development of AI systems and tools will improve or worsen the following:

Job security and progression · Relationships · Autonomy and flexibility · Nature of work tasks · Earnings and benefits · Risk, health, and safety

GREATLY WORSEN · MODERATELY WORSEN · NO CHANGE · MODERATELY IMPROVE · GREATLY IMPROVE

Source: Survey of 507 job seekers in the US who are 18 years or older, conducted in September 2023 by Censuswide.

FIGURE 11-2

Worker Beliefs on AI's Impact on Workplace Wellbeing

To what extent do you think the development of AI systems and tools will improve or worsen the following:

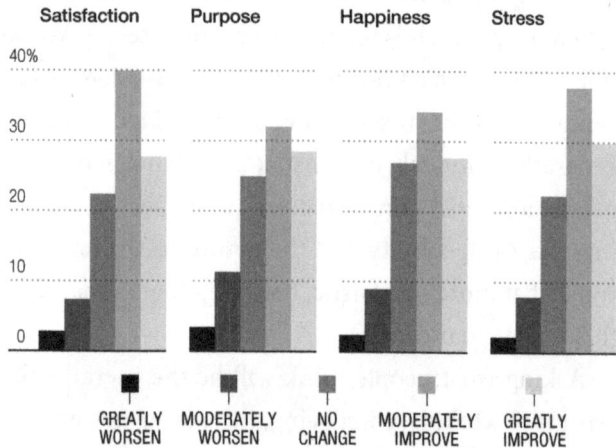

Source: Survey of 507 job seekers in the US who are 18 years or older, conducted in September 2023 by Censuswide.

also a split—in line with the idea that things could go either way. Over half think things will improve to some extent, with around a quarter saying they will stay the same, and just over 10 percent believing that AI will likely reduce workplace wellbeing (see figure 11-2).

Though in line with what we have discussed in terms of the potential for further polarizing of wages and job quality in the labor market, we find that the most optimistic tend to be those who already have high levels of workplace wellbeing and income. Nevertheless, we note that this survey exercise ought to be taken with a strong grain of salt. If technologists and others researchers cannot agree on the potential impacts of automation, it seems unlikely that the opinions of job seekers and employees would necessarily be more reliable. It is certainly worth monitoring both sides of the equation in order to best understand how people are feeling, which is in itself an important outcome of potential technological change.

It's Not What You've Got, It's How You Use It

One overarching theme from this discussion is that technology's impact on each of the drivers is neither wholly positive nor negative.[25] The extent to which technology will affect the drivers of workplace wellbeing—and indeed is already doing so—is theoretically ambiguous. It is shaped not only by the characteristics of the technology in question, but also by a series of choices that organizations, policy makers, and individuals make. These choices will determine whether the future of work enhances wellbeing or detracts from it. We turn to these choices in the next chapter.

Chapter 12

Shaping the Future of Work

Tthere are two main approaches to the conversation about the future of work. The first is based around predictions and asks what kinds of technologies are likely to arise, how many jobs will be created or lost as a result, and so on. The second approach is currently less prevalent but is, we believe, much more useful. It is a discussion based instead around the question of how we can shape the future of work and direct the development of technologies so that they work better for us.

Technology Is Neither Good Nor Bad

Historian of technology Melvin Kranzberg famously noted that "technology is neither good nor bad; nor is it neutral."[1] Indeed, there is nothing inherently positive or negative about a particular technology when it comes to its likely effects on workplace wellbeing, as we found in the previous chapter. Ultimately, technology's role in the future of work hinges on the decisions we make. It's a tool that can either enhance the drivers of workplace wellbeing or undermine them, depending on its design and how we adopt and implement it.[2]

The view that technology autonomously dictates the future of work is a misconception. Instead, it's a dynamic landscape shaped by human decisions, policies, and strategies. We might be tempted to think about the kinds of technologies we expect to be developed over time, or even to look at existing technologies and assess the extent to which they may—for better or worse—affect worker wellbeing. But in doing so, we are taking an overly passive stance, essentially assuming that technology comes out of nowhere and that we have to then react.

Much of the existing literature on the (un)employment effects of technological change, for example, has taken technology as a given and then focused on skills retraining as one key—if not the only—policy prescription to alleviate problems surrounding technologically induced job loss. This approach assumes that technology develops by itself and that humans need to adapt to technology.

But technology is not deterministic, and the way in which technologies will affect how jobs are designed and organized is not inevitable—it depends on a range of factors. These include the nature of the technologies and how they have been developed, but also—importantly—how organizations choose to bring them into the workplace and implement them.[3] AI and robotics exemplify this dual potential. When integrated thoughtfully, they can augment human capabilities and improve wellbeing. But when used solely for efficiency, there is a strong risk of simplifying jobs, eroding autonomy, and diminishing worker wellbeing. The critical factor in technology's impact lies in how it is aligned with organizational goals and human skills.

Managerial choices about technology are key. These are active choices, with important consequences. The effect of a particular technology on an aspect of the workplace depends on the extent to which firms take a human-centered approach in the way it is designed and adopted within the firm.[4] Do managers involve workers in the process of strategizing about how to bring technology into the workplace? Is their mindset one of looking to replace labor or thinking about ways to use technologies to enhance it and make work better? Unfortunately, the former approach currently seems to be winning out, and we need a step change in how we think about technological design and adoption.

Putting Away the Crystal Ball

The economist (and, as it happens, Jan's former landlord) John Kenneth Galbraith once famously said that there are two types of forecasters—those who know they can't predict the future, and those who don't know they can't predict the future. While hugely interesting and engaging, the conversation about how many jobs will be lost or what technology will look like in the future typically does not lead us very far.

When we started to think about writing this book, for example, OpenAI had not yet released ChatGPT—an event that has already significantly changed the way people think about the potential for large language models to substitute for or augment a range of tasks. Trying to guess what technologies will exist in twenty or thirty years and the kinds of tasks they might have an impact on is a fool's game or, at the very least, is one better left to technologists. If our view of what may be possible is somewhat different now than it was a year ago, trying to envision what technology will look like in decades from now is fraught with difficulty.

Instead, the more pertinent conversation is about how we can shape the future of work. And shape it so that technology is more human-centric and works to make the experience of work better, by which we mean, of course, more satisfying, enjoyable, purposeful, and less stressful. It is up to humans to decide how we develop various forms of it, not to mention how we choose to implement it within workplaces. The question is, do we design it to maximize efficiency, workplace wellbeing, or something else?

As we saw in the previous chapter, with regard to the six drivers of workplace wellbeing, many are theoretically ambiguous when it comes to the effects of new technological advancements. One running theme throughout the discussion, though, was that automation has the potential to take away much mundane or boring work. While we cannot predict the future, we can look at existing jobs in order to shed light on this and assess the extent to which it is actually true.

The Wellbeing of Jobs Currently Exposed to Automation

Here we consider the extent to which new technologies are likely to affect—that is, replace, supplant, change, or otherwise have an impact on—the jobs and tasks that we are most (un)happy doing. We rely on two primary sources of data. The first will be familiar by now. Our measures of workplace wellbeing are drawn from the Indeed data we have relied on throughout the book, which we aggregate to the level of fine-grained occupations.[5] To look at automation, we use data collected by the Occupational Information Network, commonly known as O*NET, maintained by the US Department of Labor.

Through extensive and ongoing surveys of workers in hundreds of occupations, O*NET offers detailed and informative statistics on a broad array of work tasks, job characteristics, and skill sets. Most importantly for our purposes, the data also contains an indicator of which jobs are currently most automatable—or more specifically, what percent of tasks inherent to each occupation are currently capable of being automated.

The data shown in figure 12-1 suggests that jobs with the highest degree of automation are also those that workers, at least in today's labor market, tend to be the least happy performing, across all four measures of workplace wellbeing. At least at first pass, this appears to be good news. It implies that the activities we as human beings are best suited for are also those that bring us the most joy, fulfillment, and satisfaction. The clearest examples of this are critical thinking, creative expression, and social interaction, yet there are many more examples to choose from.

However, even if our analysis does indicate that automation is least likely to affect occupations and activities that most support wellbeing today, that does not necessarily mean that it will promote wellbeing at work in the future. For one, this analysis does not rule out potentially adverse effects of job displacement. There is no guarantee that those who currently do these unhappy tasks will find jobs doing more meaningful or enjoyable work.

Perhaps even more importantly, exactly *how* automation will affect the roles and responsibilities of workers employed in particularly susceptible

FIGURE 12-1

More Automated Professions Have Lower Workplace Wellbeing

Occupational wellbeing (on a 1–5 scale) by current level of automation

Based on O*NET, which provides data on work context and quantifies—using a combination of worker and expert surveys—the current degree of automation in the occupation, on a 0–100 scale.

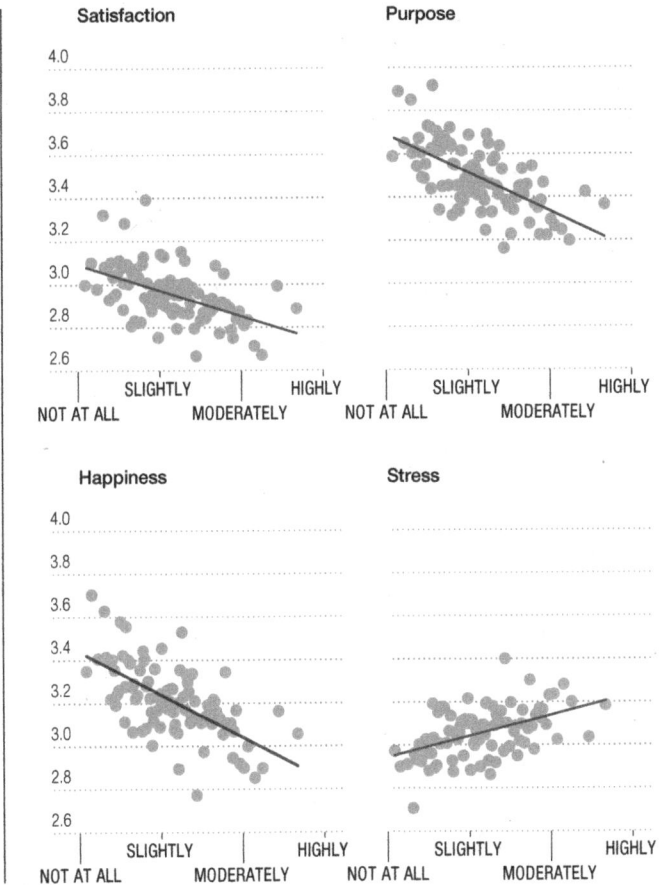

Satisfaction

Purpose

Happiness

Stress

Note: Indeed data on workplace wellbeing is aggregated to 6-digit occupational codes and matched to data on Work Context collected by O*NET.
Source: Indeed data on workplace wellbeing (October 2019 to May 2024); O*NET data on automation; Micah Kaats and George Ward, "Artificial Intelligence and Job Quality," Working Paper, 2024.

professions remains somewhat unclear. Much of popular discussion and academic literature is very careful to use phrases like occupations "exposed to AI" or "susceptible to robotics." Words like "exposed" do a lot of heavy lifting here. It could be that these technologies replace these tasks, a process usually referred to as substitution of labor. Or it could be that they augment those tasks by combining with humans in different ways to do the task in different ways.

Exposure to Technology: Substitution or Augmentation?

Consider the example of writers. Among the most important tasks managers work on are email correspondence, desk research, and of course, writing. The data suggests that these are precisely the sorts of tasks likely to be affected by generative AI. But does that mean writers will increasingly find themselves out of work? Will businesses begin to pay more for data servers than they do for staff writers? Or will employees of the future be able to work fewer hours for the same amount of income and dedicate their remaining time to leisure and other personal projects? Or, perhaps most intriguing of all, will the rise of automation lead to new forms of collaborative and cooperative efforts between humans and machines? In the present context, will generative AI instead increasingly take on the role of research assistants, allowing them to spend more of their time actually writing and less time looking for sources and conducting desk research? If so, then being exposed to automation may not be a bad thing after all.

Some evidence has already begun to emerge that work conducted in collaboration with AI is more enjoyable than work conducted independently. In one cleverly designed experiment, two economics PhD students at MIT, Shakked Noy and Whitney Zhang, were particularly quick out of the blocks once ChatGPT was released and started to make waves. With impressive speed, they saw an opportunity and put together a relatively simple but powerful experiment where they asked over four hundred study participants to complete a series of assignments.[6] Half of the participants were randomly assigned to work on the task independently, while the other half were given access to and shown how to use generative AI for assistance.

Those in the AI group not only produced more work of higher quality—that is, both productivity and performance increased—but also reported higher levels of job satisfaction and self-efficacy. The greatest gains accrued to those most likely to struggle with the tasks to begin with, reducing over-all inequality in productivity and performance between workers. The mechanism was precisely what we discussed earlier as well as in the previous chapter. The authors found that the use of ChatGPT "restructures tasks towards idea-generation and editing and away from rough-drafting." In other words, automation freed participants to focus on more enjoyable tasks that they were better suited for to begin with.

These kinds of dynamics have also played out in real-world workplace settings. Economists Erik Brynjolfsson, Danielle Li, and Lindsey Raymond found when they looked at the introduction of a generative AI system to help customer support agents, those who had access to it were generally more productive in terms of resolving more issues per hour—an effect that was particularly strong for workers with lower levels of skill at the outset. But it also appears to improve how workers experience the job, with fewer of them ultimately quitting the organization.

The Perils of Unemployment

Recent research by economist Daron Acemoglu and colleagues has looked extensively at the introduction of robots into different industries and labor markets in the United States and generally has found strong evidence of substitution—with labor shares going down in areas most exposed.[7] Ultimately, even if augmentation is possible and desirable, substitution is also commonplace, and we cannot simply wave it away.

It is true that technological change over the long run has yet to lead us to a situation of widespread technological unemployment, with more jobs being created than lost when we look at things in aggregate.[8] But we should be careful about using this fact to excuse ourselves from facing up to any dangers. For one, with such major technological change happening, historians have rightly pointed out that the only really valid comparison in terms of scope and scale, if there is one, is the First Industrial Revolution.[9] Moreover, even looking at more recent technological change, the aggregate numbers certainly do not mean that some groups of people have not lost their jobs or had the value of their skills degraded, often with devastating and long-lasting consequences, both for individual workers as well as entire communities and even regions.

Job loss is hugely detrimental to subjective wellbeing as a whole, as we saw at length earlier in the book. Not only does losing a job lead to a sharp drop in life satisfaction, but it is also a life event that we do not tend to adapt to.[10] Unemployment is miserable, and policy makers as well as business leaders should do everything they can to avoid it. Not only do people not adapt to unemployment, but some studies have also identified lingering effects on wellbeing even after returning to work—so-called scarring effects of unemployment.

One analysis found that, after finding a new job, German men who reported longer periods of unemployment in the previous three years were still 0.5 points less satisfied with their lives than counterparts who stayed employed during the same period.[11] These effects remained significant even after controlling for the influence of differential working conditions and salaries between both groups. Taking an even longer-term perspective, some research has found long-lasting effects of youth unemployment on wellbeing levels in adulthood.[12] Young people who come of age during a recession are also more likely to value financial security and less likely to value job meaning later in life.[13] All of these effects go beyond what can be explained by lost income and provide a potentially cautionary tale for those arguing that ever-more frequent job loss is tolerable so long as other jobs are being created elsewhere in the economy.

The Example of Working from Home

One way of exploring and underscoring a number of these dynamics is to take a prominent example, that of new technologies allowing for much more remote working and other flexible working arrangements. Technology has developed over time, from phones to flash drives, to the internet and email, to video-conferencing, cloud storage, and remote access to all sorts of data and analytics tools. In some form, relevant technology existed for quite some time and did not diffuse immediately. Its impact on the drivers of workplace wellbeing is somewhat ambiguous from a theoretical standpoint. Different firms have used it in very different ways. They have implemented it to maximize different kinds of outcomes. And they have thought about its success in terms of very different measures.

In 2019, around 7 percent of days worked in the United States were at home.[14] This skyrocketed during the pandemic to be well over half of all days worked—a development that can be seen when looking at data collected by the US Census, tailored surveys by researchers interested in remote working trends, all the way to data on traffic and footfall in city centers and business districts. Since then, that share has fallen, of course, as social distancing mandates eased. But working from home is far from being back to prepandemic levels. Although newspaper headlines frequently tout the great return to the office, the level of remote working seems to have stabilized at around 25 to 30 percent.[15]

In among all of this, companies gleaned huge amounts of data on working from home; they tried all sorts of different arrangements—fully remote, hybrid, mandating certain days in the office, and so on—as well as different modes of doing things. This included different video-conferencing software, modes of collaboration, ways of trying to maintain social ties and connections, and everything else in between. There was no predetermined way that the technology is used, and firms and their managers made a range of choices.

Thinking about remote working from the perspective of the driver framework, it seems clear that it will raise flexibility. People can work from where they choose and, depending on the kinds of tasks involved, decide when to do them. Among other things, this has helped mothers stay in the workforce.[16] Beyond this, other benefits are likely to arise. For example, allowing for more flexible working arrangements will help cut down on commuting times, which is widely documented to be one of the unhappiest activities people engage in daily.[17]

However, think about other drivers as well—some of which may run in the opposite direction, complicating the picture somewhat. Maxing out one driver of workplace wellbeing at the expense of another is unlikely to be a successful strategy to achieving happiness at work. Even within independence and flexibility, the dangers to autonomy arising from firms increasing their surveillance and monitoring of remote employees can threaten any gains from flexibility. The pressure to always be "on" can also become overwhelming, and even though people have the flexibility to work whenever they choose, they can end up working more hours and experiencing overload.[18]

We can also look at development and security. One large-scale experiment at a Chinese travel agency found that employees who were randomly assigned to work from home were both more productive and more satisfied with their work.[19] This is very encouraging, but the study also found that employees in the treatment group were ultimately less likely to be promoted than their peers as time went on. If the continued expansion of flexible working arrangements is not complemented by an equivalent expansion of policies and frameworks to promote job security and professional development, then sustaining employee wellbeing in the future may prove increasingly difficult.

At the same time, we also need to keep an eye on the relationships driver as well. Relationships with colleagues and managers can be crucially important for employee wellbeing, even more so than the other drivers. Because these relationships become weaker or more difficult to manage, the transition to more flexible working arrangements could decrease wellbeing in the long run. There is emerging evidence to suggest that workers are starting to feel the effects of these trade-offs in real time. One survey found, for example, among adults who transitioned to work from home since Covid-19, that even though 64 percent reported having an easier time balancing their work and personal lives, 60 percent also reported feeling less connected to coworkers.[20]

In addition to the direction of any potential effects—positive or negative—that technologies may have on the drivers of wellbeing, there is also the time horizon to think about. For example, the flexibility benefits of cutting out the commute were immediate for many among us who worked from home during the pandemic. However, our social relationships at work, and the sense of belonging that comes with them, gradually eroded. What was often lost were the informal interactions—impromptu watercooler moments—and as colleagues moved on, there were no real opportunities to bond with new recruits. For those joining the organization, it was even harder to properly get to know all their new colleagues. One way to try to mitigate these losses are things like in-person retreats, which companies like Dropbox have found to drastically reduce the turnover of remote employees.[21]

One useful way to think about social (and indeed intellectual) capital is as stocks, which were slowly being depleted during the pandemic while working fully remotely.[22] The development of this capital happens through the flow of shared experiences and chance interactions that can spark connection and creative ideas. Even part-time office-based jobs for one or two days a week provide workers with the routine, social network and identity that are often essential for wellbeing. Arrangements that combine flexibility with ways to collaborate and socialize may well be enough to generate the in-flows needed to maintain social and intellectual capital stock.

Indeed, models of hybrid working—whereby people work some days in the office and some at home—appear to be becoming the default approach for those not working fully on-site.[23] Recent experimental work has shown that this may well provide the best of both worlds. One study in a large Chinese technology company, for example, randomly assigned employees to full-time office or hybrid work and found that hybrid work increased job satisfaction, reduced turnover, and had no effect on performance. After accounting for savings in office space, in this case, it was reasonable to conclude that hybrid work should increase firm profits.[24]

Using a similar design, another group of researchers was able to test the comparative effects of a low, medium, and high version of working from home at another company.[25] Ultimately, they found the intermediate position to be most beneficial—indeed, those in the middle group ended up reporting higher job satisfaction and greater work-life balance, and feeling lower levels of isolation compared to workers in both high- and low-treatment groups who were working from home.

As new forms of technology are developed and firms experiment with different forms of implementation, one of the biggest and most important questions in management in the coming years is about how to balance the benefits and drawbacks of remote work. Currently, hybrid schedules are leading the way forward, though they mean employees do not get the key benefit from being able to live and work from anywhere, as in fully remote arrangements. Ultimately, a major challenge is how we can design work that allows for the flexibility afforded by remote work but also maintains strong social connections, which are important for wellbeing, but also for other outcomes like innovation and fusing new ideas through collective collaboration.[26]

Play an Active Role and Give Workers a Voice

There is nothing inherently good or bad about technology, and it is not inevitable that technological developments will undermine worker wellbeing (or, indeed, improve it).[27] We can be sure, though, that they will have an impact on a whole range of aspects of jobs and workplaces. In the previous chapter, we surveyed some of the ways that tools like robots and AI may affect the key drivers of workplace wellbeing. In each case, there is potential to improve but also a clear risk of degradation.

The critical task ahead is to steer technological development toward desired futures of work, ones that ultimately work for wellbeing. This requires an active approach. We need a mindset that goes beyond the existing passive mentality whereby we see ourselves as having to adapt to technological changes. It involves thoughtful integration of technology with a focus on enhancing rather than replacing human work. The effective implementation of technology in the workplace should aim not only for increased efficiency but also for improved worker wellbeing.

This is not going to be easy, and we are arguably already behind. Going forward, organizations must actively consider work design and human-centered principles when introducing new technologies.[28] In doing so, they should involve workers, give them a voice, and enable them to play a part in the design and adoption of technology. A collaborative approach that engages with unions and workers not only smooths the transition to new work practices but also ensures that these practices are aligned with the workers' needs and wellbeing.

Policy makers must also play a crucial role in shaping the future landscape of work.[29] Regulations and policies need to ensure that technological advancements do not lead to increased inequality or compromised worker wellbeing. This might involve legislating for higher minimum wages, guaranteed benefits for gig economy workers, or safeguards against excessive surveillance and work intensification. Equally, governments can play a role in incentivizing (for example, through the tax system) certain types of research and technology development above others.

Shaping the Future of Work

The key question is not so much a matter of whether technology will change the world, but when and how. Digital technologies have already begun to change the way we work. Machine learning, artificial intelligence, and robotics will no doubt continue to transform the economy. Yet the rate at which these technologies are developed, adapted, and adopted at scale is crucial. Despite the hype, the effects of technological change take decades to unravel, even in our modern world of accelerating progress. As David Autor and his colleagues at MIT have described, these are "momentous impacts, unfolding gradually."[30]

As a result, whether or not automation serves as a boon or impediment to future shared prosperity is not a foregone conclusion. It is in our control to shape the future of work. It can be positive or negative depending on what we make of it. Let's not leave it to technologists alone to decide. In this, policy makers, business leaders, union officials, human resource professionals, journalists, academics, and workers themselves all have essential roles to play. How we choose to shape and distribute the benefits and burdens of automation will determine the extent to which the future of work is appealing or threatening to most workers.

If we are serious about building a better future for work, we should think about the challenges and opportunities we face in terms of wellbeing. Supporting wellbeing at work implies promoting and protecting that which drives wellbeing. We need to keep a keen eye on productivity and performance, but just as important, we need to be thinking about job security, earnings and benefits, career development, relationships at work, variety and fulfillment, independence and flexibility, and risks to health and safety. In doing so, we can ensure that the conversation focuses on the quality of work and not just the quantity of work. In short, we can build a future that we actually want to be employed in.

Notes

Introduction

1. Chris Newlands, "Companies Reap Bigger Dividends from Happier Staff," *Financial Times*, May 21, 2024, https://www.ft.com/content/044fc5f3-e4b4-4b0d-9849-939d8c4f73da; Shawn Achor, "Is Happiness the Secret of Success?," CNN, March 19, 2012, https://edition.cnn.com/2012/03/19/opinion/happiness-success-achor/index.html; Emma Seppälä and Kim Cameron, "Proof That Positive Work Cultures Are More Productive," hbr.org, December 1, 2015, https://hbr.org/2015/12/proof-that-positive-work-cultures-are-more-productive; Sarah Malcolm, "If You Want to Be More Productive at Work, Get Happy," *Forbes*, December 10, 2021, https://www.forbes.com/sites/forbesagencycouncil/2021/04/16/if-you-want-to-be-more-productive-at-work-get-happy.

2. HBR Analytic Services, "Cultivating Workforce Well-Being to Drive Business Value," 2020, https://hbr.org/sponsored/2020/07/cultivating-workforce-well-being-to-drive-business-value.

3. Nandil Bhatia and Stephan Meier, "Strategic Salience of Employees in Executive Narratives—Using Machine Learning to Conceptualize Stakeholder Strategic Salience," Columbia Business School research paper no. 4215010, 2024, https://doi.org/10.2139/ssrn.4215010.

4. Jan-Emmanuel De Neve and George Ward, "Measuring Workplace Wellbeing," University of Oxford Wellbeing Research Centre Working Paper 2303, 2023.

5. Andrew E. Clark et al., *The Origins of Happiness* (Princeton, NJ: Princeton University Press, 2018); Ed Diener et al., "Findings All Psychologists Should Know from the New Science on Subjective Well-Being," *Canadian Psychology/Psychologie Canadienne* 58 (2017): 87–104, https://doi.org/10.1037/CAP0000063; Andrew E. Clark, "Four Decades of the Economics of Happiness: Where Next?," *Review of Income and Wealth* 64, no. 2 (2018): 245–69.

6. T. A. Judge and R. Ilies, "Affect and Job Satisfaction: A Study of Their Relationship at Work and at Home," *Journal of Applied Psychology* 4, no. 4 (2004): 661–73, https://doi.org/10.1037/0021-9010.89.4.661.

7. Clément Bellet, Jan-Emmanuel De Neve, and George Ward, "Does Employee Happiness Have an Impact on Productivity?," *Management Science* 70, no. 3 (2023): 1656–79.

8. George Ward, "Workplace Wellbeing and Employee Turnover," University of Oxford Working Paper, 2024.

9. George Ward, "Workplace Happiness and Job Search Behavior: Evidence from a Field Experiment," MIT Sloan Working Paper 6607-22, 2022.

10. The survey was carried out in 2023 by Forrester Consulting, commissioned by Indeed. The survey was done using nationally representative samples (from an online panel) in the United States, United Kingdom, Canada, India, Netherlands, France, Germany, and Japan. For an earlier set of findings using the same question in 2020, using data from the

United States only, see George Ward, "Happiness at Work: Essays on Subjective Wellbeing in the Workplace and Labor Market" (thesis, Massachusetts Institute of Technology, 2022), https://dspace.mit.edu/handle/1721.1/144621.

11. For more details, see "Indeed Workplace Happiness Report," based on a commissioned survey conducted by Forrester Consulting. The full question wording was "Do you believe your expectations about wellbeing (including feeling happy at work most of the time, a manageable stress level, a sense of satisfaction, and purpose) at work have changed compared to five years ago?"

12. Jan-Emmanuel De Neve, Micah Kaats, and George Ward, "Workplace Wellbeing and Firm Performance," University of Oxford Wellbeing Research Centre Working Paper 2304, 2023.

13. See https://www.youtube.com/watch?app=desktop&v=dnGV6cJRHlk.

14. George Ward, "The Wellbeing of Workplaces: Organization-Level Differences Between and Within Industries," University of Oxford Working Paper, 2024; George Ward, "Workplace Wellbeing and Employee Turnover," University of Oxford Working Paper, 2024.

15. See discussion and figures presented in chapter 5.

16. For more details, see "Indeed Workplace Happiness Report," based on a commissioned survey conducted by Forrester Consulting.

17. Milena Nikolova, Femke Cnossen, and Daniel L. Bennett, "Robots, Meaning, and Self-Determination," *Research Policy* 53, no. 5 (2024): 104987; Sharon K. Parker and Gudela Grote, "Automation, Algorithms, and Beyond: Why Work Design Matters More Than Ever in a Digital World," *Applied Psychology* 71, no. 4 (2022): 1171–1204, https://doi.org/10.1111/apps.12241; Jilles Smids, Sven Nyholm, and Hannah A. Berkers, "Robots in the Workplace: A Threat to—or Opportunity for—Meaningful Work?," *Philosophy & Technology* 33 (2020), https://doi.org/10.1007/S13347-019-00377-4.

Chapter 1

1. N = 698,343 (satisfaction); 41,490 (meaningfulness); 684,127 (positive affect); 679,176 (negative affect). The question on meaningfulness was fielded in 2021 only. The question wordings were as follows: Life satisfaction: "Please imagine a ladder with steps numbered from 0 at the bottom to 10 at the top. The top of the ladder represents the best possible life for you and the bottom of the ladder represents the worst possible life for you. On which step of the ladder would you say you personally feel you stand at this time?" Meaningfulness: "In general, how often do you feel each of the following? Always, often, rarely, or never? The things you do are meaningful" (Always = 1, Often = 2, Rarely = 3, Never = 4) Positive emotion: Average of answers to the following 4 questions: "Did you smile or laugh a lot yesterday?" "Did you feel well-rested yesterday?" "Did you experience the following feelings during a lot of the day yesterday? [Happiness] [Enjoyment]" Negative emotion: Average of answers to the following 5 questions: "Did you experience the following feelings during a lot of the day yesterday? [Worry] [Anger] [Stress] [Sadness]"

2. Satisfied with your job: Measures whether the respondent answered "Yes" to the question "Are you satisfied with your job? (Yes/No)" N = 156,833, 155 countries. Things you do are meaningful: "Yes" if respondent answered "Always" or "Often" to "In general, how often do you feel each of the following? Always, often, rarely or never? The things you do are meaningful" N = 35,310, 121 countries, 2021 only. Enjoy the work you do: "Do you enjoy the work you do in your job every day, or not? (Yes/No)" N = 73,984, 125 countries. Felt a lot of stress yesterday: "Did you experience the following feelings during a lot of the day yesterday? Stress" N = 554,463, 165 countries.

3. For a much more in-depth discussion and empirical evidence, see George Ward, "The Wellbeing of Workplaces: Organization-Level Differences Between and Within Industries," University of Oxford Working Paper, 2024; George Ward, "Workplace Wellbeing and Employee Turnover," University of Oxford Working Paper, 2024.

4. Ward, "The Wellbeing of Workplaces."

5. See George Ward, "Happiness at Work: Essays on Subjective Wellbeing in the Workplace and Labor Market" (thesis, Massachusetts Institute of Technology, 2022), https://dspace.mit.edu/handle/1721.1/144621.

6. Estimated by regressing company happiness scores on NAICS industry categories. On an individual level, industry differences explain even less—only about 1 percent. See Ward, "The Wellbeing of Workplaces."

7. Whole Foods (N = 9,706), Walmart (N = 134,839), HSBC (N = 691), Trader Joe's (N = 3,176), Costco Wholesale (N = 6,545), Santander (N = 1,258).

8. According to data from Gallup, Connecticut and Utah are among the happiest states in the country, while Alabama and Tennessee are among the unhappiest. As a result, one might expect that people living in the former states would be happier at work than those in the latter. Not quite. In Connecticut, workers at Walmart and Target are actually less happy than those in Alabama, even though UPS workers are equally happy in both states. At the same time, UPS workers in Utah are unhappier than those in Alabama or Connecticut, even though Target employees in Utah are happier than counterparts in either one. Walmart employees in Tennessee are just as happy as those in Connecticut and Alabama, but happier than those in Utah. McDonald's workers are particularly unhappy in Connecticut and Utah, while those in Alabama are happier than those in Tennessee. In other words, when mapped across state lines, differences in workplace wellbeing simply do not line up in the way we might intuitively expect them to.

9. See, e.g., María Josefina Peláez Zuberbuhler, Marisa Salanova, and Isabel M. Martínez, "Coaching-Based Leadership Intervention Program: A Controlled Trial Study," *Frontiers in Psychology* 10 (January 30, 2020): 3066, https://doi.org/10.3389/fpsyg.2019.03066; Anthony M. Grant, Linley Curtayne, and Geraldine Burton, "Executive Coaching Enhances Goal Attainment, Resilience and Workplace Well-Being: A Randomised Controlled Study," *Journal of Positive Psychology* 4, no. 5 (2009): 396–407, https://doi.org/10.1080/17439760902992456.

10. For a discussion and evidence of the importance of mental health for subjective wellbeing, see Andrew E. Clark et al., *The Origins of Happiness* (Princeton, NJ: Princeton University Press, 2018). Within organizations, mental health may be helped by having a number of employees trained in "mental health first aid" that may be able help those in need and steer more serious cases toward outside support, and we hope to see more research on the effectiveness of such programs. For a discussion, see Amy J. Morgan, Anna Ross, and Nicola J. Reavley, "Systematic Review and Meta-Analysis of Mental Health First Aid Training: Effects on Knowledge, Stigma, and Helping Behaviour," *PLOS ONE* 13, no. 5 (May 31, 2018): e0197102, https://doi.org/10.1371/journal.pone.0197102.

11. For an extended discussion of the evidence surrounding the effectiveness of different forms of mental health care, see Richard Layard and David M. Clark, *Thrive: How Better Mental Health Care Transforms Lives and Saves Money* (Princeton, NJ: Princeton University Press, 2014).

12. Damon Jones, David Molitor, and Julian Reif, "What Do Workplace Wellness Programs Do? Evidence from the Illinois Workplace Wellness Study," *Quarterly Journal of Economics* 134, no. 4 (2019): 1747–91, https://doi.org/10.1093/QJE/QJZ023.

13. Our Oxford colleague William Fleming showed something very similar as part of his doctoral thesis when estimating the impact of individual-level interventions across 143

organizations in the UK. He failed to find an effect for a number of common wellness initiatives such as mindfulness, lifestyle apps, and resilience training. See William J. Fleming, "Employee Well-Being Outcomes from Individual-Level Mental Health Interventions: Cross-Sectional Evidence from the United Kingdom," *Industrial Relations Journal* 55, no. 2 (2024): 162–82.

14. Clément Bellet, Jan-Emmanuel De Neve, and George Ward, "Does Employee Happiness Have an Impact on Productivity?," *Management Science* 70, no. 3 (2023): 1656–79; George Ward, "Workplace Wellbeing and Employee Turnover," University of Oxford Working Paper, 2024; George Ward, "Workplace Happiness and Job Search Behavior: Evidence from a Field Experiment," MIT Sloan Working Paper 6607-22, 2022.

15. Clark et al., *The Origins of Happiness*, 2018.

16. Jan-Emmanuel De Neve, Micah Kaats, and George Ward, "Workplace Wellbeing and Firm Performance," University of Oxford Wellbeing Research Centre Working Paper 2304, 2023; Christian Krekel, George Ward, and Jan-Emmanuel De Neve, "Employee Wellbeing, Productivity and Firm Performance," Saïd Business School Working Paper 4 (2019), https://doi.org/10.2139/SSRN.3356581. The figure includes publicly traded firms with minimum ten responses only.

Chapter 2

1. Sarah Malcolm, "If You Want to Be More Productive at Work, Get Happy," *Forbes*, 2021, https://www.forbes.com/sites/forbesagencycouncil/2021/04/16/if-you-want-to-be-more-productive-at-work-get-happy/; Te-Ping Chen and Ray A. Smith, "American Workers Are Burned Out, and Bosses Are Struggling to Respond," *Wall Street Journal*, December 21, 2021, https://www.wsj.com/articles/worker-burnout-resignations-pandemic-stress--11640099198; Andrew Hill, "Six Ways to Improve the Wellbeing of Workers," *Financial Times*, December 16, 2019, https://www.ft.com/content/89948270-1ce1-11ea-97df-cc63de1d73f4; Shawn Achor, "Is Happiness the Secret of Success?," CNN, 2012, https://edition.cnn.com/2012/03/19/opinion/happiness-success-achor/index.html; Emma Seppälä and Kim Cameron, "Proof That Positive Work Cultures Are More Productive," hbr.org, December 1, 2015, https://hbr.org/2015/12/proof-that-positive-work-cultures-are-more-productive; Liz Hilton Segel, "The Priority for Workplaces in the New Normal?," McKinsey, 2021, https://www.mckinsey.com/featured-insights/world-economic-forum/davos-agenda/perspectives/the-priority-for-workplaces-in-the-new-normal; E. Hampson and A. Jacob, "Mental Health and Employers: Refreshing the Case for Investment," Deloitte, 2020.

2. HBR Analytic Services, "Cultivating Workforce Well-Being to Drive Business Value," https://Bg.Hbr.Org/Resources/Pdfs/Comm/Workplacewellbeing.Pdf, 2020.

3. Ed Diener and Robert Biswas-Diener, *Happiness: Unlocking the Mysteries of Psychological Wealth* (Hoboken, NJ: John Wiley & Sons, 2011).

4. See Ed Diener, "Guidelines for National Indicators of Subjective Well-Being and Ill-Being," *Journal of Happiness Studies* 7, no. 4 (2006): 397–404.

5. For relevant discussions surrounding the history and conceptualization of wellbeing in philosophy, psychology, and economics, see: Roger Crisp, "Well-Being," in *The Stanford Encyclopedia of Philosophy*, ed. Edward N. Zalta, Winter 2021 (Metaphysics Research Lab, Stanford University, 2021), https://plato.stanford.edu/archives/win2021/entries/well-being/; Dan Haybron, "Happiness," in *The Stanford Encyclopedia of Philosophy*, ed. Edward N. Zalta, Summer 2020 (Metaphysics Research Lab, Stanford University, 2020), https://plato.stanford.edu/archives/sum2020/entries/happiness/.

6. Jan-Emmanuel De Neve and George Ward, "Measuring Workplace Wellbeing," University of Oxford Wellbeing Research Centre Working Paper 2303, 2023.

7. See, for example, Richard B. Freeman, "Job Satisfaction as an Economic Variable," *American Economic Review* 68, no. 2 (1978): 135–41; Timothy A. Judge and Ryan Klinger, "Job Satisfaction," in *The Science of Subjective Well-Being*, ed. Michael Eid and Randy J. Larsen (London, UK: Guildford Press, 2008), 393–413; Thomas A. Wright, "The Emergence of Job Satisfaction in Organizational Research: A Historical Overview of the Dawn of Job Attitude Research," *Journal of Management History* 12 (2006): 262–77 for more detailed discussion of the history of job satisfaction research.

8. Sigal G. Barsade and Andrew P. Knight, "Group Affect," *Annual Review of Organizational Psychology and Organizational Behavior* 2, no. 1 (2015): 21–46; Arthur P. Brief and Howard M. Weiss, "Organizational Behavior: Affect in the Workplace," *Annual Review of Psychology* 53, no. 1 (2002): 279–307, https://doi.org/10.1146/ANNUREV.PSYCH.53.100901 .135156; Andrew P. Knight, Jochen I. Menges, and Heike Bruch, "Organizational Affective Tone: A Meso Perspective on the Origins and Effects of Consistent Affect in Organizations," *Academy of Management Journal* 61, no. 1 (2018): 191–219, https://doi.org/10.17863/CAM.12156. For earlier work, see, e.g., Rexford B. Hersey, *Workers' Emotions in Shop and Home: A Study of Industrial Workers from the Psychological and Physiological Standpoint* (Philadelphia: University of Pennsylvania Press, 1932). While much of the twentieth century was dominated by research in job satisfaction, very early work on the topic did in fact focus on the emotional aspects of work. So, the recent turn in the literature might be better characterized as a return to affect.

9. See, e.g., Teresa M. Amabile et al., "Affect and Creativity at Work," *Administrative Science Quarterly* 50, no. 3 (2005): 367–403, https://doi.org/10.2189/ASQU.2005.50.3.367; Amir Erez and Alice M. Isen, "The Influence of Positive Affect on the Components of Expectancy Motivation," *Journal of Applied Psychology* 87, no. 6 (2002): 1055, https://doi.org/10.1037/0021 -9010.87.6.1055; Andrew J. Oswald, Eugenio Proto, and Daniel Sgroi, "Happiness and Productivity," *Journal of Labor Economics* 33, no. 4 (2015): 789–822, https://doi.org/10.1086 /681096; Howard M. Weiss and Russell Cropanzano, "Affective Events Theory," *Research in Organizational Behavior* 18, no. 1 (1996): 1–74.

10. Lea Cassar and Stephan Meier, "Nonmonetary Incentives and the Implications of Work as a Source of Meaning," *Journal of Economic Perspectives* 32, no. 3 (2018): 215–38, https://doi.org/10.1257/JEP.32.3.215; Claudine Gartenberg, Andrea Prat, and George Serafeim, "Corporate Purpose and Financial Performance," *Organization Science* 30, no. 1 (2019): 1–18.

11. Richard M. Ryan and Edward L. Deci, "On Happiness and Human Potentials: A Review of Research on Hedonic and Eudaimonic Well-Being," *Annual Review of Psychology* 52, no. 1 (2001): 141–66; Carol D. Ryff, "Happiness Is Everything, or Is It? Explorations on the Meaning of Psychological Well-Being," *Journal of Personality and Social Psychology* 57, no. 6 (1989): 1069.

12. Gartenberg, Prat, and Serafeim, "Corporate Purpose and Financial Performance."

13. The growing scholarship on subjective wellbeing as a whole has inspired the field of positive psychology, which owes much to the work of Marty Seligman as well as others and goes beyond the study of mental illness and instead sees psychology as a discipline to study ways to foster wellbeing. Similarly, in the management world, the positive organizational scholarship (POS) movement has grown significantly in recent years, focusing on important concepts such as positive meaning and purpose at work as well as thriving at work more generally. See, for example, A. Wrzesniewski, "Finding Positive Meaning in Work," in *Positive*

Organizational Scholarship: Foundations of a New Discipline, ed. K. S. Cameron, J. E. Dutton, and R. E. Quinn (Oakland, CA: Berrett-Koehler, 2003), 296–308; F. Luthans, "Positive Organizational Behavior: Implications for Leadership and HR Development and Motivation," in *Motivation and Work Behavior*, ed. L. W. Porter, G. A. Bigley, and R. M. Steers (New York: McGraw Hill, 2003), 178–95; M. G. Pratt and B. E. Ashforth, "Fostering Positive Meaningful-ness at Work," in *Positive Organizational Scholarship: Foundations of a New Discipline*, ed. K. S. Cameron, J. E. Dutton, and R. E. Quinn, 309–27.

14. OECD, "Guidelines on Measuring Subjective Wellbeing," https://www.Oecd.Org/Statistics/Oecd-Guidelines-on-Measuring-Subjective-Well-Being-9789264191655-En.Htm, 2013.

15. For a more in-depth discussion, see De Neve and Ward, "Measuring Workplace Wellbeing."

16. See Oscar Kjell et al., "Towards Well-Being Measurement with Social Media Across Space, Time and Cultures: Three Generations of Progress," in *World Happiness Report*, ed. Jeffrey Sachs et al., 2023.

17. See De Neve and Ward, "Measuring Workplace Wellbeing."

18. We are hugely grateful to Janeane Tolomeo for the partnership with Indeed, as well as to her lieutenants Rae Albee, Anna Choi, and Jane Neiman. More generally at Indeed, we have benefited greatly from the insight and support of others including Ryan Kaminsky, Gemma Deveney, LaFawn Davis, and, ultimately, the CEO Chris Hyams, who has allowed this forward-thinking initiative to thrive.

Chapter 3

1. The story of Marienthal presented here draws heavily from Marie Jahoda, Paul F. Lazarsfeld, and Hans Zeisel, *Marienthal: The Sociography of an Unemployed Community* (London, UK: Routledge, 1933).

2. Quoted from Clemens Hetschko, Andreas Knabe, and Ronnie Schöb, "Happiness, Work, and Identity," *Handbook of Labor, Human Resources and Population Economics*, 2020, 1–26.

3. In the mid-1930s, Jahoda was imprisoned for her political activities but later managed to emigrate to the United Kingdom, where she continued her research, which would develop and become hugely influential. Among other topics, she continued to study the benefits of work, including looking more closely at social connections, routine and time structure, attitudes, and psychological wellbeing—and in doing so, laying the groundwork for what is now known to sociologists and social psychologists as the latent and manifest benefits (LAMB) of work.

4. One of us (George), over eighty years later, began his PhD at the MIT Sloan School of Management—focusing on the theme of work and wellbeing. It was a case of interesting happenstance to find out that Lazarsfeld and Jahoda's only child, Lotte Bailyn, a social psychologist born in 1930, was a renowned professor in the department.

5. "The value of any commodity, therefore, to the person who possesses it, and who means not to use or consume it himself, but to exchange it for other commodities, is equal to the quantity of labour which it enables him to purchase or command. Labour, therefore, is the real measure of the exchangeable value of all commodities. The real price of everything, what everything really costs to the man who wants to acquire it, is the toil and trouble of acquiring it." Adam Smith, *An Inquiry into the Nature and Causes of the Wealth of Nations*, ed. Edwin Cannan (Chicago: University of Chicago Press, 1977), 50, https://press.uchicago.edu/ucp/books/book/chicago/I/bo3637045.html.

6. Nathan Rosenberg, "Some Institutional Aspects of the Wealth of Nations," *Journal of Political Economy* 68, no. 6 (1960): 557–70.

7. David Spencer, *The Political Economy of Work* (London, UK: Routledge, 2008), 80.

8. Spencer, *The Political Economy of Work*.

9. Spencer, *The Political Economy of Work*.

10. As noted by the political economist David Spencer, "the Austrian formulation became a legitimating force for all kinds of workplace policies that in reality were highly damaging to the wellbeing of workers." Spencer, *The Political Economy of Work*, 91.

11. T. A. Kochan, "What Is Distinctive about Industrial Relations Research?," in *Researching the World of Work*, ed. K. Whitfield and G. Strauss (Ithaca, NY: ILR Press, 1998), 31–50; Bruce E. Kaufman, "The Institutional and Neoclassical Schools in Labor Economics," in *The Institutionalist Tradition in Labor Economics*, ed. Dell P. Champlin and Janet T. Knoedler (London, UK: Routledge, 2004), 13–38.

12. John R. Commons, *Institutional Economics* (Madison, WI: University of Wisconsin Press, 1934).

13. Commons, *Institutional Economics*.

14. The Cantril Ladder asks respondents to imagine life as a ladder with ten steps, the bottom rung representing the worst possible life and the top rung representing the best possible life, and report where on the ladder they felt they presently stood. This is today referred to as a measure of evaluative subjective wellbeing, often likened to life satisfaction.

15. Number of observations varies by measure: life satisfaction = 1,703,464, 166 countries; meaningfulness = 92,619, 121 countries (2021 only); positive emotions = 1,685,746, 165 countries; negative emotions = 1,672,344, 165 countries.

16. Though we are constrained for space and cannot break down the analyses here by country, it is worth noting that the relationships are generally stronger in materially richer countries. One likely explanation for this phenomenon is the porousness of employment classifications in less economically developed regions. In Africa, for example, it is thought that around 85 percent of all employment is informal (using data from the ILO). In Asia, this figure is roughly 70 percent. Particularly in countries without strong worker protections or formal labor market institutions, the concept of unemployment itself becomes hard to define. Almost all working adults end up working for themselves and rarely interact with public-sector agencies and authorities. As a result, it can be difficult to distinguish workers in these regions using "standard" labor market classifications.

Unfortunately, to this day, the relationship between work and wellbeing in low-income countries remains woefully understudied. The dynamics of work and wellbeing in developing regions are wholly deserving of more research. Part of the difficulty in conducting this type of research lies in the inherent challenges in collecting sufficient data upon which to base empirical analyses. In most low-income countries, the Gallup World Poll remains the only reliable source of information on population wellbeing. This is a good start, but truly understanding the dynamics of wellbeing at work ultimately requires surveying large segments of a given population at multiple points in time, a process that can be exceedingly difficult without a sufficient data collection infrastructure already in place. Throughout this book, we rely heavily on this type of large-scale empirical data, and, as a result, our focus will be inevitably and regrettably limited to higher-income regions of the world.

17. Andrew E. Clark et al., *The Origins of Happiness* (Princeton, NJ: Princeton University Press, 2018); Andrew E. Clark and Andrew J. Oswald, "Unhappiness and Unemployment," *Economic Journal* 104, no. 424 (1994): 648–59; Liliana Winkelmann and Rainer Winkelmann,

"Why Are the Unemployed So Unhappy? Evidence from Panel Data," *Economica* 65, no. 257 (1998): 1–15.

18. Clemens Hetschko, "On the Misery of Losing Self-Employment," *Small Business Economics* 47, no. 2 (2016): 461–78; S. C. Kassenboehmer and J. P. Haisken-DeNew, "You're Fired! The Causal Negative Effect of Entry Unemployment on Life Satisfaction," *Economic Journal* 119, no. 536 (2009): 448–62.

19. See, for example: Andrew E. Clark, "Work, Jobs, and Well-Being across the Millennium," *International Differences in Well-Being* (Oxford: Oxford University Press, 2010), 436–68; Clark and Oswald, "Unhappiness and Unemployment"; Kassenboehmer and Haisken-DeNew, "You're Fired!"

20. N = 248,536 person-years; 35,626 individuals. Controls included for log income, marital status, age, age-squared, number of children, individual and year fixed effects. Coefficients and 95 percent confidence intervals shown for lags and leads in unemployment. See also Jan-Emmanuel De Neve and George Ward, "Happiness at Work," in *World Happiness Report*, ed. Jeffrey Sachs, John F. Helliwell, and Richard Layard (Columbia Earth Institute, 2017), we update the analysis here to include subsequent years of data.

21. P. Brickman, D. Coates, and R. Janoff-Bulman, "Lottery Winners and Accident Victims: Is Happiness Relative?," *Journal of Personality and Social Psychology* 36 (1978): 917–27; Andrew E. Clark and Yannis Georgellis, "Back to Baseline in Britain: Adaptation in the British Household Panel Survey," *Economica* 80, no. 319 (2013): 496–512; Nathan Kettlewell et al., "The Differential Impact of Major Life Events on Cognitive and Affective Wellbeing," *SSM - Population Health* 10 (April 1, 2020): 100533, https://doi.org/10.1016/j.ssmph.2019.100533.

22. Ivana Anusic, Stevie C. Y. Yap, and Richard E. Lucas, "Testing Set-Point Theory in a Swiss National Sample: Reaction and Adaptation to Major Life Events," *Social Indicators Research* 119, no. 3 (2014): 1265–88; Clark and Georgellis, "Back to Baseline in Britain: Adaptation in the British Household Panel Survey"; Paul Frijters et al., "Can the Large Swings in Russian Life Satisfaction Be Explained by Ups and Downs in Real Incomes?," *Scandinavian Journal of Economics* 108, no. 3 (2006): 433–58; Robert Rudolf and Sung-Jin Kang, "Lags and Leads in Life Satisfaction in Korea: When Gender Matters," *Feminist Economics* 21, no. 1 (2015): 136–63.

23. Clark and Georgellis, "Back to Baseline in Britain: Adaptation in the British Household Panel Survey."

24. Alan B. Krueger and Andreas I. Mueller, "Time Use, Emotional Well-Being, and Unemployment: Evidence from Longitudinal Data," *American Economic Review* 102, no. 3 (2012): 594–99.

25. Andreas Knabe et al., "Dissatisfied with Life but Having a Good Day: Time-Use and Well-Being of the Unemployed," *Economic Journal* 120, no. 547 (2010): 867–89.

26. Winkelmann and Winkelmann, "Why Are the Unemployed So Unhappy?"

27. David G. Blanchflower and Andrew J. Oswald, "Well-Being over Time in Britain and the USA," *Journal of Public Economics* 88, no. 7 (July 1, 2004): 1359–86, https://doi.org/10.1016/S0047-2727(02)00168-8.

28. Andreas Knabe and Steffen Rätzel, "Quantifying the Psychological Costs of Unemployment: The Role of Permanent Income," *Applied Economics* 43, no. 21 (2011): 2751–63.

29. This is a Blinder-Oaxaca decomposition. Jan Goebel et al., "The German Socio-Economic Panel (SOEP)," *Jahrbücher für Nationalökonomie und Statistik (Journal of Economics and Statistics)* 239, no. 2 (2019): 345–60, https://doi.org/10.1515/jbnst-2018-0022.

30. De Neve and Ward, "Happiness at Work."

31. Clark et al., *The Origins of Happiness*; Rafael Di Tella, Robert J. MacCulloch, and Andrew J. Oswald, "Preferences over Inflation and Unemployment: Evidence from Surveys of Happiness," *American Economic Review* 91, no. 1 (2001): 335–41.

32. Andrew E. Clark, "Unemployment as a Social Norm: Psychological Evidence from Panel Data," *Journal of Labor Economics* 21, no. 2 (2003): 323–51.

33. Michael A. Shields and Stephen Wheatley Price, "Exploring the Economic and Social Determinants of Psychological Well-Being and Perceived Social Support in England," *Journal of the Royal Statistical Society: Series A (Statistics in Society)* 168, no. 3 (2005): 513–37; Nattavudh Powdthavee, "Are There Geographical Variations in the Psychological Cost of Unemployment in South Africa?," *Social Indicators Research* 80, no. 3 (2007): 629–52; Andrew E. Clark et al., "Lags and Leads in Life Satisfaction: A Test of the Baseline Hypothesis," *Economic Journal* 118, no. 529 (2008): F222–43; Andrew E. Clark, Paul Frijters, and Michael A. Shields, "Relative Income, Happiness, and Utility: An Explanation for the Easterlin Paradox and Other Puzzles," *Journal of Economic Literature* 46, no. 1 (2008): 95–114.

34. Maximilian Kasy and Lukas Lehner, "Employing the Unemployed of Marienthal: Evaluation of a Guaranteed Job Program," IZA Discussion Paper No. 16088, 2023.

35. MAGMA stands for *Modellprojekt Arbeitsplatzgarantie Marienthal* or "model project job guarantee Marienthal."

36. Wellbeing scale is the WHO-5 Well-Being Index, constructed from participants' ratings of the following statements, on a 5-item scale relating to the past two weeks: "I was happy and in a good mood"; "I felt calm and relaxed"; "I felt energetic and active"; "I felt fresh and rested when I woke up"; "My everyday life was full of things that interest me." Fieldwork conducted in 2020–2022.

37. Clark et al., *The Origins of Happiness*.

38. Maria Cotofan, Jan-Emmanuel De Neve, Marta Golin, Micah Kaats, and George Ward, "Work and Well-Being during Covid-19: Impact, Inequalities, Resilience, and the Future of Work," *World Happiness Report 2021*, 2021, 153–90.

Chapter 4

1. Day Reconstruction Method (DRM) was used to measure emotional experience of the different activities the respondent engaged in on the prior day. The chart plots average levels of wellbeing for all one-digit activity codes with 30 or more survey responses.

2. For research using this data, see George MacKerron, "Happiness Economics from 35,000 Feet," *Journal of Economic Surveys* 26, no. 4 (2012): 705–35; George MacKerron and Susana Mourato, "Life Satisfaction and Air Quality in London," *Ecological Economics* 68, no. 5 (2009): 1441–53; George MacKerron and Susana Mourato, "Happiness Is Greater in Natural Environments," *Global Environmental Change* 23, no. 5 (2013): 992–1000; Alex Bryson and George MacKerron, "Are You Happy While You Work?," *Economic Journal* 127, no. 599 (2017): 106–25.

3. Bars represent the percent change in happiness while engaging in any one particular activity relative to individual baselines recorded throughout the study period. That is, the figures shown are coefficients on activities in an individual fixed effects regression model of happiness on activity type. The sample includes 20,949 individuals completing 1,321,279 surveys over the course of 13 months from August 2010 to September 2011 in the United Kingdom. For additional details, see Bryson and MacKerron, "Are You Happy While You Work?" One important innovation was that the authors could study not only the levels of people's affective wellbeing but also the changes over time. Given the variety of ways in which different people may respond differently to happiness scales, these sorts of so-called

within-person changes in wellbeing are generally considered to be more reliable in uncovering meaningful relationships between activities and emotions.

4. Jon Clifton, *Blind Spot: The Global Rise of Unhappiness and How Leaders Missed It* (New York: Simon and Schuster, 2022).

5. See American Psychological Association, "Stress in America," press release, November 2023, https://www.apa.org/news/press/releases/stress.

6. Mark Le Fevre, Jonathan Matheny, and Gregory S. Kolt, "Eustress, Distress, and Interpretation in Occupational Stress," *Journal of Managerial Psychology* 18, no. 7 (2003): 726–44.

7. For a more extended discussion and further resources on the measurement of stress, see University of California, San Francisco, National Institute on Aging, Stress Measurement Network, https://www.stressmeasurement.org/.

8. George Ward and Ashley Whillans, "When Valuing Work Predicts Employee Wellbeing: The Role of Work Centrality in the Relationship Between Stress and Wellbeing," Working Paper, 2024.

9. N = 8,473,819, including all current and former employees in the US who answered the stress question.

10. From a practical standpoint, this again underscores the importance of measuring and monitoring multiple domains of workplace wellbeing in organizations simultaneously.

11. As one of us has recently become a parent, we are all too familiar with this exact dynamic.

12. This dynamic is discussed at length in Paul Dolan, *Happy Ever After: Escaping the Myth of the Perfect Life* (London: Penguin UK, 2019).

13. Paul Dolan, *Happiness by Design Finding Pleasure and Purpose in Everyday Life* (London: Penguin, 2015).

14. Countries included in the figure: (West) Germany, Great Britain, United States, Hungary, Norway, Sweden, Czechia, New Zealand, Japan, Spain, France, Denmark, and Switzerland.

15. Robert Dur and Max van Lent, "Socially Useless Jobs," *Industrial Relations: A Journal of Economy and Society* 58, no. 1 (2019): 3–16; Magdalena Soffia, Alex J. Wood, and Brendan Burchell, "Alienation Is Not 'Bullshit': An Empirical Critique of Graeber's Theory of BS Jobs," *Work, Employment and Society* 36, no. 5 (October 1, 2022): 816–40, https://doi.org/10.1177/09500170211015067.

16. Dur and van Lent, "Socially Useless Jobs."

17. Soffia, Wood, and Burchell, "Alienation Is Not 'Bullshit.'"

18. Of course, this is global data covering about 150 countries and may thus hide further regional variation, which would take large amounts of time and space to cover with sufficient detail. For a longer discussion and further evidence, see Jan-Emmanuel De Neve and George Ward, "Happiness at Work," in *World Happiness Report*, ed. Jeffrey Sachs, John F. Helliwell, and Richard Layard (Columbia Earth Institute, 2017).

In the figure, N = 158,087 (job satisfaction); 35,432 (work meaning); 74,324 (enjoyment); 558,074 (stress). Satisfied with your job: Measures whether the respondent answered "Yes" to the question "Are you satisfied with your job? (Yes/No)" Things you do are meaningful: "Yes" if respondent answered "Always" or "Often" to "In general, how often do you feel each of the following? Always, often, rarely or never? The things you do are meaningful." 2021 only: Enjoy the work you do: "Do you enjoy the work you do in your job every day, or not? (Yes/No)" Felt a lot of stress yesterday: "Did you experience the following feelings during a lot of the day yesterday? Stress."

19. Vanessa C. Burbano et al., "The Gender Gap in Meaningful Work," *Management Science*, 2023. For discussion of gender differences more broadly in wellbeing, see David Blanchflower and Alex Bryson, "The Gender Well-Being Gap," *Social Indicators Research*, June 3, 2024, https://doi.org/10.1007/s11205-024-03334-7; Rafael Lalive, Maha Manai, and Alois Stutzer, "Gender Differences in Well-Being and Equal Rights," in *Encyclopedia of Quality of Life and Well-Being Research*, ed. Alex C. Michalos (Dordrecht: Springer Netherlands, 2014), 2420–24, https://doi.org/10.1007/978-94-007-0753-5_4181.

20. David G. Blanchflower and Andrew J. Oswald, "Is Well-Being U-Shaped over the Life Cycle?," *Social Science & Medicine* 66, no. 8 (2008): 1733–49. However, recent evidence suggests deteriorating mental health of young people means the classic and widely studied U-shape is increasingly no longer the age-wellbeing profile. See David G. Blanchflower, Alex Bryson, and Xiaowei Xu, "The Declining Mental Health of the Young and the Global Disappearance of the Hump Shape in Age in Unhappiness," National Bureau of Economic Research Working Paper 32337, 2024. Given this, our findings here comparing workplace wellbeing and overall subjective wellbeing may be less contradictory than at first glance.

21. In general, past research has suggested that visitors of online job marketplaces are likely to have more years of education and earn higher levels of income than the general population. Niels Beerepoot and Bart Lambregts, "Competition in Online Job Marketplaces: Towards a Global Labour Market for Outsourcing Services?," *Global Networks* 15, no. 2 (2015): 236–55, https://doi.org/10.1111/glob.12051; Behrooz Mansouri et al., "Online Job Search: Study of Users' Search Behavior Using Search Engine Query Logs," in *The 41st International ACM SIGIR Conference on Research & Development in Information Retrieval*, 2018, 1185–88.

22. George Ward, "Workplace Happiness and Job Search Behavior: Evidence from a Field Experiment," MIT Sloan Working Paper 6607-22, 2022; George Ward, "The Wellbeing of Workplaces: Organization-Level Differences Between and Within Industries," University of Oxford Working Paper, 2024.

23. Ward, "The Wellbeing of Workplaces." Additionally, the study reveals a strong correlation between job satisfaction levels in the Indeed data and those from a nationally representative sample collected by the Bureau of Labor Statistics (the National Longitudinal Survey of Youth 97) at the two-digit industry level. While job satisfaction reported on Indeed is generally lower—consistent with the intuition that platform users who respond to the survey may be less satisfied than the broader workforce—the high correlation between the two data sets across industries supports the use of Indeed data for research, and suggests that it is well suited for studies like ours, which focus on comparative analysis rather than estimating absolute levels.

24. Responses from current and former employees on Indeed platform October 2019 to May 2024. Happiness = 12,163,678, satisfaction = 10,449,397, purpose = 12,540,870, stress = 8,468,784. See figure 2-1 for survey wording.

25. Ward, "The Wellbeing of Workplaces."

26. Ward, "The Wellbeing of Workplaces"; George Ward, "Happiness at Work: Essays on Subjective Wellbeing in the Workplace and Labor Market" (thesis, Massachusetts Institute of Technology, 2022), https://dspace.mit.edu/handle/1721.1/144621.

Chapter 5

1. Achyuta Adhvaryu, Teresa Molina, and Anant Nyshadham, "Expectations, Wage Hikes, and Worker Voice: Evidence from a Field Experiment," *Economic Journal*, 2024.

2. We are very grateful to Sarah Cunningham, Micah Kaats, Cherise Regier, and Will Fleming for their extensive work on this project and to the World Wellbeing Movement for disseminating the findings.

3. See chapter 3 of George Ward, "Happiness at Work: Essays on Subjective Wellbeing in the Workplace and Labor Market" (thesis, Massachusetts Institute of Technology, 2022), https://dspace.mit.edu/handle/1721.1/144621.

4. For more details, see "Indeed Workplace Happiness Report," based on a commissioned survey conducted by Forrester Consulting.

5. See, for example, Andrew J. Oswald and Stephen Wu, "Well-Being across America," *Review of Economics and Statistics* 93, no. 4 (2011): 1118–34.

6. Data from a nationally representative survey of employees in the United States in 2022. For more details, see "Indeed Workplace Happiness Report," based on a commissioned survey conducted by Forrester Consulting.

7. Our own first instinct as researchers is typically to ask as much as possible, but sometimes it is important to rein it in and instead try to collect as much information as efficiently as possible. By asking four main questions, it is possible to get a good picture of overall levels of wellbeing in a nuanced way.

8. S&P Global, *CSA Handbook 2023*, https://portal.s1.spglobal.com/survey/documents /CSA_Handbook.pdf, 2023.

9. While in some cases, spillovers may be so pervasive as to render the experiment itself meaningless—like trying to enforce "quiet reflection hours" in an open plan office—in other cases, they may simply be best thought of as features of the intervention itself, like providing a job training program to one group of workers and monitoring the extent to which the skills employees learn to develop in the program have positive spillover effects on the wellbeing and productivity of those who didn't undergo the training.

Chapter 6

1. Katherine Baicker, David Cutler, and Zirui Song, "Workplace Wellness Programs Can Generate Savings," *Health Affairs* 29, no. 2 (February 2010): 304–11, https://doi.org/10.1377 /hlthaff.2009.0626.

2. Timothy Gubler, Ian Larkin, and Lamar Pierce, "Doing Well by Making Well: The Impact of Corporate Wellness Programs on Employee Productivity," *Management Science* 64, no. 11 (2018): 4967–87, https://doi.org/10.1287/MNSC.2017.2883.

3. Susanne Buecker et al., "Physical Activity and Subjective Well-Being in Healthy Individuals: A Meta-Analytic Review," *Health Psychology Review* 15, no. 4 (October 2, 2021): 574–92, https://doi.org/10.1080/17437199.2020.1760728.

4. Zirui Song and Katherine Baicker, "Effect of a Workplace Wellness Program on Employee Health and Economic Outcomes: A Randomized Clinical Trial," *JAMA* 321, no. 15 (April 16, 2019): 1491–1501, https://doi.org/10.1001/jama.2019.3307.

5. Damon Jones, David Molitor, and Julian Reif, "What Do Workplace Wellness Programs Do? Evidence from the Illinois Workplace Wellness Study," *Quarterly Journal of Economics* 134, no. 4 (2019): 1747–91, https://doi.org/10.1093/QJE/QJZ023.

6. In this sense, wellness programs may be better conceptualized not as efforts to improve worker wellbeing and health but rather to attract workers who will have lower health-care costs.

7. Florencio F. Portocarrero and Vanessa C. Burbano, "The Effects of a Short-Term Corporate Social Impact Activity on Employee Turnover: Field Experimental Evidence," *Management Science*, October 19, 2023, https://doi.org/10.1287/mnsc.2022.01517.

8. Andrew E. Clark et al., *The Origins of Happiness* (Princeton, NJ: Princeton University Press, 2018).

9. Advik Shreekumar and Pierre-Luc Vautrey, "Managing Emotions: The Effects of Online Mindfulness Meditation on Mental Health and Economic Behavior," in Pierre-Luc

Vautrey, PhD dissertation, Massachusetts Institute of Technology, 2022, https://dspace.mit
.edu/handle/1721.1/144494.

10. There is by now a very large literature on mindfulness and meditation, to which we
cannot aim to do justice. For recent work, see, e.g., Lea Cassar, Mira Fischer, and Vanessa
Valero, "Keep Calm and Carry On: The Short- vs. Long-Run Effects of Mindfulness Meditation on (Academic) Performance," IZA Discussion Paper No. 15723, 2022.

11. Clark et al., *The Origins of Happiness*.

12. Christian Krekel, George Ward, and Jan-Emmanuel De Neve, "What Makes for a
Good Job? Evidence Using Subjective Wellbeing Data," in *The Economics of Happiness*, ed.
Mariano Rojas, (Switzerland: Springer, 2019) 241–68.

13. Maria Cotofan et al., "Work and Well-Being during Covid-19: Impact, Inequalities,
Resilience, and the Future of Work," *World Happiness Report 2021*, 2021, 153–90.

14. The figure reports the results of 5 multivariate linear regression analyses, one on each
of the data sets available. In each case, the outcome variable is job satisfaction, normalized to
have a scale from 0–10 in all data sets. Each data set has a different set of survey questions,
which are grouped into the 6 driver categories based on a clustering analysis. Each driver is the
mean of all the relevant variables in that data set, after first standardizing each to have a mean
of 0 and a standard deviation of 1. Each non-bolded marker reports the coefficient of that driver
group in the job satisfaction regression. The bolded markers show the mean coefficient (and
mean 95 percent confidence intervals) across the 5 datasets, giving equal weight to each data
set. Controls vary across data sets but include where available: gender, age, occupation,
industry, time, location, marital status, education. Controls are included for date, current
employee status, logged in status, region, industry (Indeed); gender, age, education, marital
status, immigrant status, number of children, age, age-squared, country, hours (ESS); working
hours, union status, age, age-squared, gender, marital status, education, industry, number of
children, occupation, country (ISSP); gender, age, age-squared, tenure, education, year, country,
public/private sector indicator (EWCS); gender, wage, marital status, immigrant status,
education, ethnicity, occupation, industry, age, age-squared, date (AWCS).

15. The findings are broadly similar to other carefully done analyses of this type. See,
e.g. Andrew Clark, "What Makes a Good Job? Evidence from OECD Countries," in *Job
Quality and Employer Behaviour* (London: Springer, 2005), 11–30; Andrew E. Clark, "Work,
Jobs, and Well-Being across the Millennium," *International Differences in Well-Being*
(Oxford: Oxford University Press, 2010), 436–68; Thomas Cornelissen, "The Interaction of
Job Satisfaction, Job Search, and Job Changes. An Empirical Investigation with German
Panel Data," *Journal of Happiness Studies* 10, no. 3 (June 2009): 367–84, https://doi.org/10.1007
/s10902-008-9094-5; Sonja Drobnič, Barbara Beham, and Patrick Präg, "Good Job, Good
Life? Working Conditions and Quality of Life in Europe," *Social Indicators Research* 99, no. 2
(2010): 205–25.

16. For a more detailed overview and discussion, including a thoughtful critique of each,
see Paul Osterman, "Introduction to the Special Issue on Job Quality: What Does It Mean
and How Might We Think about It?," *Industrial and Labor Relations Review* 66, no. 4 (2013):
739–52 and the rest of the special issue it is an introduction to.

17. See, e.g., Simon Jäger, Benjamin Schoefer, and Jörg Heining, "Labor in the Board-
room," *Quarterly Journal of Economics* 136, no. 2 (May 1, 2021): 669–725, https://doi.org/10.1093
/qje/qjaa038; Jarkko Harju, Simon Jäger, and Benjamin Schoefer, "Voice at Work," National
Bureau of Economic Research, March 2021, https://www.nber.org/papers/w28522.

18. T. A. Kochan, "What Is Distinctive about Industrial Relations Research?," in
Researching the World of Work, ed. K. Whitfield and G. Strauss, 1998, 31–50.

19. Paul Osterman et al., *Working in America: A Blueprint for the New Labor Market*
(Cambridge, MA: MIT Press, 2001).

20. The data was collected by Forrester Research, commissioned by Indeed. We are very grateful to both for their patience in dealing with academic researchers, their collaboration, and data sharing.

21. This is a maxDiff analysis, which is a type of best-worst scaling investigation. On a series of screens during the survey, respondents are presented with four statements at a time. These are chosen from the full list of potential drivers. In each round, they are asked to select the most important and the least important statements.

22. HBR Analytic Services, "Cultivating Workforce Well-Being to Drive Business Value," 2020, https://hbr.org/resources/pdfs/comm/workplacewellbeing.pdf.

23. HBR Analytic Services, "Cultivating Workforce Well-Being."

Chapter 7

1. Results are plotted from two multivariate regression analyses, one with job satisfaction as the outcome and the other with life satisfaction. The main predictor is perceived job satisfaction. Plotted are the predictive margins of each outcome at different levels of perceived job security, adjusted for gender, age, age-squared education, immigrant status, marital status, number of children, country, work hours.

2. Andreas Knabe and Steffen Rätzel, "Better an Insecure Job Than No Job at All? Unemployment, Job Insecurity and Subjective Wellbeing," *Economics Bulletin* 30, no. 3 (2010): 2486–94; Nicholas Rohde et al., "Is It Vulnerability or Economic Insecurity That Matters for Health?," *Journal of Economic Behavior & Organization* 134 (2017): 307–19.

3. Statistics reported in this section are drawn from Eurofound, "Working Conditions and Sustainable Work: An Analysis Using the Job," Challenges and Prospects in the EU Series (Publications Office of the European Union, 2021), https://www.eurofound.europa.eu /publications/flagship-report/2021/working-conditions-and-sustainable-work-an-analysis -using-the-job-quality-framework; Alexander Hijzen and Balint Menyhert, "Measuring Labour Market Security and Assessing Its Implications for Individual Well-Being" (Paris: OECD, 2016), https://doi.org/10.1787/5jm58qvzd6s4-en; and authors' estimates using data from the ESS, EWCS, AWCS, and ISSP.

4. Jan-Emmanuel De Neve et al., "The Asymmetric Experience of Positive and Negative Economic Growth: Global Evidence Using Subjective Well-Being Data," *Review of Economics and Statistics* 100, no. 2 (2018): 362–75.

5. Hijzen and Menyhert, "Measuring Labour Market Security. "

6. T. Luo, A. Mann, and R. Holden, "The Expanding Role of Temporary Help Services from 1990 to 2008," *Monthly Labor Review* (August 2010): 3–16.

7. Estimates from the OECD. For more information, see: data.oecd.org/emp/temporary -employment.html.

8. Hans De Witte, Tinne Vander Elst, and Nele De Cuyper, "Job Insecurity, Health and Well-Being," in *Sustainable Working Lives: Managing Work Transitions and Health throughout the Life Course*, ed. Jukka Vuori, Roland Blonk, and Richard H. Price (Dordrecht: Springer Netherlands, 2015), 109–28, https://doi.org/10.1007/978-94-017-9798-6_7.

9. Jarkko Harju, Simon Jäger, and Benjamin Schoefer, "Voice at Work," National Bureau of Economic Research Working Paper 28522, 2021, https://doi.org/10.3386/w28522.

10. Related analyses have looked into similar reforms in Germany and other European countries, finding mostly similar effects. See Simon Jäger, Shakked Noy, and Benjamin Schoefer, "Codetermination and Power in the Workplace," *Journal of Law and Political Economy* 3, no. 1 (2022).

11. Tinne Vander Elst et al., "The Role of Organizational Communication and Participation in Reducing Job Insecurity and Its Negative Association with Work-Related Well-Being," *Economic and Industrial Democracy* 31, no. 2 (2010): 249–64.

12. Cheryl L. Adkins, James D. Werbel, and Jiing-Lih Farh, "A Field Study of Job Insecurity during a Financial Crisis," *Group & Organization Management* 26, no. 4 (2001): 463–83.

13. David M. Schweiger and Angelo S. DeNisi, "Communication with Employees Following a Merger: A Longitudinal Field Experiment," *Academy of Management Journal* 34, no. 1 (1991): 110–35, https://doi.org/10.2307/256304.

14. The other two main factors identified were having stayed in the role for more than fifteen months already and not receiving a raise (or receiving an insufficient one). See Morgan Smart and A. Chamberlain, "Why Do Workers Quit? The Factors That Predict Employee Turnover," Glassdoor, 2016, https://www.glassdoor.com/research/why-do-workers-quit/.

15. In 2015, men were 13 percent more likely to report good prospects for advancement than women. While still a significant gap, this also represented a decline from 19 percent in 2010. Eurofound, "Working Conditions and Sustainable Work."

16. Authors' calculations using the ECWS data.

17. Eurofound, "Working Conditions and Sustainable Work."

18. Wen Ci et al., "Wage Returns to Mid-Career Investments in Job Training through Employer Supported Course Enrollment: Evidence for Canada," *IZA Journal of Labor Policy* 4, no. 1 (May 15, 2015): 9, https://doi.org/10.1186/s40173-015-0035-8.

19. For more information, see: Connie Chen, "Everything You Need to Know about Career Choice, Amazon's Education Benefit That Pre-pays Tuition for Degrees and Skills Development," Amazon, September 5, 2023, https://www.aboutamazon.com/news/workplace/career-choice.

20. For more information, see: Accenture, "Leading a National Apprenticeship Movement," https://www.accenture.com/us-en/about/company/apprenticeships.

21. For more information, see: Careers, "Connect Engineering Apprenticeship," https://careers.airbnb.com/connect-engineering-apprenticeship/.

22. For more information, see: Doug Wintemute, "7 Companies That Offer Apprenticeship Programs," Bootcamps, June 12, 2023, https://www.bestcolleges.com/bootcamps/guides/companies-offer-tech-apprenticeship-programs/.

23. Frank Dobbin and Alexandra Kalev, "Why Diversity Programs Fail," *Harvard Business Review*, July–August 2016, https://hbr.org/2016/07/why-diversity-programs-fail.

24. Haley Glatthorn, "University Community Remembers Prof. Peterson," *Michigan Daily*, October 10, 2012, http://www.michigandaily.com/uncategorized/10-university-psychology-professor-christopher-peterson-dies-unexpectedly-10/.

25. Ed Diener, Shigehiro Oishi, and Louis Tay, "Advances in Subjective Well-Being Research," *Nature Human Behaviour* 2, no. 4 (April 2018): 253–60, https://doi.org/10.1038/s41562-018-0307-6; Jessica Kansky and Ed Diener, "Benefits of Well-Being: Health, Social Relationships, Work, and Resilience," *Journal of Positive School Psychology* 1, no. 2 (2017): 129–69; Olga Stavrova and Maike Luhmann, "Social Connectedness as a Source and Consequence of Meaning in Life," *Journal of Positive Psychology* 11, no. 5 (2016): 470–79.

26. Joan Domènech-Abella et al., "Anxiety, Depression, Loneliness and Social Network in the Elderly: Longitudinal Associations from The Irish Longitudinal Study on Ageing (TILDA)," *Journal of Affective Disorders* 246 (March 1, 2019): 82–88, https://doi.org/10.1016/j.jad.2018.12.043; Julianne Holt-Lunstad et al., "Loneliness and Social Isolation as Risk Factors for Mortality: A Meta-Analytic Review," *Perspectives on Psychological Science* 10, no. 2 (2015): 227–37; Julianne Holt-Lunstad, Theodore F. Robles, and David A. Sbarra, "Advancing Social Connection as a Public Health Priority in the United States," *American*

Psychologist 72, no. 6 (2017): 517; Julianne Holt-Lunstad and Timothy B. Smith, "Social Relationships and Mortality," *Social and Personality Psychology Compass* 6, no. 1 (2012): 41–53; Lisa M. Jaremka et al., "Pain, Depression, and Fatigue: Loneliness as a Longitudinal Risk Factor," *Health Psychology* 33, no. 9 (2014): 948; Conor Ó Luanaigh and Brian A. Lawlor, "Loneliness and the Health of Older People," *International Journal of Geriatric Psychiatry: A Journal of the Psychiatry of Late Life and Allied Sciences* 23, no. 12 (2008): 1213–21; Yuval Palgi et al., "The Loneliness Pandemic: Loneliness and Other Concomitants of Depression, Anxiety and Their Comorbidity during the Covid-19 Outbreak," *Journal of Affective Disorders* 275 (October 1, 2020): 109–11, https://doi.org/10.1016/j.jad.2020.06.036; Nicole Valtorta and Barbara Hanratty, "Loneliness, Isolation and the Health of Older Adults: Do We Need a New Research Agenda?," *Journal of the Royal Society of Medicine* 105, no. 12 (2012): 518–22.

27. Relationships here are measured using responses to the following two questions: "How would you describe relations at your workplace between: (a) management and employees? (b) workmates and colleagues?" Answers are recorded on a 5-point scale from "very good" to "very bad" and then standardized.

28. Indeed Workplace Happiness Report, a commissioned study (N = 4,033 US adults) conducted by Forrester Consulting on behalf of Indeed, 2021.

29. Lisa A. Giacumo, Jie Chen, and Aurora Seguinot-Cruz, "Evidence on the Use of Mentoring Programs and Practices to Support Workplace Learning: A Systematic Multiple-Studies Review," *Performance Improvement Quarterly* 33, no. 3 (2020): 259–303.

30. Sameer B. Srivastava, "Network Intervention: Assessing the Effects of Formal Mentoring on Workplace Networks," *Social Forces* 94, no. 1 (2015): 427–52.

31. Vivian Lewis et al., "A Randomized Controlled Trial of Mentoring Interventions for Underrepresented Minorities," *Academic Medicine: Journal of the Association of American Medical Colleges* 91, no. 7 (2016): 994.

32. Jason Sandvik et al., "Should Workplace Programs Be Voluntary or Mandatory? Evidence from a Field Experiment on Mentorship," National Bureau of Economic Research Working Paper 29148, 2021, https://doi.org/10.3386/w29148.

33. Dobbin and Kalev, "Why Diversity Programs Fail."

34. Edward H. Chang et al., "The Mixed Effects of Online Diversity Training," *Proceedings of the National Academy of Sciences* 116, no. 16 (2019): 7778–83.

35. Dobbin and Kalev, "Why Diversity Programs Fail."

36. Sean Fath, "When Blind Hiring Advances DEI—and When It Doesn't," *Harvard Business Review*, June 1, 2023, https://hbr.org/2023/06/when-blind-hiring-advances-dei-and-when-it-doesnt; Claudia Goldin and Cecilia Rouse, "Orchestrating Impartiality: The Impact of 'Blind' Auditions on Female Musicians," *American Economic Review* 90, no. 4 (2000): 715–41; David Neumark, "Age Discrimination in Hiring: Evidence from Age-Blind vs. Non-Age-Blind Hiring Procedures," *Journal of Human Resources*, 2021; Ulf Rinne, "Anonymous Job Applications and Hiring Discrimination," *IZA World of Labor*, 2018; Daryl G. Smith et al., "Interrupting the Usual: Successful Strategies for Hiring Diverse Faculty," *Journal of Higher Education* 75, no. 2 (2004): 133–60; Iris Bohnet, Alexandra Van Geen, and Max Bazerman, "When Performance Trumps Gender Bias: Joint vs. Separate Evaluation," *Management Science* 62, no. 5 (2016): 1225–34.

37. Frank Dobbin and Alexandra Kalev, "The Promise and Peril of Sexual Harassment Programs," *Proceedings of the National Academy of Sciences* 116, no. 25 (2019): 12255–60.

38. Ilke Inceoglu et al., "Leadership Behavior and Employee Well-Being: An Integrated Review and a Future Research Agenda," *Leadership Quarterly* 29, no. 1 (February 2018): 179–202, https://doi.org/10.1016/j.leaqua.2017.12.006.

39. Fabian Kosse and Michela M. Tincani, "Prosociality Predicts Labor Market Success around the World," *Nature Communications* 11, no. 1 (October 20, 2020): 5298, https://doi.org/10.1038/s41467-020-19007-1; David J. Deming, "The Growing Importance of Social Skills in the Labor Market," *Quarterly Journal of Economics* 132, no. 4 (2017): 1593–1640, https://doi.org/10.1093/QJE/QJX022.

40. Ben Weidmann and David J. Deming, "Team Players: How Social Skills Improve Team Performance," *Econometrica* 89, no. 6 (2021): 2637–57, https://doi.org/10.3982/ECTA18461.

41. Mitchell Hoffman and Steven Tadelis, "People Management Skills, Employee Attrition, and Manager Rewards: An Empirical Analysis," *Journal of Political Economy* 129, no. 1 (January 1, 2021): 243–85, https://doi.org/10.1086/711409.

42. Sule Alan, Gozde Corekcioglu, and Matthias Sutter, "Improving Workplace Climate in Large Corporations: A Clustered Randomized Intervention," *Quarterly Journal of Economics* 138, no. 1 (2023): 151–203, https://doi.org/10.1093/qje/qjac034.

43. For further evidence on supportive leadership behaviors, see Simone Haeckl and Mari Rege, "Effects of Supportive Leadership Behaviors on Employee Satisfaction, Engagement, and Performance: An Experimental Field Investigation," *Management Science*, April 4, 2024, https://doi.org/10.1287/mnsc.2022.02170.

44. See Phyllis Moen et al., "Does a Flexibility/Support Organizational Initiative Improve High-Tech Employees' Well-Being? Evidence from the Work, Family, and Health Network," *American Sociological Review* 81, no. 1 (February 2016): 134–64, https://doi.org/10.1177/0003122415622391.

45. Yuye Ding and Mark (Shuai) Ma, "Return-to-Office Mandates," SSRN Working Paper, https://doi.org/10.2139/ssrn.4675401.

46. Alexandre Mas and Amanda Pallais, "Valuing Alternative Work Arrangements," *American Economic Review* 107, no. 12 (2017): 3722–59.

47. Daniel Schneider and Kristen Harknett, "Consequences of Routine Work-Schedule Instability for Worker Health and Well-Being," *American Sociological Review* 84, no. 1 (2019): 82–114.

48. Karen Albertsen et al., "Work-Life Balance among Shift Workers: Results from an Intervention Study about Self-Rostering," *International Archives of Occupational and Environmental Health* 87, no. 3 (2014): 265–74. Another related experiment found similar results among nurses working on psychiatric wards. After the implementation of a collaborative, open-rota scheduling system, the researchers in that case found that nurses in the intervention group were "more satisfied with their work hours, less likely to swap their shift when working within the open-rota system, and reported significant increases in work–life balance, job satisfaction, social support and community spirit when compared with nurses in the control groups." Joanna Pryce, Karen Albertsen, and Karina Nielsen, "Evaluation of an Open-Rota System in a Danish Psychiatric Hospital: A Mechanism for Improving Job Satisfaction and Work–Life Balance," *Journal of Nursing Management* 14, no. 4 (2006): 282–88.

49. Controls included for gender, age, age-squared education, immigrant status, marital status, number of children, country, and work hours.

50. Erin L. Kelly and Phyllis Moen, *Overload: How Good Jobs Went Bad and What We Can Do about It* (Princeton, NJ: Princeton University Press, 2020).

51. Laura M. Giurge and Kaitlin Woolley, "Working during Non-Standard Work Time Undermines Intrinsic Motivation," *Organizational Behavior and Human Decision Processes* 170 (May 1, 2022): 104134, https://doi.org/10.1016/j.obhdp.2022.104134.

52. Daniel S. Hamermesh, Daiji Kawaguchi, and Jungmin Lee, "Does Labor Legislation Benefit Workers? Well-Being after an Hours Reduction," *Journal of the Japanese and International Economies* 44 (2017): 1–12.

53. Anthony Lepinteur, "The Shorter Workweek and Worker Wellbeing: Evidence from Portugal and France," *Labour Economics* 58 (2019): 204–20.

54. Inés Berniell and Jan Bietenbeck, "The Effect of Working Hours on Health," *Economics and Human Biology* 39 (December 2020): 100901, https://doi.org/10.1016/j.ehb.2020.100901.

55. Authors' calculations using ISSP data.

56. Erin L. Kelly, Phyllis Moen, and Eric Tranby, "Changing Workplaces to Reduce Work-Family Conflict: Schedule Control in a White-Collar Organization," *American Sociological Review* 76, no. 2 (2011): 265–90.

57. Phyllis Moen, Erin L. Kelly, and Rachelle Hill, "Does Enhancing Work-Time Control and Flexibility Reduce Turnover? A Naturally Occurring Experiment," *Social Problems* 58, no. 1 (February 1, 2011): 69–98, https://doi.org/10.1525/sp.2011.58.1.69. Other studies of employee wellbeing in firms that have introduced ROWE policies and procedures have documented similarly positive effects on organizational commitment, psychological stress, and even sleep. Brigid Schulte, *Overwhelmed: How to Work, Love, and Play When No One Has the Time* (New York: Macmillan, 2015).

58. N = 130,438 (job improves lives of others); N = 65,489 (how often you feel enthusiastic); N = 65,823 (things you do are meaningful). Job improves lives of others: "Do you think the work you do in your job significantly improves the lives of other people outside of your own household, or not? Yes/No." How often you feel enthusiastic: "In general, how often do you feel each of the following? Always, often, rarely or never? Enthusiastic." Things you do are meaningful: "In general, how often do you feel each of the following? Always, often, rarely or never? The things you do are meaningful."

59. Interestingly, overall performance improved for the firm, largely because lower performers either left, transitioned to other roles, or increased their productivity—leaving a more engaged and efficient workforce. See Nava Ashraf et al., "Meaning at Work," Working Paper, 2024.

60. Vanessa C. Burbano, "Social Responsibility Messages and Worker Wage Requirements: Field Experimental Evidence from Online Labor Marketplaces," *Organization Science* 27, no. 4 (2016): 1010–28.

61. Daniel Hedblom, Brent R. Hickman, and John A. List, "Toward an Understanding of Corporate Social Responsibility: Theory and Field Experimental Evidence" (National Bureau of Economic Research, 2019).

62. Dan Ariely, Emir Kamenica, and Dražen Prelec, "Man's Search for Meaning: The Case of Legos," *Journal of Economic Behavior & Organization* 67, no. 3 (September 1, 2008): 671–77, https://doi.org/10.1016/j.jebo.2008.01.004.

63. Adam M. Grant, "The Significance of Task Significance: Job Performance Effects, Relational Mechanisms, and Boundary Conditions," *Journal of Applied Psychology* 93, no. 1 (2008): 108.

64. In a similar experiment, as part of the same study, lifeguards who read stories about how their work directly benefited and saved the lives of swimmers subsequently reported higher levels of commitment to their jobs and were more willing to work longer hours for less money.

65. For comparison's sake, workers who have poor relationships with their manager are on average 3.2 points less satisfied with their jobs. It is important to note that these are simply raw average differences. In this case, we are not controlling for demographics or other job characteristics.

66. While we will mostly discuss jobs listed in ISSP data throughout this section, we obtained similar rankings of prosocial and useful jobs using data from European Working Conditions Survey, the American Working Conditions Survey, and Indeed. Our results are

also highly consistent with the findings of related studies in the academic literature. For a review of relevant studies, see Lea Cassar and Stephan Meier, "Nonmonetary Incentives and the Implications of Work as a Source of Meaning," *Journal of Economic Perspectives* 32, no. 3 (2018): 215–38.

67. Twenty-seven thousand respondents in thirty-seven countries. ISCO-08 four-digit codes. Jobs with ten observations or more included. Data drawn from the ISSP (2015).

68. Dana Chandler and Adam Kapelner, "Breaking Monotony with Meaning: Motivation in Crowdsourcing Markets," *Journal of Economic Behavior & Organization* 90 (2013): 123–33; Michael Kosfeld, Susanne Neckermann, and Xiaolan Yang, "The Effects of Financial and Recognition Incentives across Work Contexts: The Role of Meaning," *Economic Inquiry* 55, no. 1 (2017): 237–47.

69. Jaewon Yoon, Ashley Whillans, and Ed O'Brien, "How to Make Even the Most Mundane Tasks More Motivating," hbr.org, July 24, 2019, https://hbr.org/2019/07/how-to -make-even-the-most-mundane-tasks-more-motivating.

70. Adam M. Grant and Francesca Gino, "A Little Thanks Goes a Long Way: Explaining Why Gratitude Expressions Motivate Prosocial Behavior," *Journal of Personality and Social Psychology* 98, no. 6 (2010): 946.

71. Michael D. Siciliano and James R. Thompson, "A Field Experiment on the Impact of Beneficiary Contact on Federal Employee Perceptions of Prosocial Impact and Social Worth," *International Public Management Journal* (2021): 1–47.

72. This effect was observable not only among those who had the opportunity to meet face-to-face with an in-person speaker, but even among those who were only shown a video attestation.

73. Andrew M. Carton, "'I'm Not Mopping the Floors, I'm Putting a Man on the Moon': How NASA Leaders Enhanced the Meaningfulness of Work by Changing the Meaning of Work," *Administrative Science Quarterly* 63, no. 2 (2018): 323–69.

74. Florencio F. Portocarrero and Vanessa C. Burbano, "The Effects of a Short-Term Corporate Social Impact Activity on Employee Turnover: Field Experimental Evidence," *Management Science*, October 19, 2023, https://doi.org/10.1287/mnsc.2022.01517.

75. Daniel Kahneman and Angus Deaton, "High Income Improves Evaluation of Life but Not Emotional Wellbeing," *Proceedings of the National Academy of Science* 107 (2010): 16489–93.

76. Andrew T. Jebb et al., "Happiness, Income Satiation and Turning Points around the World," *Nature Human Behaviour* 2, no. 1 (2018): 33–38.

77. Data collected in 2010–2011. We exclude incomes above 250,000 euros at the time of the survey. We then inflate the income levels to 2024 prices using the European Central Bank's Harmonized Index of Consumer Prices (HICP).

78. Matthew A. Killingsworth, "Experienced Well-Being Rises with Income, Even above $75,000 per Year," *Proceedings of the National Academy of Sciences* 118, no. 4 (2021): 2.

79. Zeynep Ton, *The Good Jobs Strategy: How the Smartest Companies Invest in Employees to Lower Costs and Boost Profits* (New York: Houghton Mifflin Harcourt, 2014).

80. David Card, Alexandre Mas, Enrico Moretti, and Emmanuel Saez, "Inequality at Work: The Effect of Peer Salaries on Job Satisfaction," *American Economic Review* 102, no 6 (2012): 2981–3003.

81. For an even larger-scale example of this, see Ricardo Perez-Truglia, "The Effects of Income Transparency on Well-Being: Evidence from a Natural Experiment," *American Economic Review* 110, no. 4 (2020): 1019–54. In this case, the whole country of Norway passed a law that made all tax returns public.

82. Zoë Cullen and Ricardo Perez-Truglia, "How Much Does Your Boss Make? The Effects of Salary Comparisons," *Journal of Political Economy* 130, no. 3 (March 2022): 766–822, https://doi.org/10.1086/717891.

83. Emily Breza, Supreet Kaur, and Yogita Shamdasani, "The Morale Effects of Pay Inequality," *Quarterly Journal of Economics* 133, no. 2 (2018): 611–63, https://doi.org/10.1093/QJE/QJX041.

84. Joseph Blasi, Richard Freeman, and Douglas Kruse, "Do Broad-Based Employee Ownership, Profit Sharing and Stock Options Help the Best Firms Do Even Better?," *British Journal of Industrial Relations* 54, no. 1 (2016): 55–82; Colin Green and John S. Heywood, "Does Performance Pay Increase Job Satisfaction?," *Economica* 75, no. 300 (2008): 710–28.

85. Myeong-Hun Lim et al., "Performance-Based Pay System and Job Stress Related to Depression/Anxiety in Korea: Analysis of Korea Working Condition Survey," *International Journal of Environmental Research and Public Health* 20, no. 5 (2023): 4065.

86. Michael S. Dahl and Lamar Pierce, "Pay-for-Performance and Employee Mental Health: Large Sample Evidence Using Employee Prescription Drug Usage," *Academy of Management Discoveries* 6, no. 1 (2020): 12–38.

87. For a more in-depth treatment, see Douglas L. Kruse, Richard B. Freeman, and Joseph R. Blasi, *Shared Capitalism at Work: Employee Ownership, Profit and Gain Sharing, and Broad-Based Stock Options* (Chicago: University of Chicago Press, 2010).

88. Kruse, Freeman, and Blasi, *Shared Capitalism.*

89. Norman Frohlich et al., "Employee versus Conventionally-Owned and Controlled Firms: An Experimental Analysis," *Managerial and Decision Economics* 19, no. 4–5 (1998): 311–26.

90. Alex Bryson et al., "Share Capitalism and Worker Wellbeing," *Labour Economics* 42 (2016): 151–58.

91. For such analyses, see, e.g., Deirdre McCaughey et al., "The Relationship of Positive Work Environments and Workplace Injury: Evidence from the National Nursing Assistant Survey," *Health Care Management Review* 39, no. 1 (March 2014): 75, https://doi.org/10.1097/HMR.0b013e3182860919; Seth Ayim Gyekye, "Workers' Perceptions of Workplace Safety and Job Satisfaction," *International Journal of Occupational Safety and Ergonomics* 11, no. 3 (January 2005): 291–302, https://doi.org/10.1080/10803548.2005.11076650.

92. Data from the Bureau of Labour Statistics: https://www.bls.gov/iif/home.htm.

93. Michael J. Burke et al., "Relative Effectiveness of Worker Safety and Health Training Methods," *American Journal of Public Health* 96, no. 2 (February 2006): 315–24, https://doi.org/10.2105/AJPH.2004.059840; Lynda S. Robson et al., "A Systematic Review of the Effectiveness of Occupational Health and Safety Training," *Scandinavian Journal of Work, Environment & Health* 38, no. 3 (2012): 193–208; Michael J. Colligan and Alexander Cohen, "The Role of Training in Promoting Workplace Safety and Health," in *The Psychology of Workplace Safety* (Washington, DC: American Psychological Association, 2004), 223–48, https://doi.org/10.1037/10662-011; OSHA, "Recommended Practices for Safety and Health Programs," 2016, https://www.osha.gov/sites/default/files/publications/OSHA3885.pdf.

94. Michael S. Christian et al., "Workplace Safety: A Meta-Analysis of the Roles of Person and Situation Factors," *Journal of Applied Psychology* 94, no. 5 (September 2009): 1103–27, https://doi.org/10.1037/a0016172.

95. Johnny Dyreborg et al., "Safety Interventions for the Prevention of Accidents at Work: A Systematic Review," *Campbell Systematic Reviews* 18, no. 2 (2022): e1234, https://doi.org/10.1002/cl2.1234.

96. Laura Boudreau, "Multinational Enforcement of Labor Law: Experimental Evidence on Strengthening Occupational Safety and Health Committees," *Econometrica* 92, no. 4 (2024): 1269–1308.

97. Sarah Flèche and Richard Layard, "Do More of Those in Misery Suffer from Poverty, Unemployment or Mental Illness?," *Kyklos* 70, no. 1 (2017): 27–41, https://doi.org/10.1111/kykl.12129.

98. See World Health Organization, "Mental Health at Work," press release, September 28, 2022, https://www.who.int/news-room/fact-sheets/detail/mental-health-at-work.

99. Holly Kearl, N. E. Johns, and Anita Raj, "Measuring# MeToo: A National Study on Sexual Harassment and Assault," UC San Diego Center on Gender Equity and Health, 2019.

100. Chai R. Feldblum and Victoria A. Lipnic, "Select Task Force on the Study of Harassment in the Workplace," Washington: US Equal Employment Opportunity Commission, 2016.

101. Feldblum and Lipnic, "Select Task Force on the Study of Harassment."

102. The survey (Well Being 436) was conducted from July to October 2015 through RAND's American Life Panel. For further details see Nicole Maestas et al., "The Value of Working Conditions in the United States and Implications for the Structure of Wages," *American Economic Review* 113, no. 7 (2023): 2007–47.

103. Frank Dobbin and Alexandra Kalev, "The Promise and Peril of Sexual Harassment Programs," *Proceedings of the National Academy of Sciences* 116, no. 25 (2019): 12255–60.

104. Frank Dobbin and Alexandra Kalev, "Why Sexual Harassment Programs Backfire," *Harvard Business Review*, May–June 2020, https://hbr.org/2020/05/why-sexual-harassment-programs-backfire.

105. Lilia M. Cortina and Jennifer L. Berdahl, "Sexual Harassment in Organizations: A Decade of Research in Review," *Handbook of Organizational Behavior* 1 (2008): 469–97.

106. Lilia M. Cortina and Vicki J. Magley, "Raising Voice, Risking Retaliation: Events Following Interpersonal Mistreatment in the Workplace," *Journal of Occupational Health Psychology* 8, no. 4 (2003): 247.

107. Sandy Welsh and James E. Gruber, "Not Taking It Any More: Women Who Report or File Complaints of Sexual Harassment," *Canadian Review of Sociology/Revue Canadienne de Sociologie* 36, no. 4 (1999): 559–83, https://doi.org/10.1111/j.1755-618X.1999.tb00964.x.

108. Shereen G. Bingham, "Ombuds Work on Sexual Harassment Cases: The Power of Our Stories," *Journal of the International Ombudsman Association* 14, no. 2 (2021); Charles L. Howard, "What Happens When an Employee Calls the Ombudsman?," *Harvard Business Review*, May–June 2020, https://hbr.org/2020/05/what-happens-when-an-employee-calls-the-ombudsman.

109. See https://worldwellbeingmovement.org/playbook/.

Chapter 8

1. Thomas A. Wright and Russell Cropanzano, "The Role of Psychological Well-Being in Job Performance: A Fresh Look at an Age-Old Quest," *Organizational Dynamics* 33, no. 4 (2004): 338–51.

2. Jeffrey Muldoon, "The Hawthorne Legacy: A Reassessment of the Impact of the Hawthorne Studies on Management Scholarship, 1930–1958," *Journal of Management History* 18, no. 1 (2012): 105–19.

3. Arthur H. Brayfield and Walter H. Crockett, "Employee Attitudes and Employee Performance," *Psychological Bulletin* 52, no. 5 (1955): 396; Michelle T. Iaffaldano and Paul M. Muchinsky, "Job Satisfaction and Job Performance: A Meta-Analysis," *Psychological Bulletin* 97, no. 2 (1985): 251.

4. Iaffaldano and Muchinsky, "Job Satisfaction and Job Performance," 270.

5. Many of these limitations are discussed in more detail in Arthur P. Brief and Howard M. Weiss, "Organizational Behavior: Affect in the Workplace," *Annual Review of*

Psychology 53, no. 1 (2002): 279–307; Timothy A. Judge et al., "The Job Satisfaction–Job Performance Relationship: A Qualitative and Quantitative Review," *Psychological Bulletin* 127, no. 3 (2001): 376.

6. Judge et al., "The Job Satisfaction–Job Performance Relationship."

7. Michael Riketta, "The Causal Relation between Job Attitudes and Performance: A Meta-Analysis of Panel Studies," *Journal of Applied Psychology* 93, no. 2 (2008): 472.

8. Nancy P. Rothbard and Steffanie L. Wilk, "Waking Up on the Right or Wrong Side of the Bed: Start-of-Workday Mood, Work Events, Employee Affect, and Performance," *Academy of Management Journal* 54, no. 5 (2011): 959–80.

9. Jan-Emmanuel De Neve and Andrew J. Oswald, "Estimating the Influence of Life Satisfaction and Positive Affect on Later Income Using Sibling Fixed Effects," *Proceedings of the National Academy of Sciences* 109, no. 49 (2012): 19953–58.

10. For examples, see: Amir Erez and Alice M. Isen, "The Influence of Positive Affect on the Components of Expectancy Motivation," *Journal of Applied Psychology* 87, no. 6 (2002): 1055; Alice M. Isen, "Positive Affect and Decision Making," in *Handbook of Emotions*, ed. M. Lewis and J. M. Haviland-Jones, 2nd ed. (New York: Guilford, 1993), 417–35; Alice M. Isen and Johnmarshall Reeve, "The Influence of Positive Affect on Intrinsic and Extrinsic Motivation: Facilitating Enjoyment of Play, Responsible Work Behavior, and Self-Control," *Motivation and Emotion* 29, no. 4 (2005): 295–323, https://doi.org/10.1007/S11031-006-9019-8.

11. For reviews, see: Sonja Lyubomirsky, Laura King, and Ed Diener, "The Benefits of Frequent Positive Affect: Does Happiness Lead to Success?," *Psychological Bulletin* 131, no. 6 (2005): 803; Elizabeth R. Tenney, Jared M. Poole, and Ed Diener, "Does Positivity Enhance Work Performance?: Why, When, and What We Don't Know," *Research in Organizational Behavior* 36 (2016): 27–46.

12. Lisa C. Walsh, Julia K. Boehm, and Sonja Lyubomirsky, "Does Happiness Promote Career Success? Revisiting the Evidence," *Journal of Career Assessment* 26, no. 2 (2018): 199–219, https://doi.org/10.1177/1069072717751441.

13. Andrew J. Oswald, Eugenio Proto, and Daniel Sgroi, "Happiness and Productivity," *Journal of Labor Economics* 33, no. 4 (2015): 789–822.

14. Figure 8-1 reproduces results from their experiment 1. This involved a comedy clip and a productivity task of adding up pairs of numbers. Participants were incentivized by being paid per correct addition. N = 276. * Indicates significant differences between groups at the 5 percent level.

15. Nicholas Bloom et al., "Does Working from Home Work? Evidence from a Chinese Experiment," *Quarterly Journal of Economics* 130, no. 1 (2015): 165–218.

16. Erin L. Kelly et al., "Changing Work and Work-Family Conflict: Evidence from the Work, Family, and Health Network," *American Sociological Review* 79, no. 3 (2014): 485–516; Phyllis Moen et al., "Does a Flexibility/Support Organizational Initiative Improve High-Tech Employees' Well-Being? Evidence from the Work, Family, and Health Network," *American Sociological Review* 81, no. 1 (February 1, 2016): 134–64, https://doi.org/10.1177/0003122415 622391; Phyllis Moen et al., "Can a Flexibility/Support Initiative Reduce Turnover Intentions and Exits? Results from the Work, Family, and Health Network," *Social Problems* 64, no. 1 (2017): 53–85.

17. Clément Bellet, Jan-Emmanuel De Neve, and George Ward, "Does Employee Happiness Have an Impact on Productivity?," *Management Science* 70, no. 3 (2023): 1656–79.

18. These efforts were greatly aided by Butterfly AI, to whom we are very grateful.

19. The figure shows the relationship between sales and happiness from a regression where weekly sales are predicted by surveyed happiness, with a series of time-varying controls

as well as worker and week fixed effects. Standard errors are double-clustered on weeks and individuals. The regression is Poisson-IV, and the coefficients are presented here as percentage changes, in order to make them more interpretable. Percent effects are deduced from poisson coefficients: (exp(_b[happiness level]) − 1) * 100.

20. For extensive reviews, see: Ed Diener and Micaela Y. Chan, "Happy People Live Longer: Subjective Well-Being Contributes to Health and Longevity," *Applied Psychology: Health and Well-Being* 3, no. 1 (2011): 1–43; Jessica Kansky and Ed Diener, "Benefits of Well-Being: Health, Social Relationships, Work, and Resilience," *Journal of Positive Psychology and Wellbeing* 1, no. 2 (2017): 129–69.

21. Diener and Chan, "Happy People Live Longer"; Kansky and Diener, "Benefits of Well-Being."

22. Manfred E. Beutel et al., "Life Satisfaction, Anxiety, Depression and Resilience across the Life Span of Men," *Aging Male* 13, no. 1 (2010): 32–39; Heli Koivumaa-Honkanen et al., "Life Satisfaction and Depression in a 15-Year Follow-Up of Healthy Adults," *Social Psychiatry and Psychiatric Epidemiology* 39, no. 12 (2004): 994–99; Sabine Sonnentag, "Wellbeing and Burnout in the Workplace: Organizational Causes and Consequences," *International Encyclopedia of the Social & Behavioral Sciences* 25, no. 2 (2015): 537–40.

23. Michael T. Ford et al., "Relationships between Psychological, Physical, and Behavioural Health and Work Performance: A Review and Meta-Analysis," *Work & Stress* 25, no. 3 (2011): 185–204.

24. For a review of relevant evidence, see: Marcus Crede et al., "Job Satisfaction as Mediator: An Assessment of Job Satisfaction's Position within the Nomological Network," *Journal of Occupational and Organizational Psychology* 80, no. 3 (2007): 515–38.

25. James B. Avey, Jaime L. Patera, and Bradley J. West, "The Implications of Positive Psychological Capital on Employee Absenteeism," *Journal of Leadership & Organizational Studies* 13, no. 2 (2006): 42–60.

26. Karen M. Gil et al., "Daily Mood and Stress Predict Pain, Health Care Use, and Work Activity in African American Adults with Sickle-Cell Disease," *Health Psychology* 23, no. 3 (2004): 267; Lisa Hope Pelled and Katherine R. Xin, "Down and Out: An Investigation of the Relationship between Mood and Employee Withdrawal Behavior," *Journal of Management* 25, no. 6 (1999): 875–95.

27. Paul Hemp, "Presenteeism: At Work But Out of It," *Harvard Business Review*, October 2004, https://hbr.org/2004/10/presenteeism-at-work-but-out-of-it.

28. Mariella Miraglia and Gary Johns, "Going to Work Ill: A Meta-Analysis of the Correlates of Presenteeism and a Dual-Path Model," *Journal of Occupational Health Psychology* 21, no. 3 (2016): 261.

29. Myde Boles, Barbara Pelletier, and Wendy Lynch, "The Relationship between Health Risks and Work Productivity," *Journal of Occupational and Environmental Medicine* 46, no. 7 (2004): 737–45.

30. Miraglia and Johns, "Going to Work Ill: A Meta-Analysis of the Correlates of Presenteeism and a Dual-Path Model."

31. Gail Kinman and Siobhan Wray, "Presenteeism in Academic Employees—Occupational and Individual Factors," *Occupational Medicine* 68, no. 1 (2018): 46–50.

32. Kansky and Diener, "Benefits of Well-Being."

33. Sigal G. Barsade et al., "To Your Heart's Content: A Model of Affective Diversity in Top Management Teams," *Administrative Science Quarterly* 45, no. 4 (2000): 802–36; Roderick D. Iverson, Mara Olekalns, and Peter J. Erwin, "Affectivity, Organizational Stressors, and Absenteeism: A Causal Model of Burnout and Its Consequences," *Journal of Vocational Behavior* 52, no. 1 (1998): 1–23; Barry M. Staw, Robert I. Sutton, and Lisa H. Pelled, "Employee

Positive Emotion and Favorable Outcomes at the Workplace," *Organization Science* 5, no. 1 (1994): 51–71; Lorna Doucet, Sherry M. B. Thatcher, and Matt E. Thatcher, "The Effects of Positive Affect and Personal Information Search on Outcomes in Call Centers: An Empirical Study," *Decision Support Systems* 52, no. 3 (2012): 664–73; Evert A. Van Doorn, Marc W. Heerdink, and Gerben A. Van Kleef, "Emotion and the Construal of Social Situations: Inferences of Cooperation versus Competition from Expressions of Anger, Happiness, and Disappointment," *Cognition & Emotion* 26, no. 3 (2012): 442–61; Deanna C. Whelan and John M. Zelenski, "Experimental Evidence That Positive Moods Cause Sociability," *Social Psychological and Personality Science* 3, no. 4 (2012): 430–37; Jennifer M. George, "State or Trait: Effects of Positive Mood on Prosocial Behaviors at Work," *Journal of Applied Psychology* 76, no. 2 (1991): 299; Alicia A. Grandey et al., "Is 'Service with a Smile' Enough? Authenticity of Positive Displays during Service Encounters," *Organizational Behavior and Human Decision Processes* 96, no. 1 (2005): 38–55; Christian Krekel, George Ward, and Jan-Emmanuel De Neve, "Employee Well-Being, Productivity, and Firm Performance: Evidence and Case Studies," *Global Happiness and Wellbeing*, 2019; Peter J. Carnevale, "Positive Affect and Decision Frame in Negotiation," *Group Decision and Negotiation* 17 (2008): 51–63; Peter J. D. Carnevale and Alice M. Isen, "The Influence of Positive Affect and Visual Access on the Discovery of Integrative Solutions in Bilateral Negotiation," *Organizational Behavior and Human Decision Processes* 37 (1986): 1–13.

34. Iverson, Olekalns, and Erwin, "Affectivity, Organizational Stressors, and Absentee-ism: A Causal Model of Burnout and Its Consequences"; Staw, Sutton, and Pelled, "Employee Positive Emotion and Favorable Outcomes."

35. Patricia B. Barger and Alicia A. Grandey, "Service with a Smile and Encounter Satisfaction: Emotional Contagion and Appraisal Mechanisms," *Academy of Management Journal* 49, no. 6 (2006): 1229–38; S. Douglas Pugh, "Service with a Smile: Emotional Contagion in the Service Encounter," *Academy of Management Journal* 44, no. 5 (2001): 1018–27; Wei-Chi Tsai and Yin-Mei Huang, "Mechanisms Linking Employee Affective Delivery and Customer Behavioral Intentions," *Journal of Applied Psychology* 87, no. 5 (2002): 1001.

36. Carnevale, "Positive Affect and Decision Frame in Negotiation"; Carnevale and Isen, "The Influence of Positive Affect and Visual Access on the Discovery of Integrative Solutions in Bilateral Negotiation."

37. Van Doorn, Heerdink, and Van Kleef, "Emotion and the Construal of Social Situations: Inferences of Cooperation versus Competition from Expressions of Anger, Happiness, and Disappointment."

38. Barbara L. Fredrickson, "The Role of Positive Emotions in Positive Psychology: The Broaden-and-Build Theory of Positive Emotions," *American Psychologist* 56, no. 3 (2001): 218; Barbara L. Fredrickson, "The Broaden–and–Build Theory of Positive Emotions," *Philosophical Transactions of the Royal Society of London. Series B: Biological Sciences* 359, no. 1449 (2004): 1367–77.

39. Matthijs Baas, Carsten KW De Dreu, and Bernard A. Nijstad, "A Meta-Analysis of 25 Years of Mood-Creativity Research: Hedonic Tone, Activation, or Regulatory Focus?," *Psychological Bulletin* 134, no. 6 (2008): 779.

40. Teresa M. Amabile et al., "Affect and Creativity at Work," *Administrative Science Quarterly* 50, no. 3 (2005): 367–403.

41. Elizabeth R. Tenney, Jared M. Poole, and Ed Diener, "Does Positivity Enhance Work Performance?: Why, When, and What We Don't Know," *Research in Organizational Behavior* 36 (2016): 27–46.

42. Mark A. Davis, "Understanding the Relationship between Mood and Creativity: A Meta-Analysis," *Organizational Behavior and Human Decision Processes* 108, no. 1 (2009):

25–38; Alice M. Isen, "On the Relationship between Affect and Creative Problem Solving," *Affect, Creative Experience, and Psychological Adjustment* 3, no. 17 (1999): 3–17; Kareem J. Johnson, Christian E. Waugh, and Barbara L. Fredrickson, "Smile to See the Forest: Facially Expressed Positive Emotions Broaden Cognition," *Cognition and Emotion* 24, no. 2 (2010): 299–321; Gillian Rowe, Jacob B. Hirsh, and Adam K. Anderson, "Positive Affect Increases the Breadth of Attentional Selection," *Proceedings of the National Academy of Sciences* 104, no. 1 (2007): 383–88.

43. Alice M. Isen et al., "The Influence of Positive Affect on the Unusualness of Word Associations," *Journal of Personality and Social Psychology* 48 (1985): 1413–26; Alice M. Isen, Kimberly A. Daubman, and Gary P. Nowicki, "Positive Affect Facilitates Creative Problem Solving," *Journal of Personality and Social Psychology* 52 (1987): 1122–31; Alice M. Isen and Kimberly A. Daubman, "The Influence of Affect on Categorization," *Journal of Personality and Social Psychology* 47, no. 6 (1984): 1206.

44. Davis, "Understanding the Relationship between Mood and Creativity."

45. Matthew J. Grawitch et al., "Promoting Creativity in Temporary Problem-Solving Groups: The Effects of Positive Mood and Autonomy in Problem Definition on Idea-Generating Performance," *Group Dynamics: Theory, Research, and Practice* 7, no. 3 (2003): 200.

Chapter 9

1. HBR Analytic Services, "Cultivating Workforce Well-Being to Drive Business Value," 2020, https://hbr.org/sponsored/2020/07/cultivating-workforce-well-being-to-drive-business -value.

2. Jeanne Meister, "The Future of Work Is Employee Well-Being," *Forbes*, August 4, 2021, https://www.forbes.com/sites/jeannemeister/2021/08/04/the-future-of-work-is-worker -well-being/.

3. Qin Li et al., "Employee Turnover and Firm Performance: Large-Sample Archival Evidence," *Management Science* 68, no. 8 (August 2022): 5667–83, https://doi.org/10.1287/mnsc .2021.4199.

4. Peter W. Hom et al., "One Hundred Years of Employee Turnover Theory and Research," *Journal of Applied Psychology* 102, no. 3 (March 2017): 530–45, https://doi.org/10 .1037/apl0000103.

5. Brooks C. Holtom et al., "Turnover and Retention Research: A Glance at the Past, a Closer Review of the Present, and a Venture into the Future," *Academy of Management Annals* 2, no. 1 (January 2008): 231–74, https://doi.org/10.5465/19416520802211552.

6. Rodger W. Griffeth, Peter W. Hom, and Stefan Gaertner, "A Meta-Analysis of Antecedents and Correlates of Employee Turnover: Update, Moderator Tests, and Research Implications for the Next Millennium," *Journal of Management* 26, no. 3 (2000): 463–88; Lyman W. Porter et al., "Organizational Commitment, Job Satisfaction, and Turnover among Psychiatric Technicians," *Journal of Applied Psychology* 59, no. 5 (1974): 603; Robert P. Tett and John P. Meyer, "Job Satisfaction, Organizational Commitment, Turnover Intention, and Turnover: Path Analyses Based on Meta-Analytic Findings," *Personnel Psychology* 46, no. 2 (1993): 259–93.

7. A. E. Clark, Y. Georgellis, and P. Sanfey, "Job Satisfaction, Wages and Quits: Evidence from German Panel Data," *Research in Labor Economics* 17 (1998): 95–121; L. Levy-Garboua, C. Montmarquette, and V. Simonnet, "Job Satisfaction and Quits," *Labour Economics* 14 (2007): 2–251.

8. Caspar Kaiser and Andrew J. Oswald, "The Scientific Value of Numerical Measures of Human Feelings," *Proceedings of the National Academy of Sciences* 119, no. 42 (October 18, 2022): e2210412119, https://doi.org/10.1073/pnas.2210412119.

9. James K. Harter et al., "Causal Impact of Employee Work Perceptions on the Bottom Line of Organizations," *Perspectives on Psychological Science* 5, no. 4 (2010): 378–89, https://doi.org/10.1177/1745691610374589; Francis Green, "Well-Being, Job Satisfaction and Labour Mobility," *Labour Economics* 17, no. 6 (2010): 897–903.

10. Thomas A. Wright and Douglas G. Bonett, "Job Satisfaction and Psychological Well-Being as Nonadditive Predictors of Workplace Turnover," *Journal of Management* 33, no. 2 (2007): 141–60.

11. Joseph Blasi, Richard Freeman, and Douglas Kruse, "Do Broad-Based Employee Ownership, Profit Sharing and Stock Options Help the Best Firms Do Even Better?," *British Journal of Industrial Relations* 54, no. 1 (2016): 55–82.

12. Leslie B. Hammer et al., "Measurement Development and Validation of the Family Supportive Supervisor Behavior Short-Form (FSSB-SF)," *Journal of Occupational Health Psychology* 18, no. 3 (2013): 285; Erin L. Kelly, Phyllis Moen, and Eric Tranby, "Changing Workplaces to Reduce Work-Family Conflict: Schedule Control in a White-Collar Organization," *American Sociological Review* 76, no. 2 (2011): 265–90; Erin L. Kelly et al., "Changing Work and Work-Family Conflict: Evidence from the Work, Family, and Health Network," *American Sociological Review* 79, no. 3 (2014): 485–516; Phyllis Moen et al., "Does a Flexibility/Support Organizational Initiative Improve High-Tech Employees' Well-Being? Evidence from the Work, Family, and Health Network," *American Sociological Review* 81, no. 1 (February 1, 2016): 134–64, https://doi.org/10.1177/0003122415622391; Heather N. Odle-Dusseau et al., "The Influence of Family-Supportive Supervisor Training on Employee Job Performance and Attitudes: An Organizational Work–Family Intervention.," *Journal of Occupational Health Psychology* 21, no. 3 (2016): 296.

13. Achyuta Adhvaryu, Teresa Molina, and Anant Nyshadham, "Expectations, Wage Hikes, and Worker Voice: Evidence from a Field Experiment," *Economic Journal* 132, no. 645 (2022): 1978–93; Hugh Xiaolong Wu and Shannon X Liu, "Managerial Attention, Employee Attrition, and Productivity: Evidence from a Field Experiment," Rotman School of Management working paper 3787204, 2021.

14. George Ward, "Workplace Wellbeing and Employee Turnover," University of Oxford Working Paper, 2024.

15. Ward, "Workplace Wellbeing and Employee Turnover."

16. Ward, "Workplace Wellbeing and Employee Turnover."

17. Turnover is not a statistic that firms in the United States are required to publish. Here one of us (George) used data from DiversIQ, which has collected voluntarily disclosed turnover data from a number of sources for publicly traded companies in the US. Ward, "Workplace Wellbeing and Employee Turnover."

18. Christopher Jencks, Lauri Perman, and Lee Rainwater, "What Is a Good Job? A New Measure of Labor-Market Success," *American Journal of Sociology* 93, no. 6 (1988): 1322–57; Sherwin Rosen, "The Theory of Equalizing Differences," *Handbook of Labor Economics* 1 (1986): 641–92.

19. Vanessa C. Burbano, "Social Responsibility Messages and Worker Wage Requirements: Field Experimental Evidence from Online Labor Marketplaces," *Organization Science* 27, no. 4 (2016): 1010–28; Nicole Maestas et al., "The Value of Working Conditions in the United States and Implications for the Structure of Wages," *American Economic Review* 113, no. 7 (2023): 2007–47; Alexandre Mas and Amanda Pallais, "Valuing Alternative Work Arrangements," *American Economic Review* 107, no. 12 (2017): 3722–59; Scott Stern, "Do Scientists Pay to Be Scientists?," *Management Science* 50, no. 6 (2004): 835–53.

20. Burbano, "Social Responsibility Messages and Worker Wage Requirements."

21. George Ward, "Workplace Happiness and Job Search Behavior: Evidence from a Field Experiment," MIT Sloan working paper 6607-22, 2022

22. Reported are the percent effects on applications of showing information about workplace happiness to job seekers on Indeed, according to the score that was shown. Users were randomized into the control group (and see all company pages as normal) or the treatment group where they saw company pages with added information about workplace happiness, for ten months beginning in May 2020. N = 23,376,519 job seekers.

23. George Ward, "Happiness at Work: Essays on Subjective Wellbeing in the Workplace and Labor Market" (thesis, Massachusetts Institute of Technology, 2022), https://dspace.mit .edu/handle/1721.1/144621.

24. The figure shows the results of a willingness-to-pay (WTP) survey using a nationally representative sample in the United States. Respondents are asked to imagine two positions at companies where the job description and companies are the same other than for pay and happiness levels. They are then offered a series of choices between Position A or Position B. Position A always has a happiness score of 65 and the same pay as their current job. Position B has a happiness score of 75 (or 85) but the pay is [35, 20, 10, 5, 2] percent less than their current job. Plotted are the percentage of people saying they would choose B at different levels of salary difference. N = 4,033.

Chapter 10

1. Christian Krekel, George Ward, and Jan-Emmanuel De Neve, "Employee Wellbeing, Productivity, and Firm Performance," Saïd Business School Working Paper 4, 2019.

2. Our approach involved three steps: First, we aggregated employee wellbeing and the respective (context-specific) performance outcome at the business-unit level for each of the 339 research studies. Second, we calculated the business-unit-level correlation between employee wellbeing and performance outcomes for each study. Finally, we applied our meta-analytical toolkit to obtain a single, adjusted (i.e., non-context-specific) average correlation between employee wellbeing and the respective performance outcome.

3. Petri Böckerman and Pekka Ilmakunnas, "The Job Satisfaction-Productivity Nexus: A Study Using Matched Survey and Register Data," *ILR Review* 65, no. 2 (2012): 244–62, https://doi.org/10.1177/001979391206500203.

4. Alex Bryson, John Forth, and Lucy Stokes, "Does Employees' Subjective Well-Being Affect Workplace Performance?," *Human Relations* 70, no. 8 (2017): 1017–37, https://doi.org/10 .1177/0018726717693073.

5. Alex Edmans, "The Link between Job Satisfaction and Firm Value, with Implications for Corporate Social Responsibility," *Academy of Management Perspectives* 26, no. 4 (2012): 1–19, https://doi.org/10.5465/AMP.2012.0046; Alex Edmans, "Does the Stock Market Fully Value Intangibles? Employee Satisfaction and Equity Prices," *Journal of Financial Economics* 101, no. 3 (2011): 621–40, https://doi.org/10.1016/J.JFINECO.2011.03.021.

6. Alex Edmans et al., "Employee Satisfaction, Labor Market Flexibility, and Stock Returns around the World," *Management Science* 70, no. 7 (2023): 4167–52.

7. Andrew Chamberlain, "Does Company Culture Pay Off? Analyzing Stock Performance of 'Best Places to Work' Companies," *Glassdoor Economic Research* (blog), 2015, https://research.glassdoor.com/site-us/wp-content/uploads/sites/2/2015/05/GD_Report_1.pdf; Andrew Chamberlain and Zanele Munyikwa, "What's Culture Worth? Stock Performance of Glassdoor's Best Places to Work 2009 to 2019," *Glassdoor Economic Research* (blog), May 1, 2020, https://www.glassdoor.com/research/stock-returns-bptw-2020/.

8. However, effects were not consistent across sectors. Chamberlain and Munyikwa noted that while retail companies' stock experienced a 40.5 percent annual return on investment, returns dwindled to 4.4 percent and 3.9 percent for insurance companies and

energy companies, respectively. The relationship even turned slightly negative (–1.4 percent) among firms in construction, repair, and maintenance.

9. Chamberlain, "Does Company Culture Pay Off?"

10. Olubunmi Faleye and Emery A. Trahan, "Labor-Friendly Corporate Practices: Is What Is Good for Employees Good for Shareholders?," *Journal of Business Ethics* 101, no. 1 (2011): 1–27.

11. Minjie Huang et al., "Family Firms, Employee Satisfaction, and Corporate Performance," *Journal of Corporate Finance* 34 (2015): 108–27; Efthymia Symitsi, Panagiotis Stamolampros, and George Daskalakis, "Employees' Online Reviews and Equity Prices," *Economics Letters* 162 (2018): 53–55.

12. Andy Moniz, "Inferring Employees' Social Media Perceptions of Corporate Culture and the Link to Firm Value," SSRN Working Paper 2768091, 2017; Symitsi, Stamolampros, and Daskalakis, "Employees' Online Reviews and Equity Prices"; T. Clifton Green et al., "Crowd-sourced Employer Reviews and Stock Returns," *Journal of Financial Economics* 134, no. 1 (2019): 236–51.

13. Green et al., "Crowdsourced Employer Reviews and Stock Returns."

14. Jan-Emmanuel De Neve, Micah Kaats, and George Ward, "Workplace Wellbeing and Firm Performance," University of Oxford Wellbeing Research Centre Working Paper 2304, 2023.

15. Huang et al., "Family Firms, Employee Satisfaction, and Corporate Performance"; Andy Moniz, "Inferring Employees' Social Media Perceptions of Corporate Culture and the Link to Firm Value," 2017, http://dx.doi.org/10.2139/ssrn.2768091; Symitsi, Stamolampros, and Daskalakis, "Employees' Online Reviews and Equity Prices."

16. While we primarily rely on Tobin's q and ROA as our key indicators of firm performance, we also introduce gross profits as an outcome variable in several specifications and find consistent results. As profits vary considerably between companies of different sizes, we also control for firm assets and number of employees as well as industry fixed effects in all our regression equations.

17. At the same time, we also looked within industries by including a set of fixed effects for the firm's sector as well as a range of other variables that may be driving both wellbeing and performance. These include the number of surveys, firm size, lagged assets, and capital intensity.

18. Minimum ten responses per firm-country-year are required to be included in the analysis, in both figures 10-2 and 10-3.

19. Nicholas Kaldor, "Marginal Productivity and the Macro-Economic Theories of Distribution: Comment on Samuelson and Modigliani," *Review of Economic Studies* 33, no. 4 (1966): 309–19.

20. We also look at financial performance later, in 2021 and beyond, again using the pre-Covid wellbeing as a predictor, as a further test and find similar results.

21. These findings are consistent with a causal interpretation, but we nevertheless do not make such a claim here. Indeed, future research may look to exploit natural experiments and to leverage further changes over time within companies in order to better isolate cause and effect here.

22. We limit each year to companies with at least a hundred surveys filled in of each of the four wellbeing items and that can be matched to stock prices using the CRSP database. Using a balanced panel of firms (i.e., those that are eligible in all three years, we find similar results, with the delta (between the total wellbeing and S&P 500 returns) being slightly higher in this case.

23. There were 429 eligible firms for the 2020 list; 683 (2021); 948 (2022); and 366 (2023).

24. Since these are indexes rather than a "total return," this makes them good comparators since they too ignore the impact of dividends, as we do in this study.

25. Some estimates suggest that sustainable investments now top $30 billion, an increase of 68 percent from 2014. Witold Henisz, Tim Koller, and Robin Nuttall, "Five Ways That ESG Creates Value," *McKinsey Quarterly*, 2019, https://www.mckinsey.com/business-functions /strategy-and-corporate-finance/our-insights/five-ways-that-esg-creates-value.

26. Business Roundtable, "Business Roundtable Redefines the Purpose of a Corporation to Promote 'An Economy That Serves All Americans,'" 2019, https://www.businessroundtable .org/business-roundtable-redefines-the-purpose-of-a-corporation-to-promote-an-economy -that-serves-all-americans.

27. Pleased as we were to see the measures included, it is worth noting that none of this would have been possible without the efforts of the World Wellbeing Movement, which we have been heavily involved with and of which one of us (Jan) is a formal cofounder.

Chapter 11

1. Carl Benedikt Frey and Michael A. Osborne, "The Future of Employment: How Susceptible Are Jobs to Computerisation?," *Technological Forecasting and Social Change* 114 (2017): 254–80.

2. Erik Brynjolfsson, Tom Mitchell, and Daniel Rock, "What Can Machines Learn and What Does It Mean for Occupations and the Economy?," in *AEA Papers and Proceedings*, vol. 108 (2018), 43–47.

3. Melanie Arntz, Terry Gregory, and Ulrich Zierahn, "The Risk of Automation for Jobs in OECD Countries: A Comparative Analysis," 2016. See also Brynjolfsson, Mitchell, and Rock, "What Can Machines Learn?"; Edward Felten, Manav Raj, and Robert Channing Seamans, "The Effect of Artificial Intelligence on Human Labor: An Ability-Based Approach," *Academy of Management Proceedings* (2019), 15784; Michael Webb, "The Impact of Artificial Intelligence on the Labor Market," Stanford University Working Paper, 2019, https://doi .org/10.2139/SSRN.3482150; Tyna Eloundou, Sam Manning, Pamela Mishkin, and Daniel Rock, "GPTs Are GPTs: Labor Market Impact Potential of LLMs," *Science* 384, no. 6702 (2024): 1306–1308.

4. For a summary, see Philippe Aghion et al., "The Effects of Automation on Labor Demand," in *Robots and AI*, eds. Lili Yan Ing and Gene M. Grossman (London, UK: Routledge, 2022), 15–39, https://doi.org/10.4324/9781003275534-2.

5. Or, as Andrew Oswald once reminded us, long-term (un)employment statistics are so flat you could drive a train across them.

6. David Autor et al., "New Frontiers: The Origins and Content of New Work, 1940–2018," *Quarterly Journal of Economics* 139, no. 3 (2024): 1399–1465.

7. Daron Acemoglu and Pascual Restrepo, "Automation and New Tasks: How Technology Displaces and Reinstates Labor," *Journal of Economic Perspectives* 33, no. 2 (2019), https://doi .org/10.1257/JEP.33.2.3.

8. Daron Acemoglu and David Autor, "Skills, Tasks and Technologies: Implications for Employment and Earnings," *Handbook of Labor Economics* 4 (2011): 1043–1171.

9. For relevant discussions, see: David Autor and Anna Salomons, "Is Automation Labor Share–Displacing? Productivity Growth, Employment, and the Labor Share," Brookings Papers on Economic Activity, 2018, 1–63; Emin Dinlersoz and Zoltan Wolf, "Automation, Labor Share, and Productivity: Plant-Level Evidence from U.S. Manufacturing," working paper, September 2018, https://ideas.repec.org//p/cen/wpaper/18-39.html; James Manyika et al., "A Future That Works: AI, Automation, Employment, and Productivity," McKinsey

Global Institute Research, 2017: 1–135; Lise McQuay, "Will Robots Duplicate or Surpass Us? The Impact of Job Automation on Tasks, Productivity, and Work," *Psychosociological Issues in Human Resource Management* 6, no. 2 (2018): 86–91.

10. Duncan Gallie et al., "The Hidden Face of Job Insecurity," *Work, Employment and Society* 31, no. 1 (February 1, 2017): 36–53, https://doi.org/10.1177/0950017015624399.

11. One study using data following German workers over time suggests that the degree of computerization—the extent to which tasks in a given occupation are likely to be substitutable by computers—leads to increases in worker's' beliefs about the extent to which they might lose their job. Katharina Dengler and Stefanie Gundert, "Digital Transformation and Subjective Job Insecurity in Germany," *European Sociological Review* 37, no. 5 (October 1, 2021): 799–817, https://doi.org/10.1093/esr/jcaa066. See also Henrik Schwabe and F. Castellacci, "Automation, Workers' Skills and Job Satisfaction," *PLOS ONE*, 2020, https://doi.org/10.1371/JOURNAL .PONE.0242929.

12. Alex J. Wood et al., "Good Gig, Bad Gig: Autonomy and Algorithmic Control in the Global Gig Economy," *Work, Employment and Society* 33, no. 1 (February 1, 2019): 56–75, https://doi.org/10.1177/0950017018785616.

13. Erin L. Kelly and Phyllis Moen, *Overload: How Good Jobs Went Bad and What We Can Do about It* (Princeton, NJ: Princeton University Press, 2020).

14. For a broader discussion on technology and meaning, see Milena Nikolova, Femke Cnossen, and Daniel L. Bennett, "Robots, Meaning, and Self-Determination," *Research Policy* 53, no. 5 (2024): 104987.

15. Francis Green, *Demanding Work: The Paradox of Job Quality in the Affluent Economy* (Princeton, NJ: Princeton University Press, 2007).

16. Francis Green et al., "Working Still Harder," *ILR Review* 75, no. 2 (March 1, 2022): 458–87, https://doi.org/10.1177/0019793920977850.

17. For a deeper discussion of the important distinction between tending the machine and managing the machine, see Sarah Bankins, "The Ethical Use of Artificial Intelligence in Human Resource Management: A Decision-Making Framework," *Ethics and Information Technology* 23, no. 3 (2021), https://doi.org/10.1007/S10676-021-09619-6.

18. Daron Acemoglu and Pascual Restrepo, "Robots and Jobs: Evidence from US Labor Markets," *Journal of Political Economy* 128, no. 6 (2020): 2188–2244; Wolfgang Dauth et al., "Adjusting to Robots: Worker-Level Evidence," Opportunity and Inclusive Growth Institute working paper, August 21, 2018, https://ideas.repec.org//p/fip/fedmoi/0013.html.

19. Daron Acemoglu and Pascual Restrepo, "Automation and New Tasks: How Technology Displaces and Reinstates Labor," *Journal of Economic Perspectives* 33, no. 2 (2019): 3–30.

20. Acemoglu and Restrepo, "Robots and Jobs." See also George J. Borjas and Richard B. Freeman, "From Immigrants to Robots: The Changing Locus of Substitutes for Workers," *RSF: The Russell Sage Foundation Journal of the Social Sciences* 5, no. 5 (2019): 22–42.

21. Luísa Nazareno and Daniel Schiff, "The Impact of Automation and Artificial Intelligence on Worker Well-Being," *Technology in Society*, 2021, https://doi.org/10.1016/J .TECHSOC.2021.101679.

22. Green et al., "Working Still Harder."

23. Beth Gutelius and Sanjay Pinto, "Pain Points: Data on Work Intensity, Monitoring, and Health at Amazon Warehouses," UIC Center for Urban Economic Development, 2023.

24. The survey was carried out by Indeed in partnership with CensusWide. It included 3,700 job seekers and human resource professionals. We focus here on the job-seeker sample, collected in the UK, United States, Canada, India, France, Japan, and Germany.

25. See, e.g., Timothy F. Bresnahan, Erik Brynjolfsson, and Lorin M. Hitt, "Information Technology, Workplace Organization, and the Demand for Skilled Labor: Firm-Level Evidence," *Quarterly Journal of Economics* 117, no. 1 (2002): 339–76, https://doi.org/10.1162/003355302753399526; S. Parker and G. Grote, "Automation, Algorithms, and Beyond: Why Work Design Matters More Than Ever in a Digital World," 2020, https://doi.org/10.1111/APPS.12241; Jilles Smids, Sven Nyholm, and Hannah Berkers, "Robots in the Workplace: A Threat to—or Opportunity for—Meaningful Work?," *Philosophy and Technology* 33 (2020): 9–10.

Chapter 12

1. Melvin Kranzberg, "Technology and History: 'Kranzberg's Laws,'" *Bulletin of Science, Technology & Society* 15, no. 9 (1995): 5–13, https://doi.org/10.1177/027046769501500104.

2. Effects of automation on job quality are quite diverse and ultimately depend on the ways in which managers design and strategize technology implementation. See, e.g., Timothy F. Bresnahan, Erik Brynjolfsson, and Lorin M. Hitt, "Information Technology, Workplace Organization, and the Demand for Skilled Labor: Firm-Level Evidence," *Quarterly Journal of Economics* 117, no. 1 (2002): 339–76, https://doi.org/10.1162/003355302753399526; Sharon K. Parker and Gudela Grote, "Automation, Algorithms, and Beyond: Why Work Design Matters More Than Ever in a Digital World," *Applied Psychology* 71, no. 4 (2022): 1171–1204, https://doi.org/10.1111/apps.12241; Jilles Smids, Sven Nyholm, and Hannah Berkers, "Robots in the Workplace: A Threat to—or Opportunity for—Meaningful Work?," *Philosophy and Technology* 33 (2020): 9–10.

3. Janine Berg et al., "Risks to Job Quality from Digital Technologies: Are Industrial Relations in Europe Ready for the Challenge?," *European Journal of Industrial Relations* 29, no. 4 (2023), https://doi.org/10.1177/09596801231178904.

4. Parker and Grote, "Automation, Algorithms, and Beyond."

5. These are six-digit SOC codes.

6. Shakked Noy and Whitney Zhang, "Experimental Evidence on the Productivity Effects of Generative Artificial Intelligence," *Science* 381, no. 6654 (2023): 187–92.

7. Daron Acemoglu and Pascual Restrepo, "Robots and Jobs: Evidence from US Labor Markets," *Journal of Political Economy* 128, no. 6 (2020): 2188–2244. For further discussion, see also Daron Acemoglu and Simon Johnson, *Power and Progress: Our Thousand-Year Struggle over Technology and Prosperity* (New York: PublicAffairs, 2023).

8. David H. Autor, "Why Are There Still So Many Jobs? The History and Future of Workplace Automation," *Journal of Economic Perspectives* 29, no. 3 (2015): 3–30; Joel Mokyr, Chris Vickers, and Nicolas L. Ziebarth, "The History of Technological Anxiety and the Future of Economic Growth: Is This Time Different?," *Journal of Economic Perspectives* 29, no. 3 (2015): 31–50, https://doi.org/10.1257/JEP.29.3.31.

9. For a much deeper and important discussion than we can possibly give here of the significance of history in understanding the future of work, see Benjamin Schneider and Hillary Vipond, "The Past and Future of Work: How History Can Inform the Age of Automation," CESifo Working Paper No. 10766, 2023, https://doi.org/10.2139/SSRN.4643947.

10. Andrew E. Clark et al., *The Origins of Happiness* (Princeton, NJ: Princeton University Press, 2018); Andrew E. Clark and Andrew J. Oswald, "Unhappiness and Unemployment," *Economic Journal* 104, no. 424 (1994): 648–59; Liliana Winkelmann and Rainer Winkelmann, "Why Are the Unemployed So Unhappy? Evidence from Panel Data," *Economica* 65, no. 257 (1998): 1–15.

11. More recently, Anne C. Gielen and Jan C. Van Ours have replicated this finding using additional waves of the same data set. See Anne C. Gielen and Jan C. Van Ours, "Unhappiness and Job Finding," *Economica* 81, no. 323 (2014): 544–65.

12. David N. F. Bell and David G. Blanchflower, "Young People and the Great Recession," *Oxford Review of Economic Policy* 27, no. 2 (2011): 241–67; Andrew E. Clark and Anthony Lepinteur, "The Causes and Consequences of Early-Adult Unemployment: Evidence from Cohort Data," *Journal of Economic Behavior & Organization* 166 (2019): 107–24.

13. Maria Cotofan et al., "Macroeconomic Conditions When Young Shape Job Preferences for Life," *Review of Economics and Statistics* 105, no. 2 (2020): 1–20.

14. José María Barrero, Nicholas Bloom, and Steven J. Davis, "The Evolution of Work from Home," *Journal of Economic Perspectives* 37, no. 4 (November 1, 2023): 23–49, https://doi.org/10.1257/jep.37.4.23.

15. Barrero, Bloom, and Davis, "The Evolution of Work from Home."

16. Emma Harrington and Matthew Kahn, "Has the Rise of Work-from-Home Reduced the Motherhood Penalty in the Labor Market?," University of Virginia Working Paper, 2023.

17. Kiron Chatterjee et al., "Commuting and Wellbeing: A Critical Overview of the Literature with Implications for Policy and Future Research," *Transport Reviews* 40, no. 1 (2020): 5–34.

18. Erin L. Kelly and Phyllis Moen, *Overload: How Good Jobs Went Bad and What We Can Do about It* (Princeton, NJ: Princeton University Press, 2020).

19. Nicholas Bloom et al., "Does Working from Home Work? Evidence from a Chinese Experiment," *Quarterly Journal of Economics* 130, no. 1 (2015): 165–218.

20. Kim Parker, Juliana Menasce Horowitz, and Rachel Minkin, "Covid-19 Pandemic Continues to Reshape Work in America," Pew Research, February 2022, https://www.pewresearch.org/social-trends/2022/02/16/covid-19-pandemic-continues-to-reshape-work-in-america/.

21. Paolo Confino, "Dropbox Let Employees Work Remotely. It Saw Record-High Turnover," *Fortune*, December 6, 2022, https://fortune.com/2022/12/06/dropbox-virtual-first-model-asynchronous-work-retention-turnover-remote-work/.

22. For a more detailed discussion of these ideas, see Jan-Emmanuel De Neve, "Why It's Too Soon to Scrap the Office," CityAM, accessed June 1, 2024, https://www.cityam.com/why-its-too-soon-to-scrap-the-office.

23. Cevat Giray Aksoy et al., "Working from Home around the Globe: 2023 Report," *WFH Research*, 2023.

24. Nicholas Bloom, Ruobing Han, and James Liang, "Hybrid Working from Home Improves Retention without Damaging Performance," *Nature* 630 (2024): 920–25, https://doi.org/10.1038/s41586-024-07500-2.

25. Prithwiraj Choudhury et al., "Is Hybrid Work the Best of Both Worlds? Evidence from a Field Experiment," *Review of Economics and Statistics*, 2024, https://doi.org/10.2139/ssrn.4068741.

26. Yiling Lin, Carl Benedikt Frey, and Lingfei Wu, "Remote Collaboration Fuses Fewer Breakthrough Ideas," *Nature* 623, no. 7989 (November 2023): 987–91, https://doi.org/10.1038/s41586-023-06767-1; Longqi Yang et al., "The Effects of Remote Work on Collaboration among Information Workers," *Nature Human Behaviour* 6, no. 1 (January 2022): 43–54, https://doi.org/10.1038/s41562-021-01196-4.

27. Milena Nikolova, Femke Cnossen, and Boris Nikolaev, "Robots, Meaning, and Self-Determination," *Research Policy* 53, no. 5 (2024): 104987; Sharon K. Parker and Gudela Grote, "Automation, Algorithms, and Beyond: Why Work Design Matters More Than Ever in a Digital World," *Applied Psychology* 71, no. 4 (2022): 1171–1204, https://doi.org/10.1111/apps

.12241; Jilles Smids, Sven Nyholm, and Hannah A. Berkers, "Robots in the Workplace: A Threat to—or Opportunity for—Meaningful Work?," *Philosophy & Technology* 33 (2020), https://doi.org/10.1007/S13347-019-00377-4.

28. This is not only likely to improve worker wellbeing, but also strongly likely to improve the likelihood of technology acceptance among the workforce.

29. Berg et al., "Risks to Job Quality from Digital Technologies: Are Industrial Relations in Europe Ready for the Challenge?"

30. David H. Autor et al., *The Work of the Future: Building Better Jobs in an Age of Intelligent Machines* (Cambridge, MA: MIT Press, 2022).

Index

Our Thanks

This book is the culmination of years of our research on the topic of workplace wellbeing, all of it built on decades of research by countless others. Interest in wellbeing at work has only grown in recent years, particularly as the global pandemic began to shine a much-needed spotlight on the mental health and wellbeing of workers. As more people expressed real interest in the topic and curiosity about our research, we felt compelled to bring our work together in a way that we hope will be helpful to practitioners in the field. Our goal is not only to clarify concepts but also to arm those working on the front lines of improving workplace wellbeing with the latest evidence available.

Needless to say, this book would not be what it is without the generous support of many people. We are indebted to a long list of individuals we cannot hope to fully name here. That list includes our academic mentors and colleagues who drew us into the field of wellbeing science and who continue to inspire us, our data and industry partners who enabled much of our work, the academic institutions that supported us throughout, and the many others who helped bring the book to fruition—not to mention, of course, our partners, families, and friends who provided invaluable support and encouragement from beginning to end.

We thank Harvard Business Review Press for the opportunity to write the book and, in particular, our editor, Jeff Kehoe, for taking on and guiding the project. Thanks too to our literary agent, Tom Killingbeck. We are especially grateful to Micah Kaats for providing outstanding research assistance and to Yoel Sevi for his excellent research assistance in the latter stages of manuscript preparation.

Without our coauthors on many of the projects we discuss in the book—including Clément Bellet, Micah Kaats, Christian Krekel, and others—the work would not have been possible. We benefited greatly from the valuable feedback we received at various stages of writing, and we thank, in particular, Alex Bryson, Andrew Clark, Erin Kelly, Richard Layard, Alan Manning, and three anonymous peer reviewers for their constructive comments on earlier drafts. The book was greatly improved by their insights.

Advancing empirical research frontiers typically requires access to high-quality data, as well as the opportunity to run large-scale field experiments. Benefiting from both has been a pleasure and a privilege, and we are extremely grateful to the many data providers and industry partners who enabled our research. When we first started guiding the development of the workplace wellbeing survey in collaboration with Indeed, back in 2019, we had no idea that this effort would become the world's largest study of its kind. We are very grateful to the team at Indeed, whose dedication to collecting valid and reliable data on workplace wellbeing on a massive scale has not only helped our own work but will surely also continue to facilitate a great many research insights in the future.

We owe a debt of gratitude on this front to Janeane Tolomeo, who leads a wonderful team at Indeed, as well as to LaFawn Davis, who has been a staunch supporter and advocate for workplace wellbeing from the start of the project. Their bravery in allowing us to do academic research using their data, without the recourse to control the findings, can only be applauded. As we argue at length in the book, we hope more and more organizations will experiment and continue to build and share knowledge about best practices when it comes to workplace wellbeing. Although each of us has consulted for various technology and other companies, including Indeed, this book was written entirely outside of any paid consultancy relationship.

We thank another major partner, Gallup, which has, over the years, collected truly remarkable data on subjective wellbeing. The Gallup World Poll, which is notable not only for its extraordinary geographical breadth but also for its rigor and sophistication, provided an invaluable window into the workplace wellbeing of employees around the world. We are both (unpaid) research advisers to Gallup, and we are very grateful to that organization for sharing its data for academic research.

Finally, we are grateful to both the University of Oxford and the Massachusetts Institute of Technology for providing us with supportive professional homes. The Wellbeing Research Centre at Oxford and the Institute for Work and Employment Research at MIT, in particular, as well as Saïd Business School, Somerville College, and Harris Manchester College, have together given us a highly collegial and stimulating work environment—something that has brought us over the years a great deal of happiness, satisfaction, sense of purpose and meaning, and, only occasionally, a little bit of stress.

About the Authors

JAN-EMMANUEL DE NEVE is Professor of Economics and Behavioural Science at the University of Oxford, where he also directs the Wellbeing Research Centre. He is best known for his research on the economics of wellbeing, which has led to new insights into the relationship between happiness and income, productivity, firm performance, and economic growth. His pioneering research has been published in leading academic journals across multiple disciplines, including *Science, Nature, Review of Economics and Statistics, Psychological Science, Management Science, Journal of Political Economy*, and the *British Medical Journal*. His research was also recognized among "The Management Ideas That Mattered Most" by *Harvard Business Review*. He currently guides the world's largest study on workplace wellbeing in partnership with Indeed.

De Neve coauthored the main textbook on wellbeing science with Richard Layard. In addition, he is an editor of the *World Happiness Report* and cofounder of the World Wellbeing Movement. He is also a member of the UN's Expert Group on Wellbeing Measurement. De Neve frequently acts as a consultant to governments and major corporations, and his insights on wellbeing and policy are sought by leading global media.

GEORGE WARD earned his PhD from MIT's Sloan School of Management. He is currently the Mary Ewart Junior Research Fellow in Economics at Somerville College, University of Oxford, and he also holds the Persol Research Fellowship at Oxford's Wellbeing Research Centre. He frequently collaborates with large organizations, including Indeed and British Telecom, using field experiments alongside big data and advanced statistical techniques to address pressing challenges in both business and public policy.

Ward coauthored *The Origins of Happiness: The Science of Well-Being over the Life Course,* and his research has been published in leading academic journals such as *Management Science, Review of Economics and Statistics, Journal of Personality and Social Psychology, American Psychologist,* and *American Journal of Political Science.* His work spans a broad range of topics related to human wellbeing, including the links between economic growth and happiness, the impact of workplace wellbeing on productivity, retention, recruitment, and firm performance, the role of management practices and organizational culture in shaping employee wellbeing, and the emotional foundations of voting behavior and the rise of populism. His findings have been widely featured in major outlets such as *The Economist, Financial Times, New York Times, Harvard Business Review,* and *The Guardian.*